TAKE ME BACK TO DEAR OLD BLIGHTY

The Pottery and Glass Record.

ARKINSTALL & SON,

ARCADIAN WORKS,

STOKE-ON-TRENT.

BRITISH INDUSTRIES FAIR, LONDON,
FEB. 24th to MARCH 7th.

STAND A 88.
FANCY GOODS SECTION.

Arcadian Arms China

Over 500 Shapes. Comprising Latest Military Novelties.

SPECIAL FEATURE—COAT OF ARMS TEA WARE.

PROMPT DELIVERY NOW GUARANTEED.

"PRATT" WARE — Reproductions of Famous Old Blue Prints.
SPECIALITY 1919—BLUE CHARIOTS.

FLOWER POTS, VASES, CANDLESTICKS, SALAD BOWLS, TEAPOTS, HOT WATER JUGS, AND A COMPLETE RANGE OF USEFUL AND FANCY ARTICLES.

The same assortment is also made and shown in PRATTS BLACK "KAN-SU," and "CHERUBS" which have proved an immense success.

Advertisement for Arcadian Arms China from the Pottery and Glass Record, February 1919.

TAKE ME BACK TO DEAR OLD BLIGHTY

The First World War through the eyes of the Heraldic China Manufacturers

Robert Southall

MILESTONE PUBLICATIONS

Published by Milestone Publications
Goss & Crested China Ltd.
62 Murray Road
Horndean
Hants PO8 9JL

ISBN No. 0 903852 14 4

Design Brian Iles
Photography Michael Edwards Studio Havant

Printed and bound in Great Britain by
R.J. Ackford, Industrial Estate Chichester Sussex
Colour section printed by
Southern Press Horndean

Other Milestone Publications
Crested China *Sandy Andrews*
The Price Guide To Crested China *Nicholas Pine*
The Price Guide To Goss China *Nicholas Pine*
Goss China Arms, Decorations and Their Values *Nicholas Pine*
The Goss Record 8th Edition
The Goss Record War Edition
Goss For Collectors - The Literature
Arcadian Arms China Catalogue

This Book is:

Dedicated to David and John, my father and uncle, who though alike in so many ways, by diverse means made its completion possible.

And is for - Ruth, Lizzie and Angharad

Contents

Author's Introduction and Acknowledgements

Since my interest in Great War Crested China was aroused some ten years ago I have never ceased to be amazed by the number and variety of models that turn up in collections, dealer's lists and antique shops around the country. Inevitably I found myself asking the questions What? When? and Why? What were they copied from? When were they made? Why were they made? Wherever I turned I found only incomplete, inadequate answers. Gradually, through my own researches, I was able to piece together scraps of information and build a more complete picture of this hitherto unresearched branch of the Crested China industry.

In order to put the models into perspective I have divided each chapter into two sections. The first, the 'reality', recounts the events of the war, both general and specific, that surrounded the models' conception. The second, the 'fantasy', details the models that are found. Together I hope they will provide the reader, whether general or specialist, with a fascinating view of the greatest event of the twentieth century to date.

I wish to express my gratitude to a number of specialists who have freely provided me with information. In particular I wish to thank Colonel P. Horden, Curator of the Royal Tank Museum, Bovington, who permitted me to examine the Museum's collection of Crested China and who has provided an invaluable and tolerant source of information; Mr. Peter Cooksley for his comments on the aeroplanes; Major C.W.P. Coan of the Royal Corps of Transport; Lesley Westgate of the Naval Historical Library; S.C. Walter of the Royal Artillery Institution; Monsieur J. Lorette of the Army and Military History Museum, Brussels and to the Staff of the Departments of Photographs; Exhibits and Firearms; Printed Books and Documents; Special Collections and Art of the Imperial War Museum, London, for their responses to my many requests. In particular I would like to thank Mr. Willis of the Department of Photographs for his help in identification, Mr. J.R. Allen of the Department of Exhibits who made exhibits available to me to photograph and Miss Rose E. Coombes, Special Collections Officer, for freely supplying me with photographs.

I also wish to thank the librarians from the following towns who supplied me with information on their town's war memorials: Aylesbury, Brighton, Carlisle, Cheltenham, Clacton-on-Sea, Dartford, Derby, Dover, Dovercourt, Folkestone, Great Yarmouth, Gravesend, Harrogate, Harwich, Hertford, Ilkestone, Kirkwall, Llandudno, Loughborough, Norwich, Nottingham, Oxford, Plymouth, Portsmouth, Stoke-on-Trent, Tunbridge Wells, Walsall, Westminster and Worthing.

I have also received help from: J.N. Slater, Editor Railway Magazine; A.M. Harrison of the Manx Museum; C.J. Turner, Cranbrook Rural Council; M.Y. Ashcroft, Archivist, North Yorkshire County Council; D.E. Barnes, East Dereham Town Council; A.J. Bryce of the Sandeman Library; Mrs. J.M. Marsden, Tourist Officer, West Derby; V.H. Bourne of the Newhaven & Seaford Historical Society; Mr. J.A. Gauld of Killin Tourist Association; H. Place, Thetford Town Council; J.A.C. West of the Weymouth & Portland Local History Museum and the Registrar of the Patent Office, London.

My thanks also go to numerous fellow collectors who have willingly allowed me to examine and photograph their collections, in particular Robin and Philip Riley and John Proud whose extensive collections have provided many of the illustrations for this book; and to Sandy Andrews who, in the course of her researches into the History of Heraldic Souvenir Ware, has provided me with much valuable information.

Robert Southall

1
Introduction

'Goss china upholds the time-honoured association of ceramics with topical and historical events as a means of establishing a permanent and abiding memory. Pottery is to archeology what fossils are to geology'

Pottery Gazette 2 April 1917.

Heraldic china has its origins in the latter half of the nineteenth century when the firm of W.H. Goss started to make small, white porcelain models, embellished with the coat of arms of a particular town, city, county or country. Conceived for the souvenir market before the days of the post card and other objets d'art that today grace the shelves of shops around the country, these pieces of "fancy ware" were eagerly sought by an ever increasing band of collectors seeking to add to their collection a memento of an enjoyable holiday or an important national event. They were bought for a few shillings or less and appealed to all ages and social classes. By the dawn of the twentieth century they were an integral part of the country's souvenir trade.

Early in the twentieth century W.H. Goss was joined by other manufacturers, mostly from the Stoke-on-Trent area, in the production of this china. Some, like H.T. Robinson of Arcadian china, put most of their efforts into this line of fancy-ware while others were content to 'dabble' to a greater or lesser degree. In their search to create new and novel models to extend their range they explored the many avenues opened to them by topical as well as historical events.

When war broke out in 1914 the whole of Europe was thrown into turmoil and Great Britain became a nation at war. The following four years saw a holocaust on a scale hitherto unknown. It was a war for which no-one was prepared and the enormity of which few people at the time fully appreciated. The men of Britain had gone off to war in their thousands, smiling, cheering and in high-spirits, only to return in their hundreds, broken, blinded, shell-shocked and gassed. Those at home were only able to look on in horror at this transformation, oblivious of the circumstances that had brought it about. For the Tommy reality was in the mud and horror of the trenches; for those at home the notion of reality was gleaned from the Press in which news of the war's progress was carefully refined to maintain its 'glorious' image.

The war was, and still is, unique. None before or since have been fought in such conditions and with such casualties. The advances in science and technology that had been made in the halcyon days of Victoria and Edward were now turned in their full force against mankind. The petrol engine gave rise to the tank, armoured car, submarine and aeroplane; the advances in munitions provided more destructive 'high' explosives and the devastating machine-gun with its incredible rate of fire, while new technology permitted the construction of the awe-inspiring Zeppelins and Dreadnoughts. All too slowly the destructive powers of these new weapons were appreciated and like some voracious animal with unlimited food supply, they devoured lives by the thousand before the Generals realised that the tactics employed in previous wars were now hopelessly outdated.

In their naivety the china manufacturers saw in the glut of artefacts of war suitable bases for their models and in the years during and following the war designed a large number of models of a martial character whose origins were on the battlefields of the First World War. From the guns, grenades and tanks of the land to the aircraft and airships of the air and the ships and submarines of the sea. From the people and personalities who fought to the memorials that now remain in their memory. Individually they appear to us now as interesting objects of a by-gone era, collectively they provide a fascinating and unique view of what is one of the most important events of the twentieth century.

2
The Figures

On Sunday June 28th 1914, while on an official visit to Sarajevo, the capital of the Austrian province of Bosnia-Herzegovina, Archduke Franz Ferdinand, heir to the throne of Austria-Hungary, and his wife, the Duchess Sophie, were assassinated by student Gavrilo Princip. Within six weeks every European nation was at or preparing for war.

When Britain declared war on Germany on August 3rd 1914, the news was greeted with wild excitement in all corners of the country. Patriotic fervour was at an all time high. Statesmen, politicians and the general population all agreed on three things... it would be short, glorious and victorious. Only in the mind of one of Britain's greatest soldiers and recently appointed Secretary of State for War, Lord Kitchener, did the reality of the situation rear its ugly head for he alone was to forecast a war lasting three years. In the event all were proved wrong. The war lasted for four long years and was fought in some of the worst conditions that soldiers have ever experienced. In its wake it left Europe shocked and shattered by the years of carnage and was to make a lasting impression on the morals and values of European society.

The war was essentially one of manpower. In the first few days some six million men were brought together in mortal combat. By the end of hostilities this number had increased to an estimated 65 million. Most of the European nations fielded armies consisting of men who had been conscripted. Germans, for instance, served two years from their seventeenth birthday and then continued with lesser degrees of training until their forty-fifth year. The French served for three years from their twentieth birthday and then continued training until their forty-fifth year. At any time during the intervening years they could be called to arms in the service of their country.

In contrast the British Army was a professional one based on voluntary enlistment. By taking the 'King's shilling' Thomas Atkins committed himself to a period of seven years in the Regular Army followed by a further five years in the Army Reserve. These forces were backed up by the recently formed Territorials, or 'weekend soldiers' as Kitchener disdainfully called them, who were charged with the defence of the homeland in the absence of the regulars.

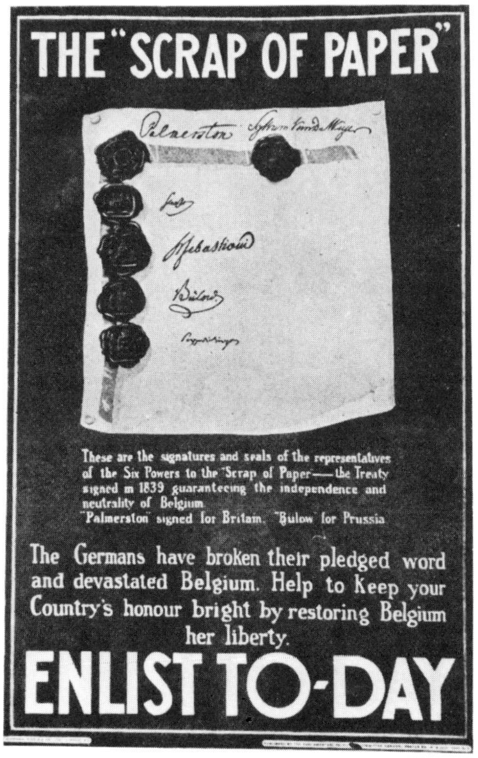

The 'Scrap of Paper' that Britain abided by - and brought about the death of a generation.

Recruiting poster designed by Alfred Leete which appeared first on the cover of the 'London Opinion' and later, in this modified version, on hoardings all over the country. Issued by the Parliamentary Recruiting Committee in September 1914, within a month half a million had answered their country's call.

For many recruits the army offered the security that was absent in civilian life. In return for their services they received three square meals a day, a roof over their heads, a bed and a pay packet. More than their counterparts in civvy street could rely upon in the difficult years at the turn of the century. Nevertheless they made a force that was respected wherever it went. What it lost in numbers it made up for in training and discipline. The 800,000 strong British Regular Army was, on paper at least, a 'contemptible little army' when compared with Germany's war strength of 5 million and France's 4 million.

In their initial advance Germany implemented a plan drawn up some ten years earlier by the then Chief of General Staff, Count Alfred von Schleiffen. Although deviated from in detail, the advance was, in general, as laid down in the original plans. German troops were to cross neutral Belgium and with a broad sweep, advance onto Paris. Once the capital had been secured and the country capitulated, troops could be transported to the Eastern Front where a much longer war was envisaged with the Russians. In the event Belgium refused passage to German troops and consequently was invaded on August 4th 1914. The defence, high in spirit, served only as a delaying tactic and the small Belgian army was soon overrun by the mighty German war machine. Rallying to this violation of neutrality Britain declared war on Germany and on 13th August contingents of the 100,000 strong British Expeditionary Force (BEF) left Southampton bound for Boulogne. The first to step ashore amid

Tommy driving a steamroller over the Kaiser. Arcadian china 120mm ins. 'To Berlin'.

David Lloyd George - Minister of Munitions and later Prime Minister. l. to r. Grafton China 140mm Reg. No. 659418 : Arcadian China 138mm ins. 'David Lloyd George: born Jan 17 1863'.

John Bull and his pack. l. to r. Arcadian China 127mm ins. 'Who said Germans' : Carlton China 122mm. John Bull and his dog : Alexandra china 127mm ins. 'Duggy Haig'.

George V. l. to r. Shelley China 125mm : Arcadian china 140mm : Grafton china 133mm.

Three models from a series brought out by the Arcadian factory in 1916.
l. to r. 'Model of Tommy in Bayonet attack' 127mm. Reg. No. 658676 : 'Model of Tommy throwing hand grenade' 123mm Reg. No. 658681 : Soldier standing to attention 133mm.

Willow Art China. l. to r. Sailor 130mm ins. 'Our Brave Defender' : Nurse 133mm ins. 'A Soldier's Friend' : Soldier 130mm ins. 'Our Brave Defender'.
Three of the earliest models made in the war. Designed soon after hostilities commenced and on sale by Christmas 1914.

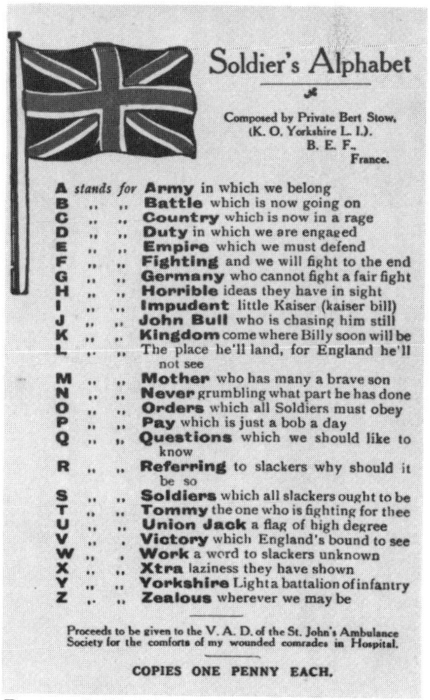

Soldier's Alphabet

Composed by Private Bert Stow,
(K. O. Yorkshire L. I.).
B. E. F.,
France.

A *stands for* **Army** in which we belong
B ,, ,, **Battle** which is now going on
C ,, ,, **Country** which is now in a rage
D ,, ,, **Duty** in which we are engaged
E ,, ,, **Empire** which we must defend
F ,, ,, **Fighting** and we will fight to the end
G ,, ,, **Germany** who cannot fight a fair fight
H ,, ,, **Horrible** ideas they have in sight
I ,, ,, **Impudent** little Kaiser (kaiser bill)
J ,, ,, **John Bull** who is chasing him still
K ,, ,, **Kingdom** come where Billy soon will be
L ,, ,, The place he'll land, for England he'll not see
M ,, ,, **Mother** who has many a brave son
N ,, ,, **Never** grumbling what part he has done
O ,, ,, **Orders** which all Soldiers must obey
P ,, ,, **Pay** which is just a bob a day
Q ,, ,, **Questions** which we should like to know
R ,, ,, **Referring** to slackers why should it be so
S ,, ,, **Soldiers** which all slackers ought to be
T ,, ,, **Tommy** the one who is fighting for thee
U ,, ,, **Union Jack** a flag of high degree
V ,, . **Victory** which England's bound to see
W ,, . **Work** a word to slackers unknown
X ,, ,, **Xtra** laziness they have shown
Y ,, ,, **Yorkshire** Light a battalion of infantry
Z ,, ,, **Zealous** wherever we may be

Proceeds to be given to the V. A. D. of the St. John's Ambulance Society for the comforts of my wounded comrades in Hospital.

COPIES ONE PENNY EACH.

Postcard: 'Soldier's Alphabet'

'Model of Tommy on sentry duty' Arcadian china Reg. No. 657213.

Carlton soldiers. l. to r. 'Are we downhearted? NO!' 153mm with a verse from 'Tipperary' on his back : Soldier wearing a bandolier 122mm : Scottish soldier 144mm Reg. No. 651139, registered in September 1915. It is probable that the other two appeared about the same time.

Grafton china. l. 'Over the top' 117mm No. 433 : r. 'The Bomb thrower' 133mm No. 425. The only models to feature steel helmets and, surprisingly, the only full length figures made by this factory.

a tumultuous welcome from the local inhabitants were companies of the Argyll & Sutherland Highlanders, in the days that followed troops poured into the town which rapidly took on the appearance of an army camp. As the new arrivals marched past the Scotsmen's barracks they were met with the old football cry, 'Are we downhearted?' to which the answer always came as a thunderous roar, 'No...o...o...o!'.

The townspeople took up the cry and shouted it to troops as they passed; the men of Buckinghamshire added their own: 'Shall we win?' to which the long drawn out answer was 'Ye...e...e...s!'

This force was under the overall command of Sir John French and was made up of two Army Corps under Sir Douglas Haig and Sir Horace Smith-Dorrien (Lieut-General Sir James Grieson had been the original corps commander but had died of natural causes en route). When the force had landed the long march to meet the enemy began. In high spirits the troops marched through the towns and villages of Northern France and Belgium, spurred on by cheering local inhabitants who thronged the wayside. No-one had any conception of what was to follow.

The Great Armies of the European nations met outside the small Belgian mining town of Mons. After a night of heavy fighting in which the British proved their worth, the commander of the French Armies, Marshal Joffre whom the British were supporting, called for a retreat. Reluctantly General French complied and the historic retreat from Mons began. For the next month the BEF fought a rearguard action as the German steamroller rolled on. When the advance was finally halted, only 50 miles from Paris, out came the entrenching tools and down went the troops. Like a vast army of moles the armies went underground. Over the following months a pattern of warfare was established that lasted until the final year of the war: a line of trenches, stretching for some 200 miles, from Ostend in the north to Belfort in the south, divided Central Europe.

By December, following the battles of Mons, Le Cateau, 1st Ypres and the Aisne, casualties were already beyond imagination. German losses stood at an estimated 700,000, French 850,000, while the BEF, that contemptible little army, had virtually ceased to exist. Battalions,

Postcard portrait of the country's most distinguished soldier and father of the modern army, Horatio Herbert Kitchener, 1st Earl of Khartoum and Aspal. Appointed Secretary of State for War in August 1914, he was killed in the sinking of HMS Hampshire off the Orkneys in June 1916.

General Joffre - the 'Papa' of the French army. Trained as a military engineer, he formulated the plans for the defence of France against German invasion. After the disasters of Verdun in 1916 he was replaced by General Nivelle.

Silk cigarette card of General, later Field Marshal, Sir Douglas Haig. Originally a Corps Commander of the BEF in 1914 he replaced Sir John French as Commander in Chief in 1916. Apart from the reference to him on the bulldog inscribed 'Duggy Haig' he seems to have escaped the notice of the china manufacturers!

Field Marshal Lord Kitchener. l. to r. Grafton china 109mm with inscription on reverse : Unmarked 120mm : Carlton china 140mm with inscription : Grafton china 132mm. with Flags of the Allies crest. Unmarked 120mm.

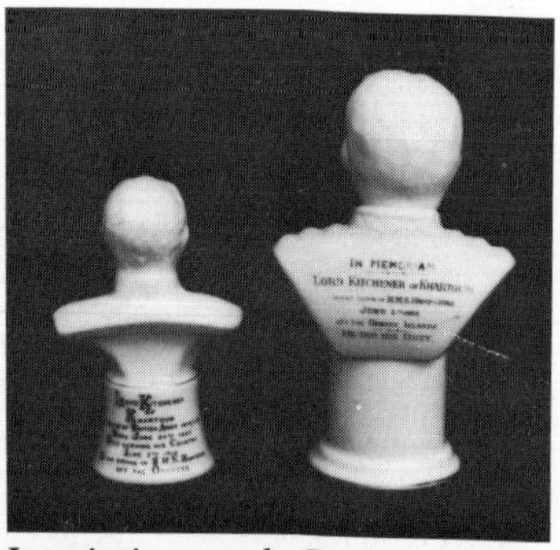

Inscriptions on l. Grafton and r. Carlton busts of Lord Kitchener. Many busts carry inscriptions detailing important events of the person's life.

King Albert of Belgium - ascended the throne in December 1909; resisted passage of German troops in 1914 and saw his country overrun. Later he commanded the Allied Army in Flanders.

Grafton china: 'Foch' 125mm : 'Allenby' 140mm : 'Albert' 122mm.

Marshal Foch - distinguished soldier and leader. He reached retiring age in 1916 but remained on the active list. Became generalissimo of the Allied forces on the Western Front and led the Peace delegation that received Germany's surrender on 11th November 1918.

originally a thousand strong, now stood in hundreds, some even in tens. Over two-thirds of the original 100,000 had become casualties. To supplement our dwindling forces many Territorial units waived the required six months notice of overseas duty and volunteered for immediate posting to France. By Christmas twenty-two Territorial Battalions (approximately 20,000 men) were in France and by February they had been joined by a further twenty-six. With the regular forces so depleted it was apparent that steps would have to be taken to raise another fighting force. From the beginning of September widespread appeals had been made for volunteers for 'Kitchener's New Army'. The response was beyond all expectation. In the first month 500,000 signed on and took the King's shilling. By the end of the year over 1 million had enlisted.

The problems of housing, feeding, clothing and training such a large force were enormous and for many of the 'New Army' men it was some time before they were fully equipped. With so few regular officers and N.C.O.s left to lead and train the men suitable candidates had to be found from amongst the volunteers. Officers who had long since retired were called back to lead the new battalions. What they lacked in training they made up for in enthusiasm and patriotism. In many parts of the country, towns, cities, firms, trades and businesses took recruitment into their own hands: forming battalions from their local lads and then presenting them to the nation. Many of these 'Pals' battalions were to suffer appalling losses on the Western Front.

In January 1916, with the supply of volunteers almost exhausted, the government finally introduced conscription. Under the 1st Military Service Act, all single men between the ages of 18 and 41 were required to enlist. The Second Act in May included married men. By 1918 eight million men had enlisted.

As the war continued, the generals of both sides produced and executed their plans for breaching the enemies' front line. Reluctant to change they stuck tenaciously to the tactics that had been tried and tested in the wars of the nineteenth century, often with a total disregard for the technological advances that had been made and their consequent effect on warfare. General French who was replaced by Haig in December 1915 as C-in-C admitted, when writing in 1919..... "It is easy to be wise after the event but I cannot help wondering why none of us realised what the most modern rifle, the machine gun, motor traction, the aeroplane and wireless telegraphy would bring about...."*

The war became one of attrition, but at tremendous cost. Thousands upon thousands of the prime of Europe's manhood were thrown into the mincing machine. Success or failure was to be measured in the relative number of casualties incurred and inflicted. Advances in yards often cost the lives of thousands of men and the losses of the early months of the war pale to insignificance when compared to those of later years... the Battle of Loos, October 1915: British casualties 50,000, French 190,000, German 140,000; Verdun February-June 1916: French casualties 315,000, German 281,000; The First Battle of the Somme, July-November 1916: British casualties 420,000 (60,000 on the first day), French 200,000, Germans about 450,000; Passchendaele, July-November 1917: British 300,000, German 200,000 .... and so the numbers go on. Whole battalions virtually ceased to exist; their numbers decimated by the murderous fire of the machine gun. Pals who had joined up together in the same burst of patriotic fervour, died within yards of each other. The cavalry, the pride of the nineteenth century was now as incongruous to trench warfare as the bow and arrow. The few charges that took place in the war almost without exception ended in a field deep with the dead and dying horses and men spread over the mud and barbed wire of no-man's land.

*1914: Field Marshal Viscount French of Ypres : pub. Constable 1919.

Vice-Admiral Sir David Beatty commanded the Battlecruisers at the Battle of Jutland. As 1st Sea-Lord he received the surrender of the German High Seas Fleet at Rosyth in November 1918.

With the Regular and Territorial Forces badly depleted it became vital that a new force was raised. Millions of civilians joined the ranks and became 'New Army Men'.

Arcadian china. l. 'Model of Drummer Boy' 143mm Reg. No. 658737 : Bugle Boy 141mm. Although only the Drummer Boy was registered it is considered that they were both brought out at the same time and sold as a pair.

Arcadian china. l. 'Model of Scotch (sic) soldier' 140mm Reg. No. 657734 r. 'Model of French soldier' 134mm Reg. No. 657733.

Arcadian china: Model of Belgian Soldier. 83mm

Arcadian china. l. 'Model of Tommy firing a machine gun' 99mm Reg. No. 657214 : r. 'Model of despatch rider' 125mm Reg. No. 657737

Grafton china 81mm No. 85. Model of American soldier. An early model from the factory, found in black, white, and painted with stars and stripes.

Although campaigns were fought in other theatres of war - in Gallipoli and Egypt against the Turks and in the German colonies in South Africa, it was on the Western Front in France that the generals thought the war would be won or lost. Germany, at great cost was subjected to a war on two fronts and it was not until 1918 when Russia, torn apart by internal revolution, made her peace with Germany, that she was able to concentrate her forces on the Western Front.

The British Dominions had been committed along with their Motherland from the beginning and all made great efforts to raise volunteer forces. Canada sent an army to France, Newfoundland a battalion. Australia and New Zealand sent troops to Egypt and Indian troops, perhaps suffering the most, found themselves in the alien environments of Northern France.

Arcadian china l. 'Model of British cavalry soldier' 120mm. Reg. No. 658680.
r. 'Model of Russian Cossack' 122mm. Reg. No. 658684.

More than a match for horses and men. The war was still very much one of horse-power - carrying, pulling and fighting. Movement for men and animals alike in the deep mud of the battlefields was at best difficult and at worst impossible. Many just sank out of sight.

1 The British Bulldog and her pups defy the German Eagle. The colonies became involved when Britain declared war.

2 Recruiting poster, 'Women of Britain say GO!'

3 'You've not said how I've growed, Daddy!' from the painting by Thomas Henry. These post-cards were issued by the National Institute for the blind. Thousands returned home with their bodies mutilated and damaged beyond imagination. Gas in particular had terribly debilitating effects, attacking skin and lungs as well as the eyes. Mustard gas, chlorine and phosgene were all used at various times.

1

2

3

1

2

3

4

5

6

1. Soldier in flat cap and puttees 153mm. On the base are the words of the old football cry: Are we downhearted? NO!' - which was shouted as the troops of the British Expeditionary Force disembarked at Boulogne in August 1914. On his back is a verse from the marching song: 'It's a long way to Tipperary'.

2. 'Yours to a cinder Old Bill' 138mm. Carlton. Bruce Bairnsfather's cartoon character featured in the 'Bystander' and 'Fragments from France' magazines and raised many official eyebrows for his unmilitary demeanour - nevertheless he was closer to reality.

3. l. Scotland for ever' 116mm. Shelley 402
r. 'Vive la France' 114mm. Shelley 406.
Two models from a range of patriotic figures brought out by the Shelley factory in early 1920s. Their link with the war is tenuous although they are usually included in Great War collections.

4. L. to r. Bust inscribed 'Territorial' 95mm. Arcadian. Bust inscribed 'Tommy Atkins' 91mm. Arcadian. Bust of sailor inscribed 'HMS Dreadnought - The Handy Man' 91mm. Carlton.
The soldier has a verse from 'It's the soldiers of the King' on his back.

5. L. 'Albert, King of Belgium '; 133mm. Savoy. Crest: Belgium. Inscription: on reverse: 'Belgium invaded by Germany August 4th 1914. Capital occupied August 20th 1914'.
R. 'George V'

6. Bulldog with Union Jack draped on back 63mm. Alexandra; ins. 'Duggy Haig'. Surprisingly the only reference to Field Marshal Sir Douglas Haig in Crested China, upon whose shoulders responsibility for the 1916 Somme offensive rested.

Women at War 1914-1918. A modern poster from the Imperial War Museum showing various occupations taken up by women during the war.

Carlton china. Model of munitions worker 140mm. Reg. No. 662105 ins. 'Doing her bit - shells and more shells'.

At home, life progressed as normally as it could for a country largely devoid of its manpower. Industry, trades and businesses had to continue and into the breach stepped the women of Britain. Jobs that had hitherto been solely a male preserve were now taken up by women. They took to the buses and factories, they became chauffeurs and drivers; they donned uniforms and patrolled the streets, maintaining law and order. They took over when their husbands were called off to war, carrying on the small businesses, delivering food, coal, etc. Many contributed directly to the war effort by working in munitions factories. In this industry in particular the work was long, arduous and dangerous. Nevertheless there was never a shortage of women who did their bit for the Country.

Others volunteered for nursing duties and were sent abroad where they found themselves in unimaginable conditions. Serving in the hospitals and casualty stations a few miles behind the front lines, they tended as best they could to wounds of hitherto unexperienced severity. Those nurses who served in the hospitals and convalescent homes on British soil had no easier task. With medical knowledge and medicines so limited, much depended on the care and attention these nurses could give to their patients. No medicines on earth could help the Tommy to live without his sight, his legs or his arms.

From the outset the Red Cross and St. John's Ambulance Brigade sent detachments of doctors, nurses and ambulances to the war zones. Throughout the war, often in very dangerous conditions, they pieced together and mended the shattered bodies that had so callously been torn apart.

When the war ended the survivors returned home. Jobs had to be found, families reformed and lives had to be lived without loved ones. For those that had played their part the horror that they had experienced was firmly imprinted on their minds and would linger with them to their dying days.

A Crested China First Aid post. l. to r. Carlton china 150mm : Arcadian china 92mm. Reg. No. 658674 ins. 'Model of nurse and wounded Tommy' : Arcadian china 134mm ins. 'Soldiers friend'.

The China

It was inevitable that the china manufacturers would seek to commemorate some of the personalities and people who fought in the war. Although many would consider that they have an inherent sadness the models of the figures are amongst the cream of Heraldic ware. Many are quite accurate in their detail, some are artistic, few are comic. Models are found of full length figures and of head and shoulders busts.

The war was only a few months old when Hewitt & Leadbeater (Willow China) were manufacturing models of a soldier and sailor, suitably inscribed, 'Our Brave Defender' and a model of a nurse, aptly called 'A Soldiers Friend'. At some later date they added a model of an airman which is found in two varieties, one with his arms at his side, the other with his right arm bent and clasping a recently awarded medal.

H.T. Robinson (Arcadian China), in characteristic form, explored many of the avenues opened up by the war, making no fewer than sixteen full figures and twelve busts of military personnel in various realistic and unrealistic poses. It appears that most of his models were inspired by the Somme offensive of 1916 - Britain's 'Big Push' - for the great majority were registered in the latter half of the year when the offensive closed in November. Models were made of a soldier at attention; in a sentry box (Reg. No. 657213); firing a machine gun (Reg. No. 657214); throwing a grenade (Reg. No. 658681); riding a motorbike (Reg. No. 657737); in a bayonet attack (Reg. No. 658676); on horseback (Reg. No. 658680); a Scottish soldier (Reg. No. 657734) and even a very imaginative model of a Tommy driving a steamroller over the Kaiser, hopefully inscribed: 'TO BERLIN'. It is a mystery as to why this model was not registered - it certainly deserved to be - and consequently no accurate dating can be given for it. Models of a Drummer Boy (Reg. No. 658737) and a Bugler were possibly designed and sold as a pair although as the latter was not registered it may have been an afterthought.

Our allies were not forgotten and are represented by models of a French soldier (Reg. No. 657733), an Australian soldier (Reg. No. 768685) and a Russian Cossack on horseback (Reg. No. 658684), all in their characteristic uniforms. Two models of sailors were made. The earlier, registered in October 1915 (Reg. No. 652243) was one of Robinson's first military models, and is of a sailor standing with his hands on his hips while the other registered in December 1916 shows a sailor winding a capstan. It is probable that the former was linked to the action involving a submarine E4 a model of which was also registered on that day (see Chapter 7). Also found from this factory is a model of a nurse inscribed, 'Soldiers Friend' and a fine model of a nurse tending a wounded Tommy (Reg. No. 658674) which even shows a roll of bandage and a pair of scissors. Many of these must have had a short production run for they are among some of the scarcest pieces to be found, only the machine gunner and despatch rider seem to have survived the war, the others being taken off the market soon after their appearance.

Wiltshaw and Robinson (Carlton China), in patriotic vein, inscribed many of their models with well known catch phrases. Their models of soldiers include two English Tommies and one Scottish. The larger of the two English soldiers has 'Are we downhearted? NO!' on his base and a verse from the marching song, 'It's a long way to Tipperary', on his back. The Scottish soldier (Reg. No. 651139) sporting kilt and glengarry, dates from September 1915. It is probable that all three models date from

Arcadian china. l. Sailor 129mm Reg. No. 652243. One of this factory's earliest military models of the war, registered in October 1915 with a model of the E4 submarine. Probably linked with the report of the dramatic rescue in which this submarine was involved (see Chapter 7) : 'Model of sailor winding capstan' 110mm Reg. No. 658675.

Old Bill plate - 'When the 'ell is it going to be strawberry' Grimwades china. 'Made by the girls of Staffordshire during the winter of 1917/18 when the "Boys" were in the trenches fighting for Liberty and Civilization'.

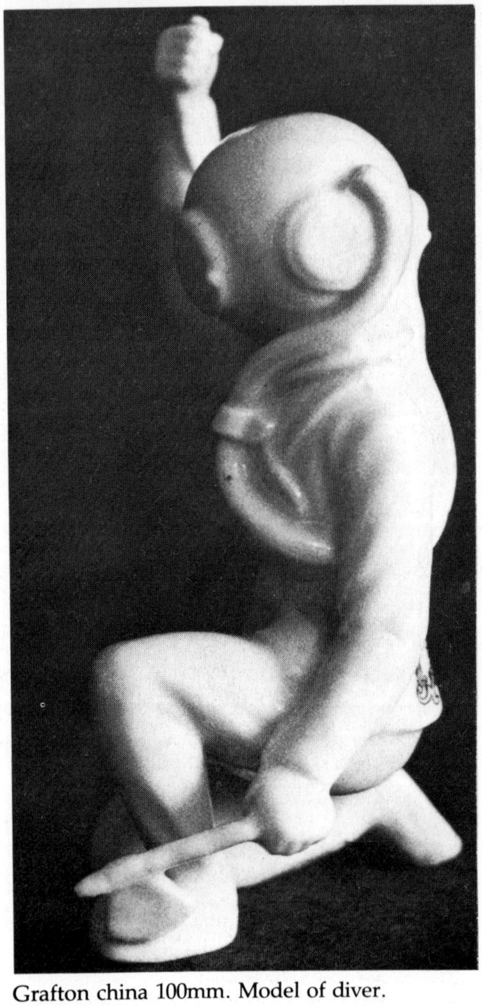

Grafton china 100mm. Model of diver.

the same time although why only one should be registered remains a mystery. Bruce Bairnsfathers' cartoon character, 'Old Bill', who appeared in 'The Bystander' magazine and later in 'Fragments from France', was modelled as a dour, mufflered figure with the inscription, 'Yours to a cinder Old Bill'. Bairnsfathers' dugout, which appeared in a spoof advertisement in the first volume of 'Fragments from France' inspired a model registered at the Patent Office in June 1917, and which is described in the Register as 'Boy in Hut' (Reg. No. 660613). The original name of 'Shrapnel View' has been changed to 'Shrapnel Villa' and a lonely little head has been put inside, looking out. Unique to this factory are the models of a nurse and munitions worker (Reg. No. 662105), the latter carrying the inscription, 'Doing her bit, shells and more shells'. Their sole contribution to the naval arm is a model of a squatting sailor holding a submarine and frequently found with the inscription, 'We've got "U" well in hand', on his hat. The pipe in the sailors mouth is turned downwards in characteristic naval fashion.

A.B. Jones & Sons (Grafton China) made few full length figures confining themselves in the main to busts of personalities, however, their two models of soldiers in trench coats and steel helmets are amongst the finest there are. One is of a soldier throwing a hand grenade and is inscribed 'The Bomb Thrower' (Grafton 425) while the other shows him climbing out of a trench inscribed 'Over the Top' (Grafton 403). The model of a squatting sailor, found with the word 'Victory' on his cap, is very similar to the Carlton one. In addition to these they made imaginative models of a 'British Territorial Bulldog' (Grafton 262) and what appears to be an American soldier smoking an enormous fat cigar (Grafton 85). However if the factory numbers are to be trusted then these models appeared well before the war. Last but not least they made an exquisite model of a diver, complete with helmet, suit and axe.

Wileman & Co's (Shelley China) only contributions date from the early twenties and consist of three models whose link with the Great War is tenuous. Their model of a Scottish soldier, carrying bagpipes and sporting a kilt and busby is inscribed, 'Scotland for Ever' (Shelley 402). The model of Britannia, complete with gold helmet and shield is inscribed, 'Rule Britannia' (Shelley 403) while their model of Marianne, the French equivalent of Britannia, has 'Vive la France' inscribed (Shelley 406). As they appear to have been part of a line of figures all made at the same time (and which includes Welsh and Irish representatives) they are not considered to have a direct relation with the war, yet are apt and interesting pieces to include in a collection should the collector be fortunate enough to acquire them.

Birks, Rawlins & Co (Savoy China) only modelled two figures, both of which stand on a circular base. One is of a Scottish soldier, the other a nurse which is found inscribed, 'Edith Cavell'.

With the exception of the Arcadian factory the china manufacturers confined themselves to producing models of busts of personalities. Lord Kitchener, Secretary of State for War and Father of the modern army, is commemorated in Arcadian, Savoy, Shelley and two Grafton models, one of which commemorates his death on the HMS Hampshire in 1916. Sir John French, commander of the BEF is found in Grafton and Shelley china and General Joffre, the 'Papa' of the French army, in Grafton, Shelley and Arcadian. Sir Edmund Allenby, commander of the Egyptian Expeditionary Force in 1917 is found in a single Grafton bust as is Marshall Foch, the generalissimo of the Allied Armies in 1918

From fact to fancy. Sandbagged dugouts provided a sanctuary from the intensive artillery bombardments. Bruce Bairnsfather was inspired to put his dug-out up 'For Let' in a spoof advertisement that appeared in Vol. 1 of 'Fragments from France'. The Carlton factory took the idea, changed the name, added a figure and registered their model in June 1917. The three models show the different wording used. The Savoy model is very rare. Carlton China 85mm Reg. No. 660613 : Savoy China 115mm.

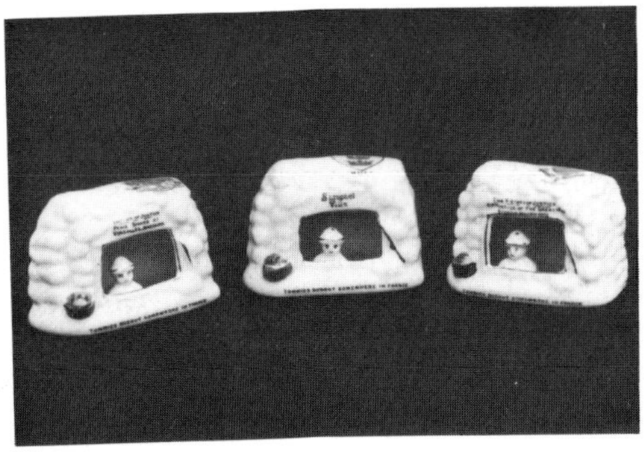

Where to Live—[ADVT.]

IN ONE OF THE CHOICEST LOCALITIES OF NORTHERN FRANCE.

TO BE LET (three minutes from German trenches), this attractive an

WELL-BUILT DUG-OUT,

containing one reception-kitchen-bedroom and UP-TO-DATE FUN HOLE (4ft. by 3ft.), all modern inconveniences, including gas and water This desirable Residence stands one foot above water level, commanding as excellent view of the enemy trenches.

EXCELLENT SHOOTING (SNIPE AND DUCK).

—Particulars of the late Tenant, Room 6, Base Hospital, Boulogne.

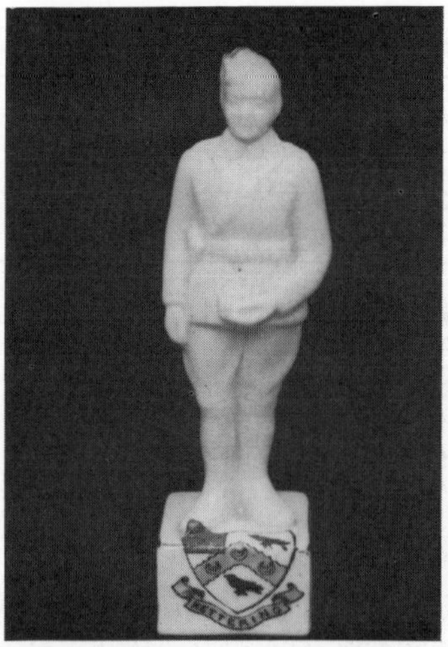

Willow Art china. 140mm. Models of airmen. One clasping a newly awarded medal.

and leader of the Peace delegation that met to sign the armistice on 11th November 1918. Lord Jellicoe, commander of the British Fleet is modelled in Grafton and Arcadian china while Lord David Beatty, commander of the British Battle cruiser fleet is commemorated in Savoy and Regis china.

John Travers Cornwell, the Boy 1st Class of HMS Chester who was posthumously awarded the Victoria Cross for his action at the Battle of Jutland, is commemorated in Savoy China. Although mortally wounded early in the action he steadfastly remained at his post until the action was over. This 'splendid instance of devotion', as it was described by Admiral Beatty, earned him nationwide admiration and his body, which had been buried privately, was exhumed and reinterred with full naval honours. Funds raised by public subscription went to present every elementary school in Britain with a special portrait of him while numerous beds bearing his name were endowed to hospitals and hostels around the country.

Busts of Sailors are found, variously inscribed with 'HMS Queen Elizabeth' (Arcadian); 'Dreadnought' (Carlton) and 'HMS Lion' or 'HMS Iron Duke' (Savoy).

An Arcadian bust of 'Tommy Atkins' carries a verse from the song, 'Tis the soldiers of the King my boy', inscribed on his back. This factory also made a very rare model of a Belgian soldier and a grotesque model of a soldier wearing a gas mask (Reg. No. 657652). It is easy to see why the latter is so scarce - only the ardent collector could steel himself to give it shelf space!

Gas was just one of the horrors that the war brought. It was first used against the French at the Battle of Ypres in April 1915 when a 'strange green vapour' rolled down onto an unsuspecting 45th Algerian Division

Arcadian china 'Model of New Gas Mask' 95mm. Reg. No. 657652. Registered in September 1916 when the Battle of the Somme was in full swing, is particularly scarce. Can you wonder why?

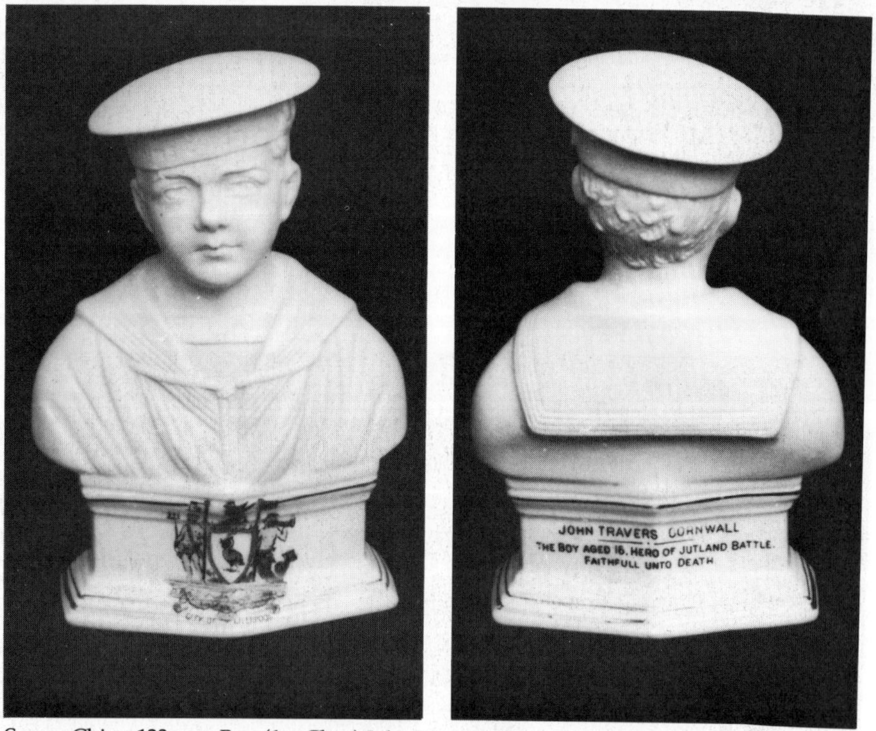

Savoy China 123mm. Boy (1st Class) John Travers Cornwell of HMS Chester who was awarded a posthumous Victoria Cross for his action during the Battle of Jutland. Although wounded and with most of his guns crew dead he remained at his post throughout the action.

Steel helmets: Top: l. Arcadian 70mm. Reg. No. 657650 ins. 'Model of steel helmet' : r. Willow China 78mm. ins. 'Tommies steel helmet'. Steel helmets were introduced in 1916 when it became apparent that the majority of casualties suffered head wounds. In the early days, when they were in short supply, troops leaving the front line gave theirs to those entering.
Bottom: l. Savoy China 84mm. ins. 'Model of French Helmet as worn by the dauntless French Poilu' : r. Porcelle 85mm. The French helmet was based on the Adrian pattern and although more comfortable to wear than the British 'Tin hat', afforded less protection. The Porcelle model resembles a German helmet although it does not carry any identification.

Peaked caps: l. to r. Devonia Art China 83mm. Carlton China 89mm. ins. 'Territorials Hat', Swan China 69mm.

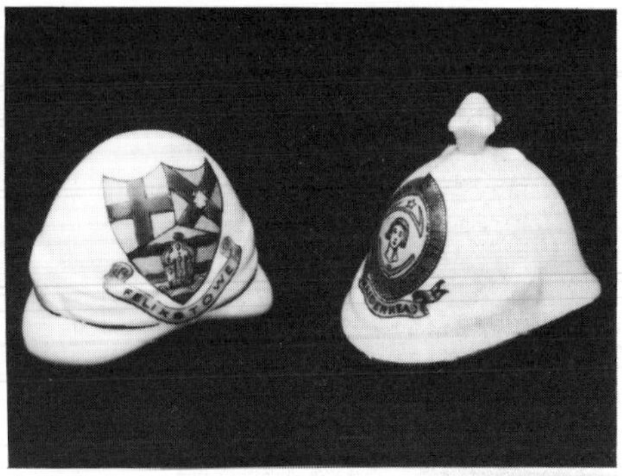

l. Pith helmet unmarked 63mm. r. Military helmet Willow Art China 64mm. The latter is frequently referred to as a 'pickelhaube' - the name given to the German helmet worn at the beginning of the war. It is more probably based on a pre-war British helmet.

Forage caps: l. to r. Shelley China 90mm. No. 176. : Carlton China 85mm, Arcadian 96mm.

Colonial hats: top l. to r. Savoy China 90mm. ins. 'Model of Anzacs Cap'; Carlton China 98mm. ins. 'Colonial Hat'; Carlton China 80mm. ins. 'Anzacs for Ever'. Bottom l. Savoy China 80mm. ins. 'Model of New Zealand Hat'; r. Arcadian China 89mm. ins. 'Model of Colonial Hat' Reg. No. 657738.

It is said that when the Australian and New Zealand troops arrived at Gallipoli they both wore their bush hats in the same, peaked manner. For ease of recognition the Australians changed the style of theirs.

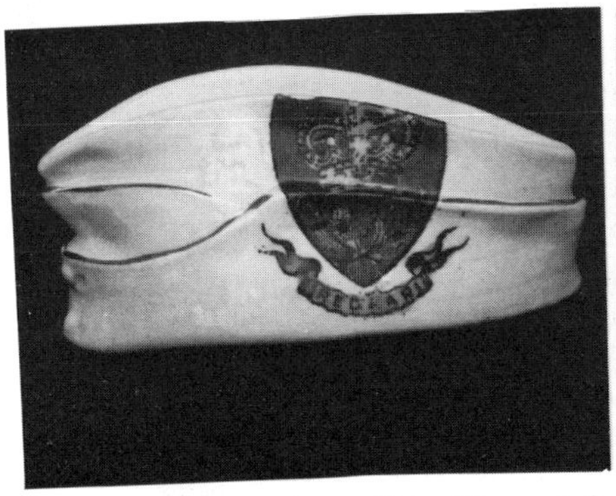

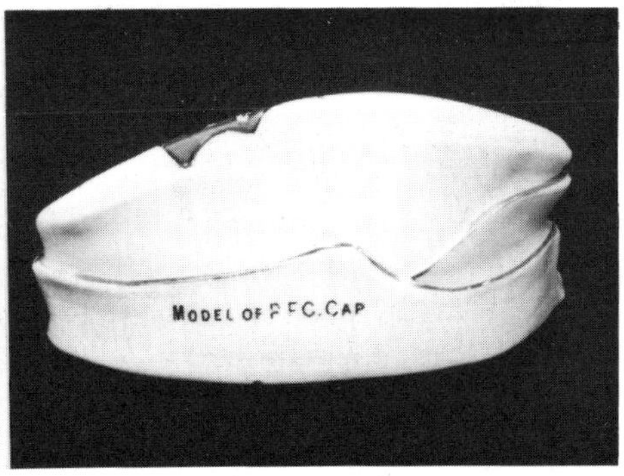

'Model of RFC cap' Savoy China 80mm. A fine and well detailed piece with the RFC badge in relief.

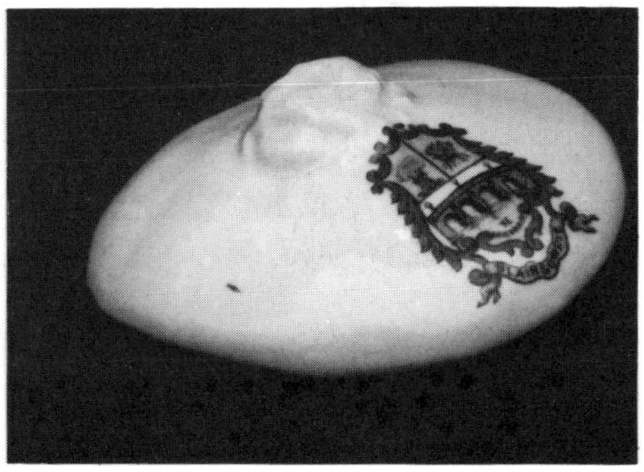

'Model of Balmoral Bonnet' Rex China 80mm.

Tents: Top l. Triood 85mm. r. Grafton 63mm. Bottom l. Shelley china 341 100mm. Reg. No. 664306 ins. 'Blighty is the place for me-e-e'. Soldier sitting at entrance to his tent playing a concertina. (Compare with design sketch in Appendix i). r. Willow Art 70mm.

Arcadian China 105mm. Reg. No. 657215. ins. 'Model of Tommies Hut'.

leaving chaos in its wake. During the war all sides experimented with chlorine, mustard gas, phosgene and tear gas with varying degrees of success. Face masks to combat the choking, lung scorching effects of gas soon appeared. The first were simply cotton soaked in chemicals and placed over the mouth, more efficient but nevertheless debilitating models followed. Stifling, inhibitors of speech and vision they at least prevented the deadly gas reaching the lungs. The model appears to be wearing an early model of a French respirator consisting of a cloth bag, pulled over the face and having ground glass eyepieces and filter box.

Amongst the many subjects modelled in china is a group labelled 'Tommies Kit'. This includes those things that the Tommy would wear, carry and live in. Caps and helmets were made in profusion and in a great variety of styles by a large number of factories. Models are found of peaked caps, Australian hats, Colonial hats. New Zealand hats, French helmets, trench helmets (introduced in 1916 when it became apparent that the majority of deaths in trench warfare were caused from head injuries), Glengarrys, Airmans hats, military helmets, forage caps, Pith helmets and even a model of a Despatch riders cap with goggles. Some date from before the war and many carry an inscription.

Bell tents that provided cover for many a soldier were made by a number of factories. Shelley china produced a splendid model of a soldier sitting outside his tent, playing a concertina. It is inscribed, 'Blighty is the place for me...e...e...e' (Shelley 341; Reg. No. 664307) and was one of the few pieces to be registered by this factory. A model of a 'Tommy's Hut' is found in Arcadian china (Reg. No. 657215).

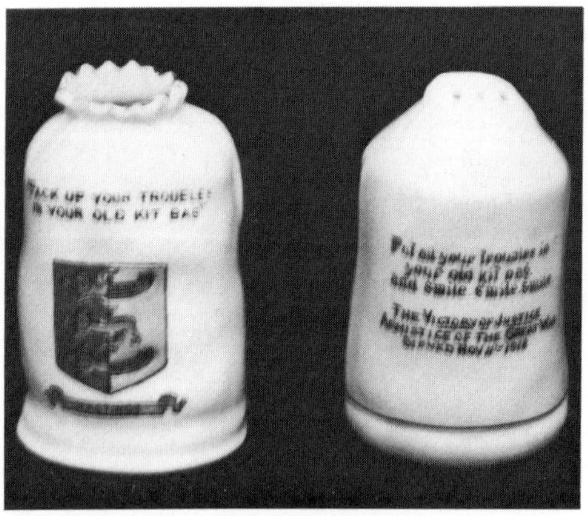

Kit bags: Carlton China 78mm. Two varieties with open and closed neck insc. 'Pack up your troubles in your old kit bag' and Peace inscription.

Two varieties of kit-bags are found, one with an open neck, the other with the string pulled tight. Both are inscribed with the line, 'Pack up your troubles in your old kit-bag'. Models of a Trench dagger (Reg. No. 657649); trench lamp (Reg. No. 657696) water bottle (Reg. No. 657695) and sandbag (Reg. No. 658678) are found in Arcadian china. Equipment such as the dagger and trench lamp were not army issue. Many enterprising private firms jumped on the bandwagon and manufactured a range of 'Trench goods' which the Tommy and his wellwishers were encouraged to buy.

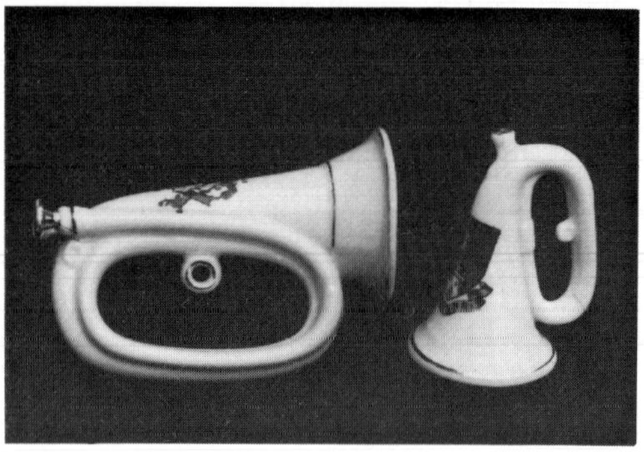

Bugles: l. Shelley China 115mm No. 354. r. Pearl Arms China 80mm.

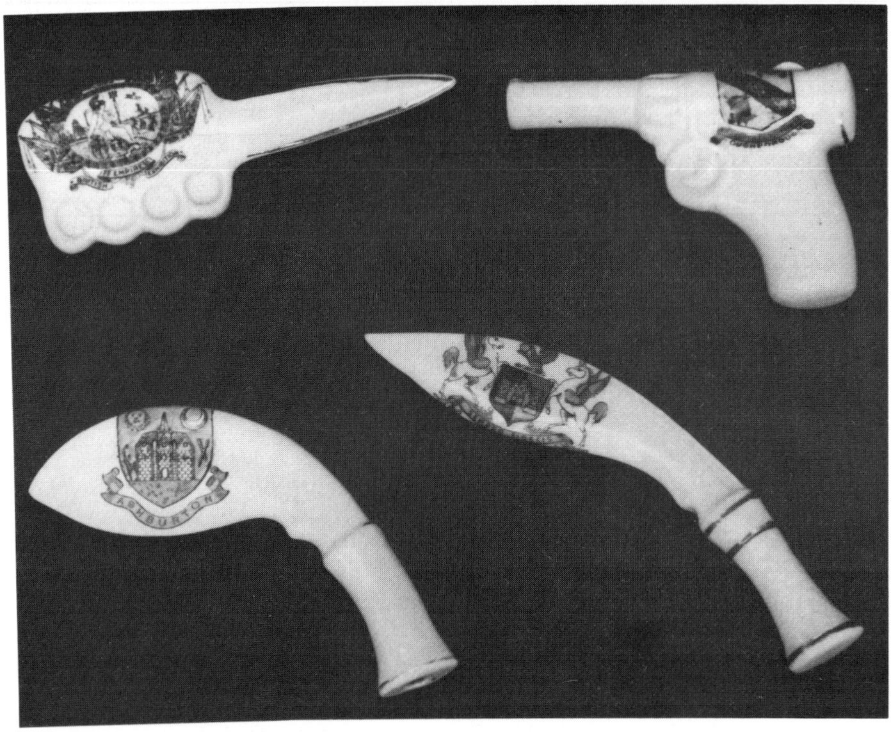

Arcadian China. Top l. 'Model of trench dagger' 115mm Reg. No. 657649. r. Model of handgun 90mm. Reg. No. 657653. A heterogeneous model although with characteristics of a Very pistol used to fire flares. Bottom l. 'Model of Ghurkha knife' 120mm Reg. No. 657698. r. Kukri Unmarked 139mm

Tommies Kit: top l. to r. Telescope. Florentine 76mm.: 'Model of pair of field glasses' Arcadian China 69mm.: Trench lamp Arcadian 72mm. Reg. No. 657696. Middle: Drum. Shelley China 66mm x 26mm.: Binoculars. Shelley China 343 92mm.: Drum. Shelley 64 x 59mm. Bottom: Water bottle. Arcadian China 72mm. Reg. No. 657695. Clip of Bullets. Arcadian China 69mm. Reg. No. 657648. Sandbag. Arcadian China 77mm. Reg. No. 658678.

Trench lamp. A non-regulation issue, fully collapsible trench lamp.

3
Armoured Cars and Tanks

Savoy China 131mm. Reg. No. 652656.

Motor cars had made their appearance in the closing years of the nineteenth century. By the time that war broke out the efficiency and reliability of the internal combustion engine, on which these machines depended, had improved tremendously and it was only a matter of time before they were adapted for a military role. Although some experimental armoured cars had been produced in the first decade of the century it was not until the war years, when the situation created a demand, that men turned their attention to their development and use. As a result the armoured car evolved, followed by the tank.

The first armoured cars that appeared in 1914 were modified fast touring cars. Chassis of various manufacturers, including Wolseley, Talbot, Lanchester, Delauney-Belleville and Rolls-Royce were requisitioned and hastily armoured, armed and strengthened so as to be fit for war. These cars were open topped and armed with a machine-gun which was able to fire over the side armour. Further development, on the basis of bitter experience, was rapid and by December the first cars with completely enclosed turrets and all-round fire appeared on the roads in France.

In the first month of hostilities, as the German Armies swept through Belgium, the armoured cars of a Naval Brigade and a Royal Naval Air Service squadron were transported across the channel to help in the defence of Antwerp. From their base in Dunkirk these and others of the Belgian army were used for hit and run attacks on the advancing enemy. While conditions were favourable the armoured cars were in their element but as the armies dug in and ground conditions worsened, the cars were no longer able to fulfil their main role. Few armoured cars were used on the Western Front after the first winter and in early 1916 the cars of the RNAS squadron were transferred to other theatres of war where conditions remained suitable enough for their use. In Palestine, Egypt, Africa and on the Eastern Front they continued in use only returning to France in 1918 when the trench line had been broken and warfare returned to the fluid state.

On the Western Front it was their descendant, the tank, that took over part of their role in France. Due mainly to the efforts and foresight of such men as Colonel E.D. Swinton, Lieut-colonel Hankey and Winston

Modified 1st Admiralty Pattern Talbot. The first armoured cars were modified touring cars. The chassis for the six cars of this pattern, made in November 1914, were supplied by Clement-Talbot Ltd. of North Kensington, London. They were open-topped and carried two maxim machine guns which fired over the side armour.

One of the first enclosed Belgian Armoured Cars, the SAVA, appeared on the roads in October 1914 and boasted fully enclosed engine and crew compartment and domed turret which was open at the rear.

The crew of this Sava fought bravely but were finally overcome.

Shelley china. 124mm. No. 329. ins. 'Model of Armoured Car'.

Churchill, then First Lord of the Admiralty, a Landship committee was formed in early 1915. It was headed by the then Director of Naval Construction, Mr. Tennyson d'Eyncourt and its main objectives were to explore the possibility of an armoured car that would climb a vertical step of 4ft. 6ins. and cross a trench ten foot wide. The prototype 'landship' first appeared in September 1915 when No. 1 Lincoln machine rumbled across Hatfield Park, its six cylinder Daimler engine dragging it along at an incredible four miles per hour. A modified version of the tank, affectionately called 'Little Willie' underwent trials on September 19th but even while it was being put through its paces work had already begun on another machine built to a design by a Major Wilson and Sir William Tritton. This tank underwent its official trials in January 1916 before Lord Kitchener, Mr. Lloyd George, Minister of Munitions, and other representatives of the War Office, at Burton Park, Lincoln. Christened 'Big Willie', 'HMLS Centipede' or, most aptly 'Mother', she was to provide the basis for the construction of all the tanks built in the war. As a result of the trials an order was made for forty machines but this was subsequently increased to one hundred and fifty.

In an attempt to stifle curiosity and to maintain secrecy various ploys were tried to explain these large tarpaulined shapes that could be seen in railway yards and on trains as they were transported from the manufacturers in Lincoln and Birmingham to their training grounds in the grounds of Lord Iveagh's Elvedon Estate near Thetford in Norfolk.

Someone had the bright idea of painting incomprehensible Russian characters on the side, which, for those who could translate, read, 'With care, to Petrograd'. Discussions followed on what they should be called and of the many suggested three found most favour: 'cisterns', 'reservoirs' and 'tanks'. When the decision was made the word 'Tank' took on a new and legendary meaning in the English language.

Ten Marks of 'Tanks' were developed in the years 1915-18. Some never existed beyond the prototype and others were completed after the armistice and were not used in war. The Mark I Heavy Tank, the direct descendant of 'Mother' was distinguished by two large rear steering wheels. One-hundred and fifty of these were supplied to the Army before being succeeded by the Marks II and III, also with steering wheels, but whose production numbers did not exceed fifty of each. The Mark IV appeared in April 1917 and was the first type without steering wheels although they had been removed from the earlier tanks when it was discovered that they formed a fragile and unnecessary appendage. Between April and December over one thousand were made and supplied to the Army. They were superceded in May 1918 by the more manouverable Mark V. Each Mark was made in two types, a 'male' which was armed with two 6 pound naval guns and three machine guns, and a 'female' armed with five machine guns. Control of these monsters was a feat in itself and of the crew of eight, four were required to steer and control the tank. Communication, so essential for smooth running, was a problem in the dark and noisy confines and although hand signals and electric lights were experimented with a loud voice was essential.

From the beginning of his offensive on the Somme in July, Field-Marshal Haig had been eager to use these new war machines and by the beginning of September fifty tanks of 'C' and 'D' companies of the newly formed Heavy Section Machine Gun Corps were in France. In the naive hope that they would break the deadlock, they were taken up to the front line and with little time for preparation or training on the new ground the crews were thrown into the fray. On 15th September, after an intensive three day bombardment, thirty two tanks (the remainder having broken down) advanced cautiously across no-man's land towards an unsuspecting enemy. They set their sights on the fortified villages of Courcelette, Marinpuich and Flers and the trench systems running down to Bouleaux Wood near Combles. (See Appendix vi)

Carlton china 129mm. ins. 'DN999' and impressed on the side: 'GLOBE THEATRE : JOHN BULL : THURSDAY : GENERAL : PUTNEY : CHARING CROSS'

London Omnibuses carrying troops to the front. In the early days military transport consisted of a "hotch-potch" of public and private vehicles. The London buses still carried their advertisements and destinations.

Tank 743 (Male) being loaded onto a railway wagon at its factory - either Fosters of Lincoln or the Metropolitan Carriage & Finance Co. at Wednesbury. The Russian lettering, added to dispel rumours, reads 'With care to Petrograd'. The sponsons - which housed the guns - have been removed for transportation. This tank took part in the first tank attack as 'D18' with the 41st Division at Delville Wood (see Appendix vi).

THE DAILY MIRROR, Wednesday, November 22, 1916.

FIRST PICTURES OF THE TANKS IN ACTION

The Daily Mirror

CERTIFIED CIRCULATION LARGER THAN THAT OF ANY OTHER DAILY PICTURE PAPER

No. 4,082 | Registered at the G.P.O. as a Newspaper | WEDNESDAY, NOVEMBER 22, 1916 | One Halfpenny.

"HUSH, HUSH"—A TANK GOES "GALUMPHANT" INTO ACTION ON THE WESTERN FRONT.

At last! To-day we are able to publish the first photograph of one of his Majesty's land ships, which have been making such successful cruises on the sea of mud on the Somme. They are the first to be published in any British newspaper, and two others will be found on pages 6 and 7. This "juggernaut," this "Diplodocus," to give it but two of the hundred and one names which have been conferred upon it, was seen "galumphing" into action, its progress being best described in the immortal language of Lewis Carroll. The tanks have been at Flers—one "led" the men down the High-street—and many of the important battles of the great "push" in France. Before them barbed wire becomes as limp as macaroni, while they mow down trees and pass casually over trenches, dealing out death as they go.—(Exclusive to *The Daily Mirror*.)

The new and mysterious 'TANK' as it first appeared to the British public on 24th November 1916. Unfortunately one of its steering wheels had been blown off in the action.

A CROWD OF GERMANS HOLDING UP THEIR HANDS TO SURRENDER
As a Tank approaches their Trench.

Postcards depicting early tank attacks. The original role of the tank was to help the infantry by clearing barbed wire and enemy trenches. One captured German said, after the first tank attack at Flers-Courcelette, that their use was 'not war but bloody butchery'.

A TANK GOING THROUGH A GERMAN BARRAGE
On its way to Attack a Sugar Factory.

BRITISH TROOPS AND A TANK
Assaulting German Trenches at Beaumont Hamel.

Mark IV Arcadian Tanks. Top l. 160mm. : r. 116mm Bottom 320mm. All inscribed 'Model of Tank' Reg. No. 658588. The large model is considered to be for shop window display.

Arcadian china. l. Tank with inset wheels 110mm. r. Mark I 145mm. ins. 'Model of Tank' Reg. No. 658588. After correcting his original mistake Robinson made a number of different sized and type tanks under the original Registration number.

Arcadian china 135mm. ins. 'Model of Tank' Reg. No. 656588. The original Crested China Tank, registered *seven* days after the first pictures appeared in the press. Unfortunately the missing wheel on the tank was by accident rather than design - the other had been blown off in action! - the first stage in correcting the design was to stick a second wheel onto this model.

Carlton tanks. l. to r. Mark IV 160mm : Mark IV 135mm : Mark I 127mm. This factory christened its tanks, 'HMLS Creme-de-Menthe' after one of the participants in the first tank attack. The number '130' was displayed on the London Tank Bank.

Within hours the news of the attack had reached the British public. Reaching for their dictionaries the journalists sought out the most suitable adjectives to portray these completely new and hitherto secret war machines. They were referred to as 'weird dragons of the slime', 'Diplodocus Galumphant', 'Polychromatic Toads' or simply 'flat footed monsters' in the press while the Tommies in the trenches preferred the simpler but amusing 'Landcrab cavalry' or 'Irish Navy'. On the trail of the journalists came the artists and cartoonists who, without photographs to copy, had a field day. Written descriptions were transformed into sketches of all manner of shapes and sizes ranging from the simply impractical to the decidedly Heath Robinson. The British public were not permitted to see an actual photograph of one of these tanks for two months until November 22nd when the 'Daily Mirror' carried the first pictures of one of these 'Hush-hush Tanks' as it trundled majestically out of action on the Somme, minus one of its steering wheels. Nevertheless the tank was firmly imprinted on peoples' minds and rapidly caught their imagination.

In reality the success of this first tank attack was limited and short-lived. Of the thirty-two tanks that started only nine proved to be of any use to the infantry (whom they were supposed to be supporting). The remainder, due largely to the crew's inexperience and lack of training failed to reach the enemy lines, either breaking down or lumbering around no-man's land like hopelessly lost giant toads until they came upon their own lines. Those that did reach the opposing trenches, not surprisingly, struck fear and terror into German hearts as they trundled along the trench sides firing on the hapless infantry with their machine guns. In the days that followed however, the gains made were lost in a series of counter attacks.

1

2

1 & 2 Contrasts in size, the largest and smallest. Ambulances: l. 157mm.; r. 90mm. Arcadian ins. 'EH 139' Whippet tanks: Top: 120mm. Grafton; Bottom: 180mm. Arcadian. The large models are thought to have been shop window display models.

3. Goss patriotic plate 150mm. sometimes found with the title: 'To Cook a German Sausage'. Possibly copied from the verse on a postcard but somewhere along the line 'scouts' became 'sprouts'.

4. Goss commemorative plate of the Hartlepool bombardment.

5. 'British Territorial Bulldog' 93mm. Grafton 262.

3

4

5

Airship and Aeroplane identification poster.

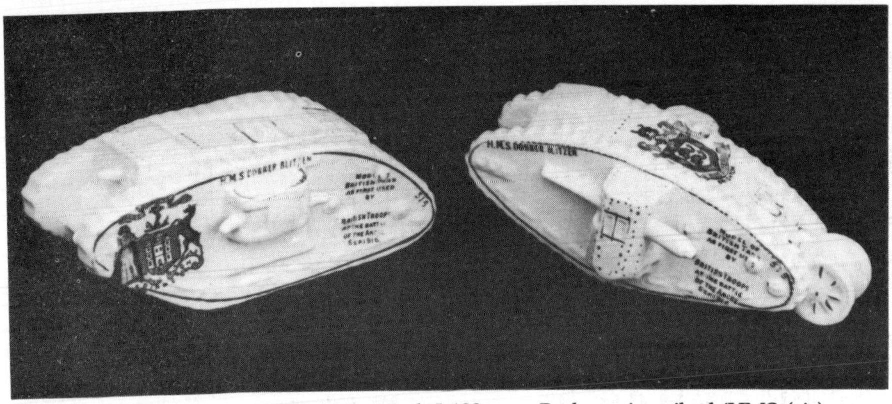

Savoy tanks. l. Mark IV 149mm : r. Mark I 132mm.: Both are inscribed 'HMS (sic) DONNER BLITZEN' and 'Model of British Tank as first used by British troops at the battle of the Ancre Sept 1916' and the number '515'. This tank was a member of 'D' Company on 15th September 1916 and its number indicates that it was a Female (armed with machine guns only). Unfortunately no battle records have been found.

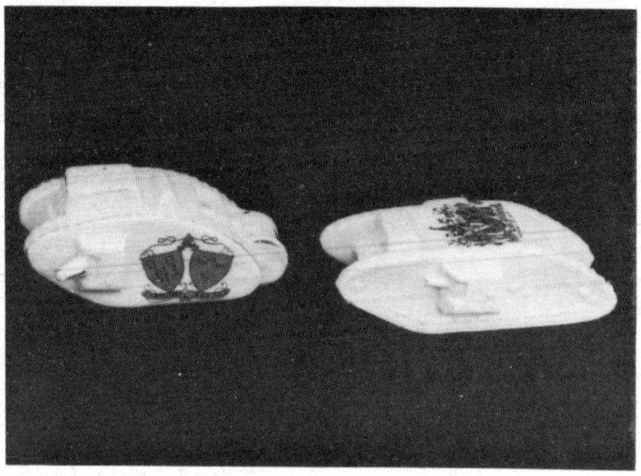

l. Alexandra 105mm.: r. Goss 113mm. The Goss Mark IV model is inscribed 'Britain expects every tank to do its damndest'.

Willow Art. l. Mark IV 98mm.: r. Mark I 127mm. Both inscribed 'Model of British Tank' Reg. No. 658588.

Grafton China. r. Mark I 120mm.: l. Mark IV 100mm. Both inscribed 'HMLS Creme-de-Menthe'.

At this early stage of their development the tanks were seen simply as an adjunct to the infantry, their function being to clear the barbed wire fortifications that so hindered advancing troops, and to traverse trenches and clear them of their occupants. It was not until the Battle of Cambrai in November 1917, when a massed force of 387 heavy tanks achieved a dramatic success, that the full potential of the tank was realised.

While the Heavy Tanks were in use a need was seen for lighter, faster tanks for use in reconnaisance; to act as the 'cavalry' of the mechanical world. In 1917 each Tank Battalion was issued with a French light tank, the Renault FT17. Armed with a machine gun or 37mm gun these fast, light tanks were used extensively for reconnoitre. They remained the main tank of the French Army until 1936, by which time over three thousand had been made. The British equivalent, the Medium Tank Mark A (nicknamed the 'Whippet' or 'Mosquito') made its debut in France in March 1918 and in the closing months of the war one hundred and ninety five saw service on the Western Front.

No other country during the First World War equalled the power and technology of the British tanks. The Germans made a few unsuccessful attempts with their own designs but relied mainly on captured British tanks. At home tanks were paraded in streets, outside town halls and in country villages all over the nation. During the winter of 1917-18 tanks visited various places as part of the War Bonds 'Tank Bank' campaign. Staying for a week at each place, where they advertised these bonds, they proved to be an unqualified success. The City of Glasgow raised £14 million; West Hartlepool an incredible £36 per head while Sunderland managed £15 per head. Londoners' chance came on March 4th 1918 when, as part of the National 'Business Man's Week', a Mark IV tank, carrying the number 130, was displayed in Trafalgar Square. At the same time a miniature fleet was launched in the fountains, while the gondola of a British Airship, anchored nearby, provided investors with souvenir leaflets. In the six days of the appeal an incredible £135 million was raised, more than half of which came from Londoners. A Battersea firm even sent their application for £250,000 of bonds by carrier pigeon; no doubt an employee had been despatched earlier in the week to purloin one of the Square's pigeons to ensure that it flew to the correct place!

This appeal, and others like it throughout the war, was a phenomenal success. In total some £6,000 million was raised to support the war

The caption reads: 'Beatty and Babs sing a song after investing in the Tank Bank at Chiswick'. This tank, a Mark IV with the number '130' was displayed at Trafalgar Square from 4th to 9th March 1918 as part of 'National Business Man's Week'. It later toured the suburbs.

The 'Tank Bank' appeal, like the earlier 'Feed the Guns' and other appeals, helped to raise much needed money to supplement the already stretched resources of the government.

effort which the Prime Minister, Herbert Asquith, had estimated in 1915 was costing the country £3 million a day.

Post-war trends made the heavy tanks obsolete. It had been conceived and designed to fulfill a very specialised role in the muddy battlefields of Northern France and, like the great dinosaurs of the past, were unable to adapt to change and faced extinction - to be replaced by the lighter, faster, medium tanks. One fact is certain however, far from being the 'pretty mechanical toys' that Kitchener chose to call them in 1916, they were one of the deciding factors in the outcome of the war. In his report to the Reichstag in October 1918, the commander of the German armies, General Ludendorff stated.... 'The supreme Army command has been compelled to take the terribly grave decision and declare that there is no longer any prospect or possibility of compelling the enemy to peace. Above all two facts have been decisive for this issue: first the tanks....'

The China

Of all the machines, equipment, guns and artillery that appeared in the war, it was the armoured cars and tanks that proved to be most popular in the china world.

No fewer than ten armoured cars and thirty different tanks were made by a variety of potteries making Heraldic Ware. Some are accurate in every detail while others are amusing results of the potter's craft. The first models appeared in the weeks following their first use on the Somme and production continued, in some cases, well into the twenties.

The Arcadian 'Model of Armoured Car' (Reg. No. 657736) is a mixture of fact and fiction. It was registered on 27th September 1916 just after the tanks had first been used and without a photograph to copy the designer had to rely upon the written descriptions of the 'Landships'. The tracks and suspension are copies of those found on the army tractors of the time but the top and body are pure fancy. In the Patent Office register it is even described as a 'Motor Vehicle "Tank" ' and is probably the earliest attempt by a manufacturer to produce a model of a tank.

The Carlton models of a Rolls Royce armoured car and 'Model of an Anti-Aircraft Motor' are good likenesses of the originals. The former, with its high turret and plated wheels resembles the 1920 version of the car, while the latter is based on the original AA motors which were built onto the chassis of London Omnibuses. The covered wheels, cylindrical turret and three guns of their other armoured car are strongly characteristic of the 1917 version of the Italian Lancia IZ armoured car. This being the case, the inscription 'RNAS' sometimes found on this model, is wrong. In the First World War they were confined to Northern Italy and, amongst other things, were used for the training of American troops in Italy. As they continued in use until the early years of World War II the model may be post-1918 although it is a mystery as to why they should put 'RNAS' on it.

Shelley china based their model on one of the first enclosed armoured cars of the war, the Belgian SAVA (named from the manufacturers of the chassis, Societe Anversoise pour fabrication de Voitures Automobiles) Shelley 329. In copying their design from a photograph (almost

The Crested China industry was not alone in the model tank field. Assorted functional and non-functional wood and metal tanks.

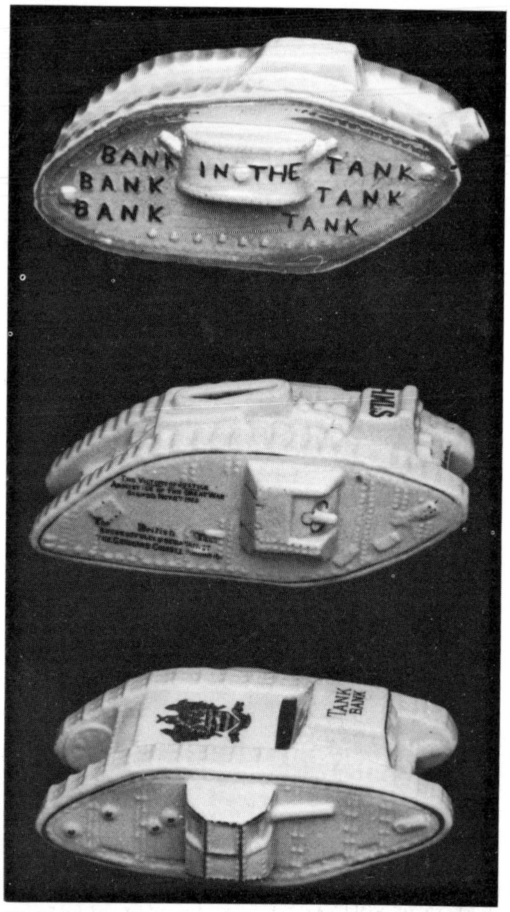

Tank Banks. Top: 'Bank in the Tank Bank' unmarked 155mm.: Middle: Carlton china 155mm. ins. 'Buy war bonds - the Tank Bank': Bottom: Shelley china 140mm No. 413 ins. 'Tank Bank' and 'Model of British Tank' Reg. No. 658588. Neither of the crested china models were very practical money boxes - both had to be smashed to extract the contents and the Shelley model has a slot so narrow that it will only take notes!

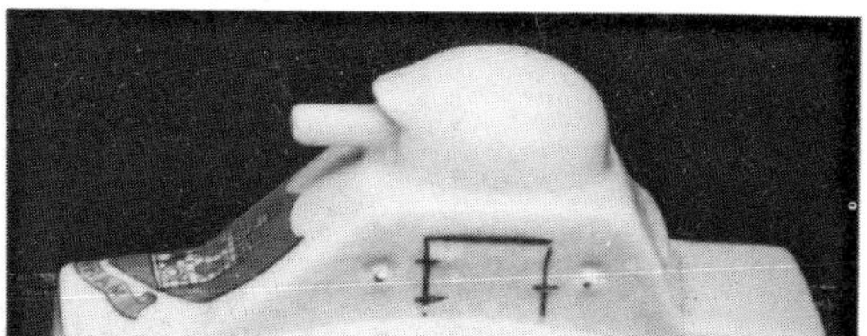

'Model of Armoured Car'. Arcadian China. 111mm. Reg. No. 657736. Registered on 27th September 1916, twelve days after the first tank attack, and described in the Register as 'Motor vehicle 'Tank' '. Without photographs the designer had to rely on written reports and rumours. The tracks and suspension are copied from Army tractors but the top is pure fiction.

Carlton china 125mm. Sometimes found with 'RNAS' on the side. Highly modified but with the characteristics - covered wheels, cylindrical turret and three guns - of the 1917 Lancia.

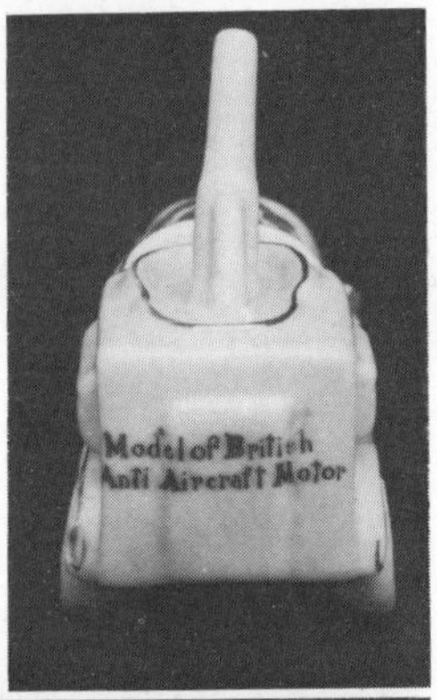

Carlton China 123mm. ins. 'Model of anti-aircraft motor'.

certainly on a postcard) in which the rear of the turret was not visible they wrongly assumed it was a fully enclosed car. In fact it was a half turret, the back being open and unprotected. Nevertheless the remaining detail is exceptional, including the tool box, entrance door and sloping front armour which characterised this car.

Savoy china modelled their car on a Modified First Admiralty pattern of the Talbot armoured car (Reg. No. 652656). This was an early, short-lived car, of which only six are thought to have been made. They were open-topped with high sided armour and equipped with two Maxim machine guns which could fire over the sides. Although they do not appear to have been used after the end of 1914 (they were replaced by a turreted version of this car) the model was not registered until November 1915.

It is with tanks that the greatest diversity in shape and size is found. Production started a few months after the first tank attack and continued, in some cases, until the mid-twenties. Within one week of their appearance in the newspapers, H.T. Robinson of the Arcadian works registered a design for a tank (Reg. No. 658588). In his haste to beat his competitors he failed to realise that the one steering wheel on the tank was accidental rather than designed. The other having been blown off in the action. How long it was before the mistake was realised is not known but certainly a number of these one-wheeled tanks appeared on the market.

This registration must have been a minor coup for Robinson for his design formed the basis for many of the models of tanks made by other manufacturers. A.B. Jones's (Grafton) design for a tank, submitted to the Patent Office in December of that year, was refused and like the others he had to beg, borrow or steal the copyright from Robinson.

All the models of Heavy tanks that followed were of two types: the Mark Is and the Mark IVs. Arcadian, Carlton, Grafton, Savoy, Shelley and Willow Art all made at least one model of each type, each manufacturer having his own characteristic design. Some carry the original registration number given for Robinson's design, others must have waited until the copyright expired (after five years) or carried on regardless and damned the consequences!

Lancia 1Z Armoured Car, 1915 pattern. Crew - 6 Armament - 3 machine guns. In the 1917 pattern the small top turret was dispensed with and the third gun mounted on the rear of the hull, facing backwards.

Robinson's first attempt to correct his design was simply to stick another wheel onto his one-wheeled tank. Very rarely tanks are found which, to the casual observer, appear to be the common two-wheeled model when they are in fact the one-wheeled tank which has had a second wheel added to it in the factory. The subsequent re-designed models of Mark I and later, Mark IV tanks are found in numerous sizes all bearing the registration number of the original one-wheel design. For reasons unknown he also produced a rather fanciful model of a Mark I tank with inset steering wheels. The scarcest Arcadian tank is undoubtedly an enormous 32cms and 15cms high model of a Mark IV which in addition to the standard colouring and crest has been found completely covered with camouflage colours! It is thought that this was made in small numbers for shop window display.

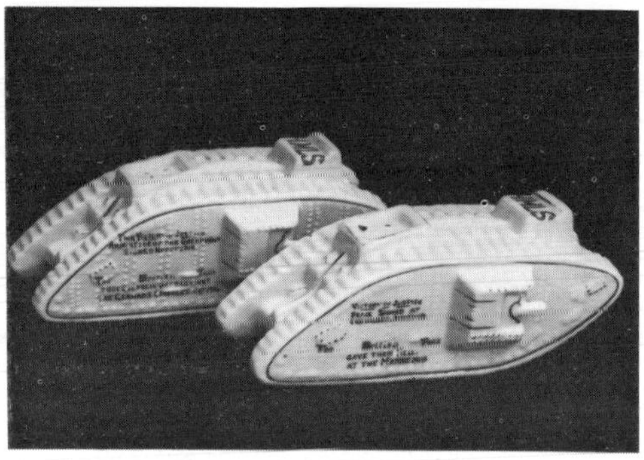

Mark IV Carlton tanks showing different inscriptions used by the factory. 'The British tank successfully used against the Germans: Combles Sept. 1916' and 'The British Tank: Gave them hell at the Marne 1918'. Combles is a small village about six miles away from the site of Creme-de-Menthe's action. Note also the two peace inscriptions, the earlier announcing the Armistice and the later, the signing of the Treaty of Versailles.

The Carlton tanks are found in a variety of sizes ranging from the tiny 80mm Mark IV model to the 160mm Mark IV. Most carry the name 'HMLS Creme-de-Menthe', the name of one of the leading tanks in the attack on a fortified sugar factory in the village of Courcelette on 15th September 1916 (see Appendix vi). Invariably they are found with the inscription, 'British tank that gave them Hell at the Marne 1918', or 'The British tank, successfully used against the Germans, Combles 1916'. At the end of hostilities they added the inscription, 'The Victory of Justice, Armistice of the Great War, signed Nov. 11th 1918', and later still, 'The Victory of Justice, peace signed at Versailles, June 28th 1919'. The Mark IV tanks carry the number '130', that of the London Tank Bank while the relatively scarce money-box tank has the additional inscription, 'Buy War Bonds, the Tank Bank, War Bonds sold £3,423,234'.

Shelley china, in addition to their Mark I and IV model (Shelley 400 and 400a) made a model inscribed 'Tank Bank' (Shelley 413) although judging from the size of the slot it was designed for very thin coins or paper money! Interestingly these models do not seem to have been made until the early twenties. Did they, one wonders, wait until Robinson's patent ran out before producing their own designs?

Grafton china made well detailed models of a Mark I and Mark IV tank and, like Carlton, christened them 'HMLS Creme-de-Menthe'. Savoy china, in a more patriotic vein, called theirs 'HMS (sic) Donner Blitzen' after one of the tanks of 'D' company. Unfortunately early records of the Tank Corps are incomplete and the battle history of this tank is not known

Anti-aircraft gunners doubling to their posts. The first anti-aircraft guns, mounted on London General Omnibuses 'B' type chassis, appeared in October 1914.

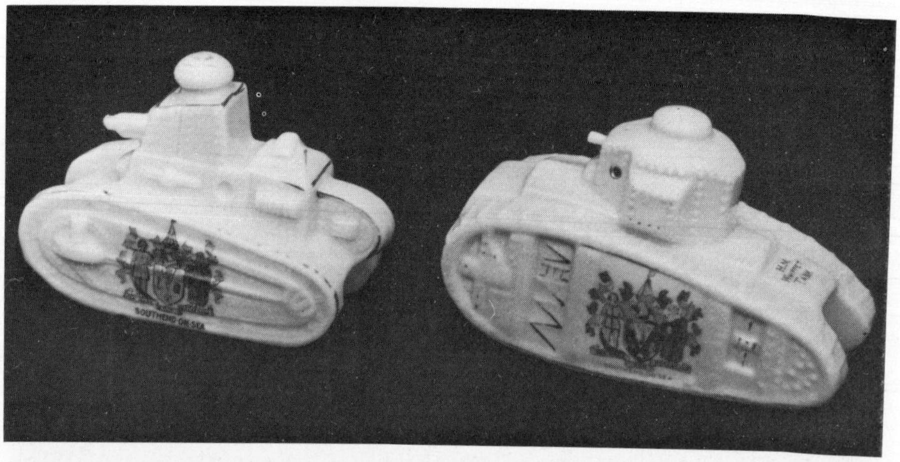

Renault Tanks: l. Grafton China 115mm. : r. Carlton China 123mm. ins. 'HM Whippet Tank' (see also postcard in colour section)

Two post war models from the Carlton factory. l. Rolls Royce Armoured Car 125mm. : r. Vickers Tank 125mm.

Medium Tank Mark A, nicknamed the 'Whippet' or 'Mosquito'. Designed by Sir William Tritton (who was also responsible for the design of the heavy tanks) as a light, fast tank (8mph) that could exploit openings made by the heavy tanks ...to act as the cavalry of the mechanical world. Armed with one Lewis machine gun, they were first seen in France in March 1918 and in the closing months of the war 195 saw action in France.

The Vickers Medium Tank Mark Two was revolutionary when it was introduced in 1922. It remained the standard British Army Tank for 16 years. Speed - 20mph : Armament - 1 three pound gun and 4 machine guns.

although the number '515' also on the model indicates that it was a female (i.e. with five machine guns) and thus the enormous guns on the model are erroneous. The Mark IV models are amazingly accurate, even down to the rivets. The inscription found on these models reads, 'Model of British Tank as first used at the Battle of the Ancre, Sept. 1916'.

Willow Art confines itself to a conservative 'Model of a British Tank' on its two models, while the father of all W.H. Goss, in true form, has, 'Model of British Tank, England expects every tank to do its damndest' inscribed on his sole model of a Mark IV tank.

Models of medium and light tanks were made. Corona and Grafton making excellent replicas of the Renault FT17 tank, although the Carlton model inscribed, 'Model of Whippet Tank' is clearly based on a Renault. It is possible that the design was copied from a postcard showing an artist's sketch of two Renaults but with the title 'Whippet Tanks'. Good copies of the Medium Tank Mark A (Whippet) are found in Arcadian and Grafton. The Arcadian model being another of these large shop window models. The Carlton model of a Vickers Medium Tank originates from the early twenties and may have been brought out at the same time as the Rolls Royce Armoured car. There is a very scarce model that resembles (if you have a good imagination) a Fiat tank although the origin of this is a complete mystery. Only two of the originals were made (only one of which left the workshop) in the closing months of the war, neither of which saw operational use.

No fewer than nineteen manufacturers put their names to a model or models of ambulances. Although there is some variation in size there is

Renault FT 17 light tank. Used for reconnaissance during the last two years of the war. It remained the standard tank of the French Army until 1936. Speed - 4.8mph; Armament - 1 eight mm machine gun or 37mm cannon.

After the battle. The crew of a Rolls Royce armoured car help with the loading of wounded onto an ambulance. This was the most famous car of the war and saw action in Egypt, Gallipoli, Russia and Africa as well as France. In the 1920 pattern the wired wheels were replaced by plated ones and the turret was heightened. Crew - 3; Armament - 1 machine gun. Note the rear wheel chains and detachable running boards. The Red Cross van is a Model 'T' Ford.

Carlton china 100mm. with 'Victory' inscription Similar to the Italian Carro Armato Fiat 2000, only two of which were made.

little in design. The models are divided into those with a flat top (based on a Model T-Ford ambulance), those with a curved top and those with a corrugated top (the originals had canvas tóps). Savoy registered a design for an Argyll ambulance on the same day they registered their Talbot armoured car (Reg. No. 652655) while the Grafton model is inscribed, 'Model of motor ambulance car given by the Staffs China Operatives; British Red Cross and St. Johns Ambulance Association; Load not to exceed 1 driver, 1 attendant and patients'. Arcadian models frequently have 'EH 139' on their radiators. A gigantic ambulance has been recorded in Arcadian china and this, like the tank, was probably made for shop window display.

Ambulances. l. to r. top. Swan china 79mm.: Clifton china 90mm.: bottom: Shelley china 97mm. No. 330.

Postcard of battered ambulance.

l. Savoy china 110mm. resembling a long-nosed Argyll ambulance.: r. Grafton china 98mm. ins. 'British Red Cross and St. John's Ambulance: Load not to exceed 1 driver, 1 attendant and patients'.

4 Guns and Grenades

Towards the end of the nineteenth century artillery and munitions technology advanced in leaps and bounds. Slow firing muzzle loaders had given way to quick firing breechloaders and the 'low' explosive, gun-powder had been replaced by 'high' explosives. The result was dramatic and totally unforeseen. The open, mobile war that was anticipated rapidly degenerated into a static, deadlocked confrontation in which opposite sides tried to pound each other into submission with colossal amounts of munitions.

British Army artillery of 1914 consisted of light field guns, firing 13 and 18 pound projectiles, field howitzers, firing a forty pound shell and heavy guns firing sixty and one hundred and twenty pound missiles. Field guns fired their shells on a flat trajectory and were of use over open ground while the howitzers and mortars fired in an arc and were of use when the enemy were obscured.

The mainstay of the field artillery was the 18 pounder Quick firing gun. The Mark I was introduced in 1904 and with little modification saw service in two World Wars. Each Infantry Division (approx. 18,000 men) was equipped with fifty-four of these and by 1918 over 10,000 had been produced. The French equivalent and perhaps the most famous of all field guns was the 75mm. The 1897 model, in use during the war, required a crew of five and had an effective range of 17,500 yds. With a rate of fire of 15 rounds per minute, twice that of the British 18 pounder, it was a highly versatile weapon and was used, not only on ground targets, but also as an anti-aircraft gun.

The heavy artillery was used with varying degrees of success, in the same way by both sides. An advance of infantry was invariably preceded by a heavy artillery bombardment in an attempt to clear the barbed wire defences of the enemy's trenches and to reduce the troops to a shambles. In the bombardment prior to the Somme Offensive the total amount of munitions used in *one week* was greater than the total made in the first eleven months of the war. It has since been calculated that by the end of the offensive, some six months later, each square yard of the battlefield had received a direct hit from three shells. The effect here and elsewhere was to turn the ground into a stinking morass of waist deep mud and corpses, making it almost impossible for the heavily laden troops to

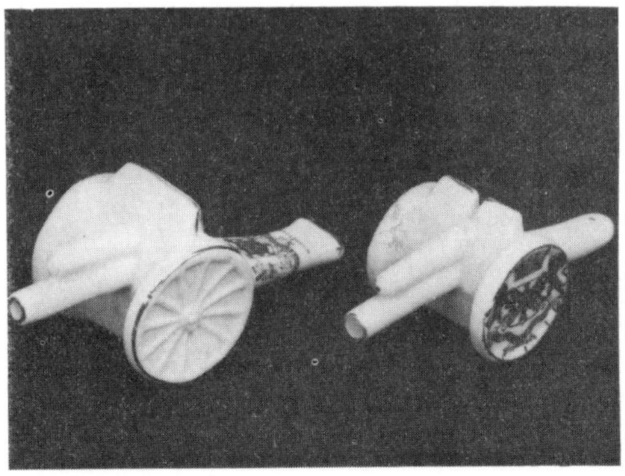

l. Wy Not china 114mm.: r. Arcadian china 110mm ins. 'Model of new field gun with screen' Reg. No. 658686. Resembling a light field gun, an 18 pounder.

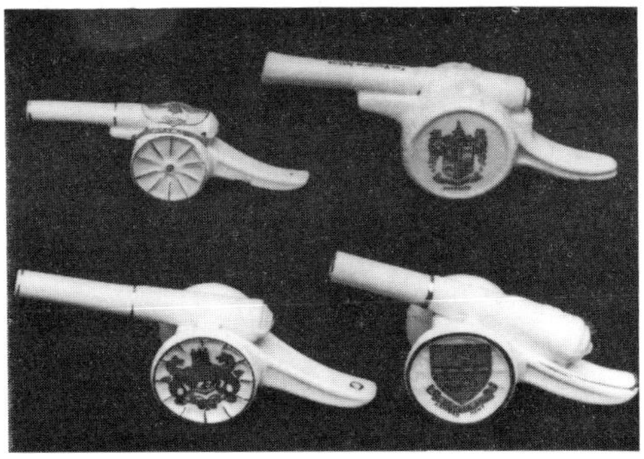

Field guns. Top. l. Arcadian china 120mm.: r. Carlton china 150mm. with 'Peace' inscription. Bottom l. Swan china 147mm. r. Alexandra china 134mm.

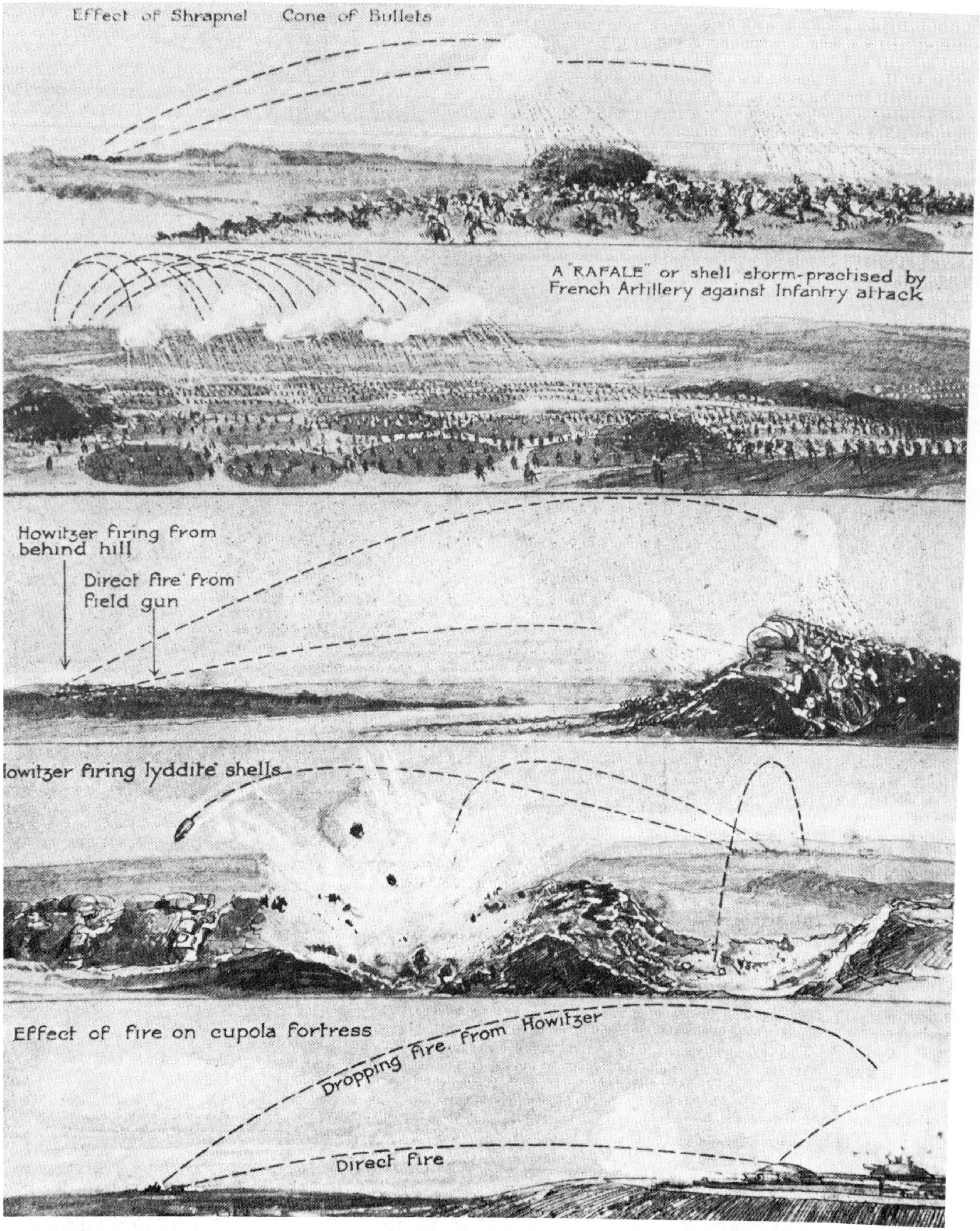

Modern artillery had dramatic and totally unforeseen effects on the war. The Armies went underground and the battlefields were turned into muddy wastelands.

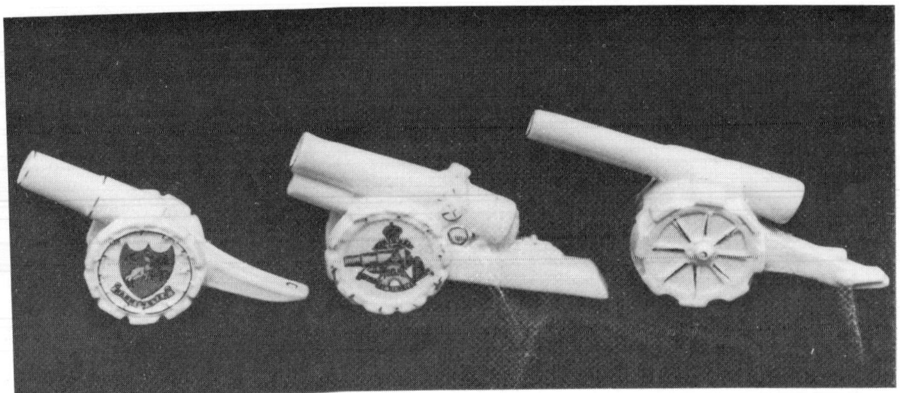

Howitzers: l. to r. Arcadian China 135mm. : Shelley China 147mm. No. 340 (with RGA crest) : Porcelle China 173mm.

British heavy gun in action.

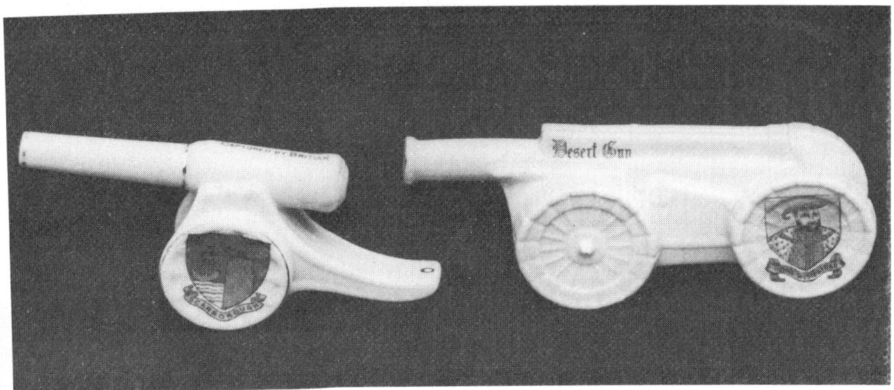

Grafton china. l. German gun captured by the British' 139mm.: r. 'Desert Gun' 154mm. resembling a 60 pounder on its transport carriage.

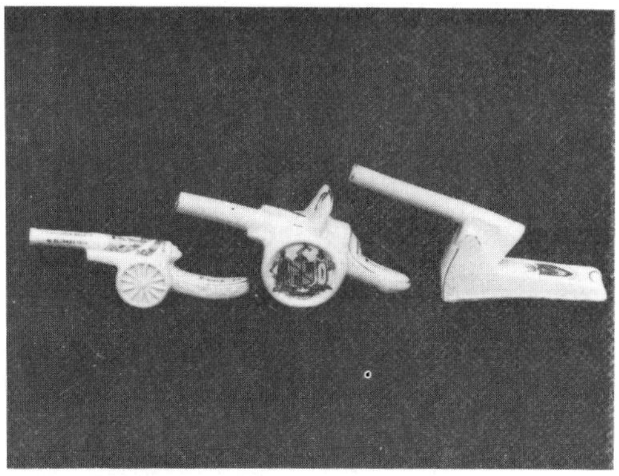

l. to r. Mother Shipton China 132mm. : Carlton china 146mm. : Grafton china 162mm. All inscribed: 'French 75'

French 75mm. field guns mounted as anti-aircraft guns. This was the original and most famous of the quick firing light artillery guns. It fired a 15 pound shot and, like its British counterpart, was a very versatile weapon.

Passschendaele 1917. The intensive artillery bombardments on the battlefields of Flanders destroyed the natural drainage system and turned the ground into a quagmire of glutinous mud.

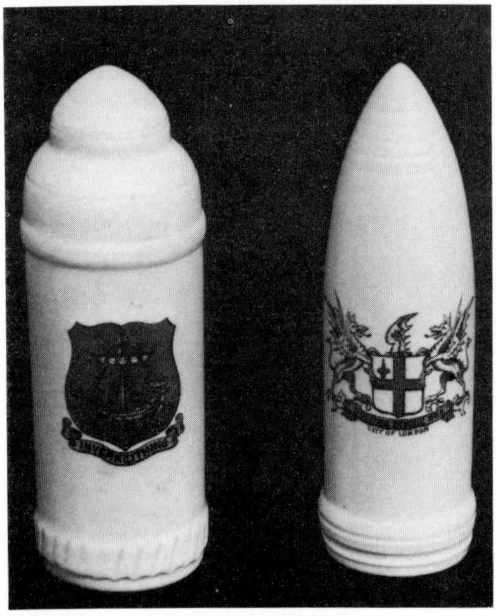

Goss china. l. 115mm. ins. 'Model of Russian shrapnel shell. The original was captured by the huns and fired by them at the British'.: r. 112mm ins. '6ins Incendiary shell'

move. Often the desired effects of the shelling were not achieved; the barbed wire remaining and the enemy emerging unscathed from deep dugouts which had provided them with a sanctuary throughout the bombardment. The advancing troops, struggling through the mud, were mown down in their thousands.

The standard shells of the time were of two types: the shrapnel and explosive. The shrapnel shell was set to explode in the air and shower the ground with thousands of pieces of shrapnel. Its main use in trench warfare was in the cutting of barbed wire. The high explosive shell, containing dynamite, TNT or the newly invented Lyddite, was used in the destruction of defensive positions. For Quick Firing guns the projectile was attached to the propellant charge, usually cordite, while for the howitzers and heavy guns, where the range was governed by the amount of charge, they were separate.

The Tommy in the trenches soon learnt to identify the shells that were being fired at him, usually by the sound they made as they approached. To these he gave nicknames - the 'Whizz-bangs', 'Flying pigs' and the 'Jack Johnsons'. The latter, also called 'Black Marias' were the high explosive shells from the German 8ins. howitzers and were named after the then negro Heavyweight Champion of the World. They exploded in a great pall of black smoke, and like their namesake, packed a big punch.

When hostilities commenced British industry was put onto a war footing. The prime concern was obviously munitions and in the early days there were shocking shortfalls in supplies. Gunners who were supposed

Products of the Crested China munitions industry - designed to break into thousands of pieces if dropped! Top l. to r. Arcadian China 98mm. ins. 'Model of anti-aircraft shell'. : Grafton China 94mm. ins. 'Jack Johnson' : Arcadian China 130mm. ins. 'Jack Johnson' : Unmarked 94mm.: Unmarked 98mm.: Bottom: l. to r. Unmarked 73mm. Arcadian China 70mm.: Savoy China ins. 'Salt' and with the crest of Lille and inscription (see Appendix ii): Grafton china 73mm No. 400 : Savoy china 110mm.
Jack Johnson was the negro heavyweight boxing champion of the time whose name was used by the Tommies to describe the German 8in. Howitzer shells.

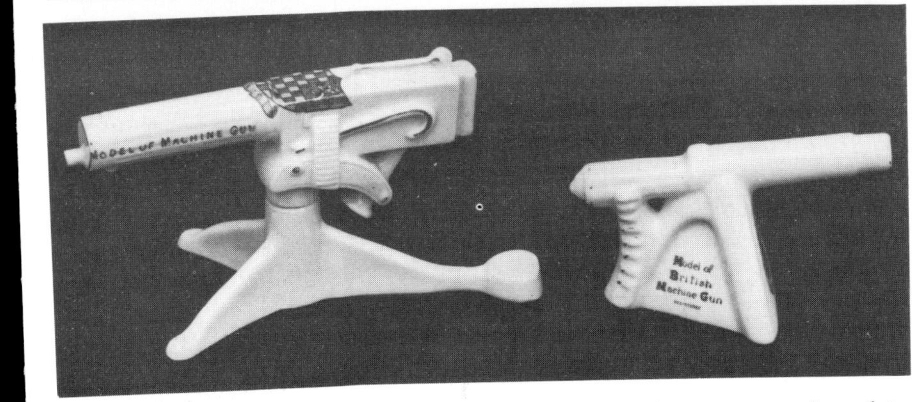

Machine guns: l. Savoy china Reg. No. 661446 ins. 'Model of British Machine Gun'. This large and impressive model comes in two parts - the top swivelling on the tripod base. : r. Carlton China 127mm.

to have reserves of 1000 rounds per gun found they were rationed to three shells a day, often when facing an enemy with unlimited supplies. The loss of the Battle of Neuve Chapelle in 1915 was blamed on the munitions workers whom, it was deemed, squandered their time and money in public houses. As a consequence Parliament hastily introduced legislation limiting the time these places were open and like so many statutes it has never been repealed. Those of us now who are unable to partake of our favourite beverage at the local hostelry in mid afternoon have the munitions workers of 1915 to thank! Possibly because of the above legislation, munitions production increased. In the period 1915-16 the output from these factories increased manyfold and at its peak the industry employed 200,000 people.

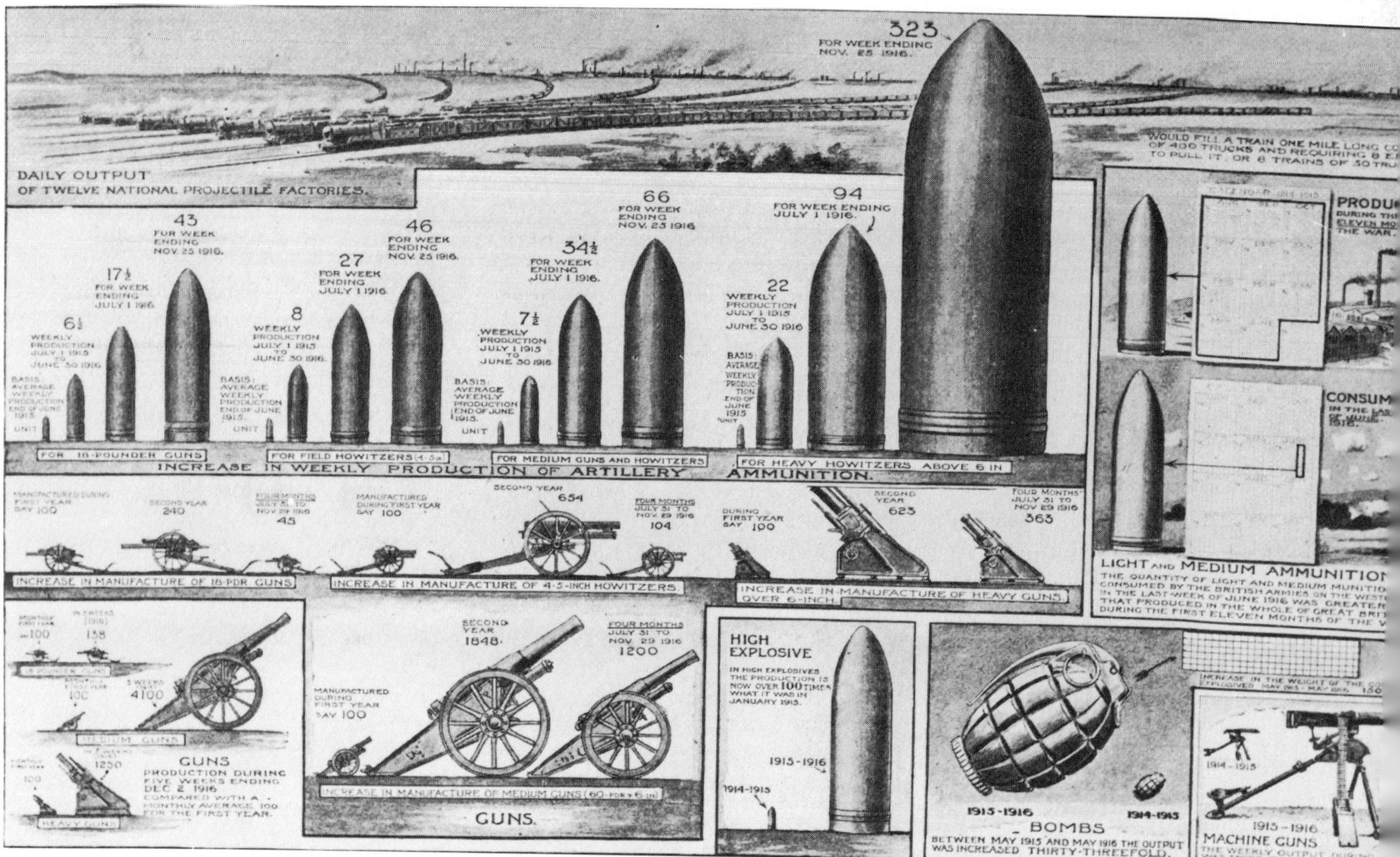

In the early stages of the war there were shocking shortfalls in the supply of munitions: gunners, rationed to three shells a day, found themselves facing an enemy with unlimited supplies. By 1916 the situation had been rectified and in the week long bombardment that preceded the Somme Offensive in July the amount of munitions used exceeded the total amount produced in the first eleven months of the war.

Vickers machine gun. Originally the Vickers-Maxim, it became the standard British machine gun of the war and was capable of a firing rate of 600 rounds per minute. At the beginning of the war each infantry battalion had 4, by the end this had increased to 43.

The standard machine-gun of the time was the Vickers-Maxim, introduced into the Army in 1891. Invented by an American, Hiram S. Maxim, it weighed only forty pounds and fired .303ins bullets at the rate of 600 per minute. The design was such that the recoil was used to load, fire and eject continuously while the trigger was being held back. The cartridges were carried on a flexible belt and the great heat produced by such a rapid rate of fire was dissipated by a water jacket surrounding the barrel. They were made in Britain by Alfred Vickers of Crayford, Kent and when Maxim's patent ran out, became known simply as 'Vickers'. With little modification to the basic model they were used by both sides in both World Wars.

The Generals were slow to realise the potential of such a gun. Haig considered it... 'a much overrated weapon' and... 'two per battalion is more than sufficient'. Kitchener thought that four per battalion would be useful and... 'any more could be counted as a "luxury" '. By the end of the war every battalion had forty-three machine guns and begged for more. With a firepower some forty times greater than the Tommy firing his Lee-Enfield at the regulation fifteen rounds per minute these guns were to wreak havoc amongst the dense formations of advancing troops. It has been estimated that the British advance on the first day of the Somme Offensive, which sustained 60,000 casualties, was stopped by just two hundred German machine guns.

Another instrument of destruction that grew out of the trenches was the hand grenade. The Germans were the first to use hand bombs in the trenches and their troops were issued with Stielhandgrnatebz (fused stick grenades) which could be thrown into the enemy trenches. Seeing the usefulness of such a device and in the absence of any official issue, the British Tommy turned his mind to inventing a suitable missile. Early attempts, ingenious though they were, often proved more dangerous to the bomber than the bombed and it was not long before they were banned and replaced by a variety of official issues. One such early grenade was known as 'Ticklers Artillery'. Tickler was a jam manufacturer who supplied the army with jam packed in tins. When the much maligned contents had been removed the tins were packed with guncotton or ammonal and fitted with a fuse. The official grenades were equally as rough and ready. The 'hairbrush grenade' (British Time-fused Hand Grenade No. 12) consisted of an explosive charge encased in a cast iron body and the whole attached to a length of wood which acted as a throwing handle.

Grenade inkwell. The grenade that established itself as the main British hand bomb was patented by Mr. William Mills of Birmingham in January 1915. On exploding the cast iron body broke into 48 pieces which covered a wide area.

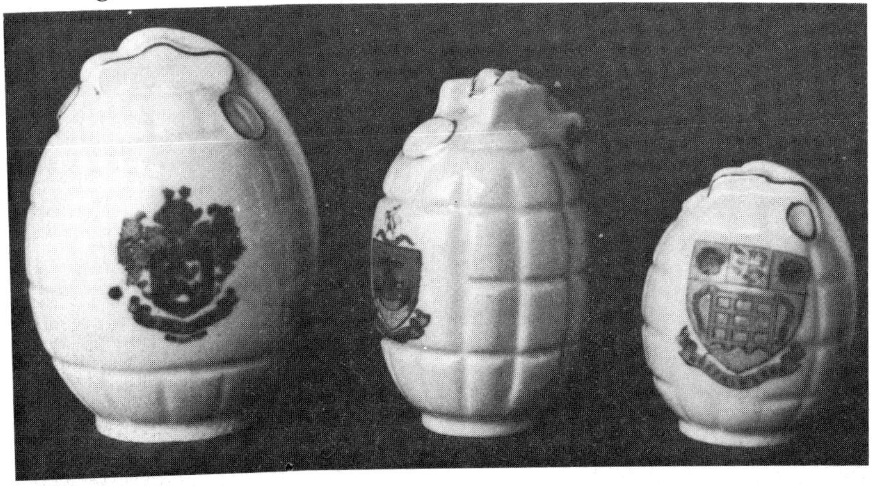

Mills bombs: l. to r. Arcadian 92mm. : Grafton china 80mm. with detachable metal pin - for practice? Arcadian china 60mm. Reg. No. 657211.

'A ticklerish question: "Funny 'ow we don't seem to get no more plum and apple these days". "They're using it for munitions now, I expect!" '

Old Bill speculating. Tickler was the manufacturer who supplied the army with jam. The empty tins were filled with ammonal and fitted with a fuse, and thrown at the enemy. These early home-made bombs, which were often as dangerous to the bomber as the bombed, were nicknamed 'Tickler's Artillery'.

Savoy china ins. 'Model of Trench Mortar bomb' Arcadian china 65mm. ins. 'Model of trench flying pig' Reg. No. 657701.

Sir Wilfred Stokes with his mortar and its projectiles. This mortar, with its variety of bombs - gas, incendiary, high explosive and burning oil - was of great use in trench warfare.

The grenade that superceded all others and was to last through two World Wars was patented by a Mr. William Mills of Birmingham in January 1915 and became known as the 'Mills bomb'. On exploding, the cast iron body, encasing the charge, broke into forty-eight pieces which covered a wide area. The removal of a safety pin started a time fuse which allowed the grenade to be thrown a distance before exploding. They were first used in the Spring of 1915 and over thirty-five million were made in the First World War alone. In the close proximity of the front-line trenches the grenade achieved an importance hitherto unappreciated and by the end of the war it was this rather than the rifle that proved more use to the Tommies.

The war saw the appearance of a large number of weapons that were specially designed and created for the unique form of warfare that was being encountered. Most were simply variations of the same theme... how to propel the largest possible charge a short distance from one trench to another. Many were conceived and built by the Tommy crouched in his dugout and ranged from the futuristic to the antiquarian in design. The main British contribution to the small, heavy projectile field came however, not from a military mind but from a civilian - Sir Wilfred Stokes; who gave his name to a short range, rapid fire trench mortar with tremendous destructive power. The gun itself was easily transported and it was the cumbersome and heavy projectiles that were the bane of Tommy's life. With its wide variety of missiles the Stokes mortar could be used for wire and trench breaking, block house destruction and as projectiles for gas, burning oil and incendiary chemicals.

The China

Most of the major manufacturers made a selection of field guns, mortars and howitzers. Although some are very good representations of the original, many have become so distorted and simplified that their origin is circumspect. To add further confusion some models are found with pedrails which were fitted to the wheels to facilitate transport over rough or muddy ground.

Models of 18 pounders are found in Corona, Willow Art and Arcadian china. The latter (Reg. No. 658586) is inscribed, 'Model of new field gun with screen'. Carlton and Grafton china both manufactured rather artistic models of a field gun which is usually found inscribed, 'French 75'. Models of larger calibre guns are found in various sizes in Arcadian (Reg. No. 652245), Carlton, Corona, Willow and Savoy. The Arcadian, Carlton and Willow models appear in two sizes and models of the first are frequently found with the inscription, 'Model of RFA gun'. The Savoy model is based on a 5in. Coastal gun on its field carriage.

No fewer than thirteen manufacturers put their name to a model or models of howitzers and mortars. Shelley china modelled a remarkable copy of 9.2in howitzer (Shelley 340) while Arcadian based theirs on an 8in. In addition to these, both made models that are found inscribed, 'Model of German Howitzer'. The similar Arcadian, Carlton, Grafton and Shelley models of trench mortars, inscribed respectively, 'War Edition 1914-15', 'Model of British Trench Mortar', 'Trench Howitzer' and 'For Freedom', belong to the decks of HMS Victory rather than the battlefields of the twentieth century. The Arcadian 'Model of a Trench Mortar' (Reg. No. 657212) is a good replica of a Krupp mortar while the Savoy model of a 'British Trench Mortar Gun' (Reg. No. 661740), and copied in Arcadian, is erroneous in name yet exact in detail. It is a copy of a German 25cm Minenwerfer that was used in the trenches. I wonder if they substituted 'British' for 'German' at the last moment in the hope that it would sell better or was it a genuine mistake? The Savoy factory also made an exceptionally accurate (and now scarce) model of a 4.5ins howitzer. The wing bomb or 'pigeon' as it was nicknamed, from the German Spigott Mortar is found in Arcadian china inscribed, 'Model of German Aerial Torpedo' (Reg. No. 657651).

The Grafton factory contributed a number of imaginative named models to the range of guns. 'Desert Gun' (Grafton 430) which is a field gun (possibly a 60 pounder) on its four wheeled transport carriage, an 'Alpine Gun' complete with two movable wheels, a model of a 'French 75' mounted on what could either be a railway carriage or sledge (Grafton 412) and a model of a 'German gun captured by the British' (Grafton 403) taken from a photograph showing the spoils of war.

German Alte Art, a large calibre (25cm) trench mortar. Putting it together and as one of the spoils of war.

l. Savoy china 142mm. resembling a 4.5ins howitzer. r. Savoy china 128mm. Reg. No. 661740 ins. 'British Trench Mortar'. Perhaps the manufacturers thought that it would not sell if they named it correctly as 'German Trench Mortar'.

Trench mortars: l. to r. Arcadian China 78mm. ins. 'War Edition 1914-1915'. Carlton China 78mm. ins. 'Model of British Trench Mortar' : Grafton china 80mm. ins. 'Trench Howitzer'. Three models that are more akin to the decks of HMS Victory than the battlefields of twentieth century France.

The German spigott mortar fired a small, but lethal, shrapnel bomb.

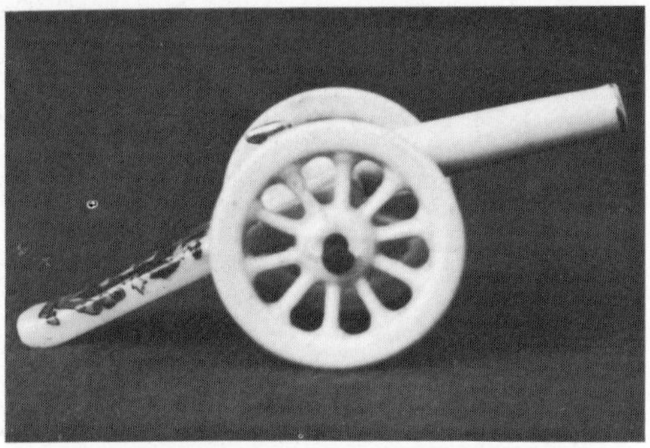

Grafton china 105mm ins. 'Model of Alpine Gun' No. 394. The wheels revolve around metal pins.

The cream of many a collection must be the Savoy model of a 'British Machine Gun' (Reg. No. 661446), a very lifelike two piece model of a Vickers (the gun is detachable from the base). A smaller, one piece model is found in two varieties in Carlton china. The Arcadian handgun (Reg. No. 657653) appears to be heterogeneous in origin, having the characteristics of several guns, although in its general shape it approximates to that of a Very pistol.

Models of Mills bombs were made in various sizes and with slight variation in design by a number of manufacturers. The Arcadian model was presumably the first to appear (Reg. No. 657211) being registered in August 1916. Grafton and Shelley factories also made models with a detachable metal pin; whether this was for practice or decoration is conjecture! A number of grenades designed by the Arcadian works in 1916 include, 'Model of Cannister bomb' (Reg. No. 657700), which may have been based on one of the original 'Jam-tin' bombs, a 'Model of Hairbrush Grenade' (Reg. No. 657702), a 'Model of German Stick Grenade' (Reg. No. 657697) which few people seem to have bought for it is very scarce and a 'German Incendiary Bomb', in addition to their model of a Mills bomb.

The Arcadian 'Plum Pudding Bomb' (Reg. No. 657699) and the Savoy 'Trench Mortar Bomb' originate from the British 2ins. (Toffee Apple)

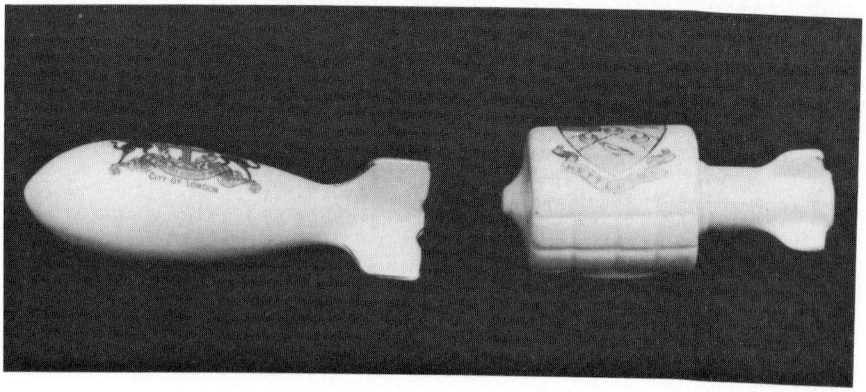

Arcadian China l. 100mm. Reg. No. 657210 ins. 'British Aerial Torpedo'. : r. 83mm. Reg. No. 657651 ins. 'German Aerial Torpedo'.

mortar but the very rare Arcadian 'Model of Trench Pig' (Reg. No. 657701) remains something of a mystery. The nickname 'Flying Pigs' was used for the projectiles of the British 9ins. howitzer and yet the model resembles one of the projectiles of the Stokes Mortar. Either way any collector who acquires one of these will be more concerned with his good fortune than the model's origin!

Shells are found in profusion. W.H. Goss made two models: one of a 'Model of a British 6ins. incendiary shell' and the other of 'A Model of Russian Shrapnel shell' which was also inscribed, 'the original was captured by the Huns and fired by them at the British'. As this was presumably a dud we can only surmise that our Russian allies took the precaution of removing the fuse before allowing it to fall into enemy hands! Arcadian china named one of their shells, 'Model of Anti-aircraft Shell' while Shelley and Carlton based theirs on a 9.2ins. shrapnel shell and a 15ins. shell respectively. Various Arcadian and Grafton models are inscribed with 'Jack Johnson' while the Savoy models are found with 'Iron Rations for Fritz' inscribed on them. As if to prove that anything could be copied the Arcadian works made a model of a clip of .303ins bullets (Reg. No. 657648).

The 'Plum Pudding bomb' alias 'Toffee Apple Mortar' alias 2in. Mortar, ready for take-off.

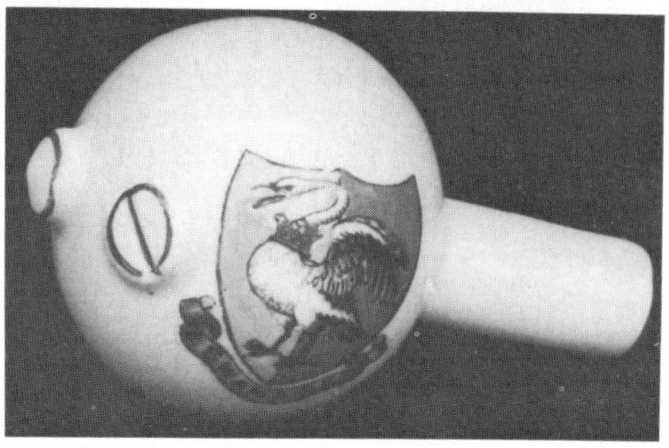

Arcadian china 70mm. Reg. No. 657699 ins. 'Model of Plum Pudding Bomb'.

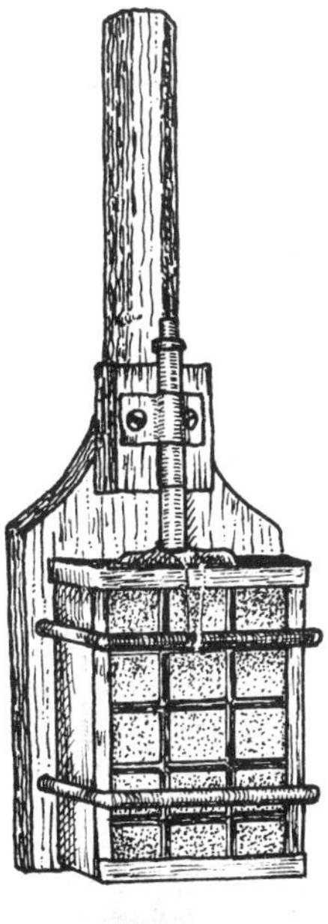

British Time fused grenade No. 12, nicknamed 'Hairbrush grenade'. This early official grenade was almost as rough and ready as the home-made ones. The explosive was attached to a wooden throwing handle.

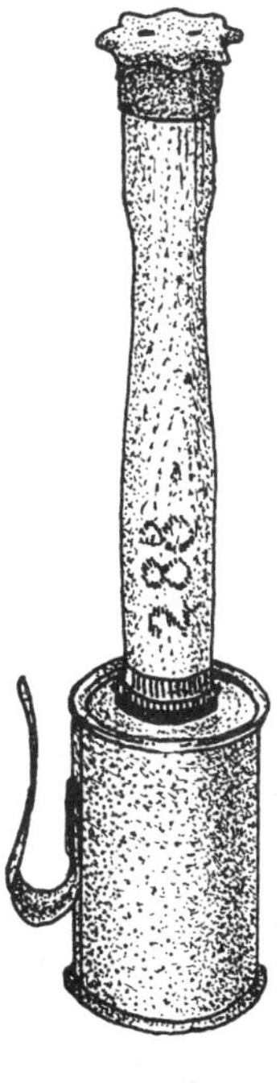

German stick grenade. The Germans were the first to realise the potential of hand bombs in trench warfare.

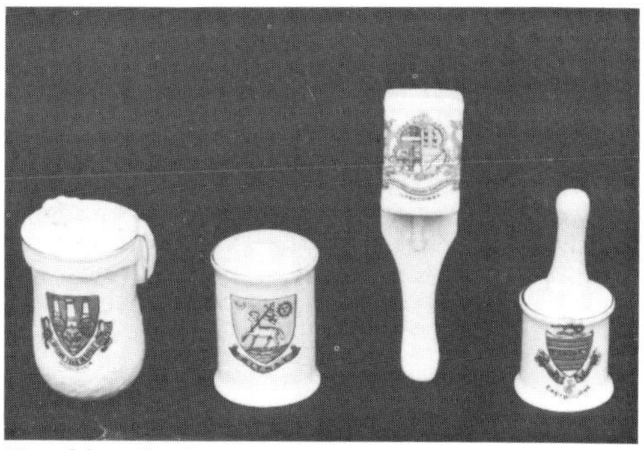

Hand bombs. l. to r. Carlton china 76mm ins. 'Model of German incendiary bomb'. Arcadian china 60mm. Reg. No. 657760 ins. 'Model of cannister bomb'.: Arcadian china 107mm. Reg. No. 657702 ins. 'Model of hairbrush grenade'.: Arcadian china 80mm. Reg. No. 657697 ins. 'Model of German stick grenade'.

5 Aeroplanes

Like the tanks on the ground and the submarines under the waves, the airships and aeroplanes were the novelty in the third and totally new dimension to warfare... war in the air. By 1914, eleven years after the Wright Brothers had made aviation history at Kitty Hawk, aeroplanes were still little more than cloth and plywood contraptions, held together by pieces of wire and flown as much by luck as skill. Military minds, not renowned for their innovatory spirit, were reluctant to accept these 'new-fangled' machines for, amongst other things, the noise of their engines would 'frighten the horses!'

Incredible as it may seem in retrospect, few people appreciated the military potential of the aeroplane. Initially it was considered that the most appropriate use the aeroplane could be put to in warfare was one of reconnaissance...' the examination by trained officers of definite tracts of territory or localities with a view to ascertaining the nature of the country, the roads, the railways, the rivers, the bridges, the battle positions, numbers and nature of enemy troops, movement of supplies, position of magazines, military depots and military deployment in progress'. It was only during the course of the war that the offensive role of the aircraft developed.

At the outbreak of hostilities France, Germany and Russia had the largest fleets of aircraft. France's Aviation Militaire had 160 aircraft and 15 airships; the Imperial German Military Air Service had 245 aircraft and 7 Zeppelins and the Imperial Naval Air Service, 36 seaplanes and 2

The RFC at Farnborough in 1914. From this small band of men equipped with a motley collection of aircraft, the RAF emerged in 1918 as a tried and tested fighting force with over a quarter of a million men.

RFC recruiting poster.

Zeppelins. The Imperial Russian Air Service could call upon an assortment of 244 planes, Germany's ally, Austro-Hungary possessed a miscellaneous collection of 36 aircraft and 1 Zeppelin while 'poor little Belgium' lost its entire fleet of twenty aircraft when it was overrun by Germany. Britain was able to muster an air force consisting of 113 assorted planes.

Military flying, in Britain, at this time was in the hands of two bodies: The Royal Flying Corps (RFC) and the Royal Naval Air Service (RNAS). When the BEF left for France in August 1914 it was accompanied by four squadrons of the RFC, numbering some 64 planes made up of Henri Farman's, Avro 504s, Bleriot XIs and BE 8s (Bleriot Experimental). The RNAS remained behind to guard the home waters and throughout the war was used extensively in anti-submarine patrols and in escorting Merchant and supply shipping.

Bleriot XI-2 Genie. Crew - 2; max. speed 68mph, bomb load - 50lbs. Used in the first two years of the war.

Bleriot XI in flight. At a time when biplanes were in vogue Louis Bleriot's epic cross channel flight in 1909 did much to popularise his monoplane design.

Willow Art china. Monoplanes 145mm. l. with movable propeller and coloured roundels : r. with fixed propeller. This model first appeared in December 1914. The roundels, introduced in 1915 as an aid to identification, appeared on later models.

l. Carlton china 135mm. r. Arcadian china 150mm.

Holt army tractor used on airfields for towing aeroplanes.

Grafton China 76mm. No. 456. ins. 'Model of airfield tractor'.

Top. l. Carlton china 135mm. r. Savoy china 127mm
Bottom l. Grafton china 140mm No. 450. r. 135mm
No. 414. The Grafton biplane has characteristics
of a BE2c and is a particularly rare model.

The very stable BE2c was used for reconnaissance in the early part of the war. Max speed - 72mph at 6,500 ft. Note the 'in line' engine as opposed to the Sopwith's 'rotary'.

The majority of aeroplanes in use at this time were biplanes and were built either with the propeller behind the pilot (pushers) or in front (tractors). The Henri Farmans were two seater pushers, the remainder tractor types. The Bleriot XIs were single seater monoplanes and were a militarised form of the aircraft used by Louis Bleriot for his epic flight across the channel in 1909. They were powered by a 70hp Gnome rotary engine which pulled the plane along at a maximum speed of 66mph and had an operational flying time of three and a half hours.

It was only a matter of time before handguns, rifles and shotguns were taken into the air, firstly for defence and later for offence. Soon ways were being looked at of mounting machine guns to aircraft. The main problem that confronted any pilot at this time was being able to fire in such a way that he did not destroy his own plane either by severing the propeller blades or by cutting his wings or wires that held them together. Guns were consequently mounted in an assortment of places: on top of wings, on the side of the fuselage, behind the pilot etc. All had the same drawback, that of having to position the aircraft for attack and the inaccessability of the gun should anything go wrong with it, as it often did. A major breakthrough was a system that allowed the gun to be fired straight ahead through the propeller arc. This was achieved initially by fitting metal sections to the propeller blades which deflected any bullets that struck them and later by an interruptor system which ensured that the gun did not fire when a propeller blade was in line with it. By mid-July 1915 the first of the German eindeckers (monoplanes) fitted with this device were in service giving them a clear advantage over the allies. The balance was not redressed until April of the following year when the RFC received their first plane with a forward firing, synchronised gun, the Sopwith 1½ Strutter.

The 1½ Strutter was superceded by what many pilots considered their favourite aeroplane of the war… the Sopwith Scout, Type 9901. It was nicknamed the 'Pup' because the pilots deemed its predecessor to have 'pupped' and entered operational service in the late summer of 1916, claiming its first enemy aircraft on 24th September. Powered by an 80hp Le Rhone engine and with a ceiling of 17,500 ft. they were armed with either a fixed, forward firing synchronised Vickers or Lewis gun or eight Le Prieur rockets. Fast, reliable and above all, highly manouverable, they remained in service until the end of the war.

Unlike the war on the ground, the aeroplane war was the place for the individual. While hundreds of thousands met their death in unjustified

l. Victoria china 160mm. r. Arcadian china 119mm. Reg. No. 658683. ins. 'Model of new aeroplane'. This model was registered in December 1916, two months after the RFC had taken charge of their first Sopwith Scouts.

One of the lucky few - shot down but survived. Propeller tip, photograph and badges of a pilot who was shot down at Oppy Wood on 4th May 1918 - less than four weeks after arriving at the front. The piece of shrapnel was removed from his back.

The Sopwith Scout ('Pup') first saw action in September 1916 and continued in service until December 1917. Its synchronised, forward firing machine gun and its maneouverability made it very popular amongst the pilots and its presence did much to redress the balance of power in the air over the Western Front.

anonymity in the mud of the trenches, the air was the place where reputations and legends were born. The era of the 'Ace' had arrived and all sides paraded their heroes... Ball, Mannock, McCudden, Fonck, Nungesser, Boeleck and of course the Rictofens. These men belonged to that breed that had... 'the cunning, the ingenuity and the mind of the hunter' and found themselves ideally suited to this new form of warfare. For others there is a different story to tell. Many young pilots, fresh and eager from training school, were thrown into a dog-fight with only a few hours flying experience behind them. With neither the time nor the opportunity to learn the tactics and manoeuvres so essential for survival they failed to return from their first operational flight and became one of the 7,589 casualties of the RFC in the four years of the war.

The majority of the early pilots were culled from cavalry units, as it was deemed that the ability to ride a horse was an asset in flying an aeroplane and consisted mainly of officers from the middle and upper classes (since at the beginning of the war the RFC did not offer any pilot training and all prospective pilots had to take, and pay for, their pilots licence privately). In the constant fight for aerial dominance over the Front Lines the turnover of pilots increased with alacrity and at its worst, in 1917, the expected life of a pilot at the front was 14 days.

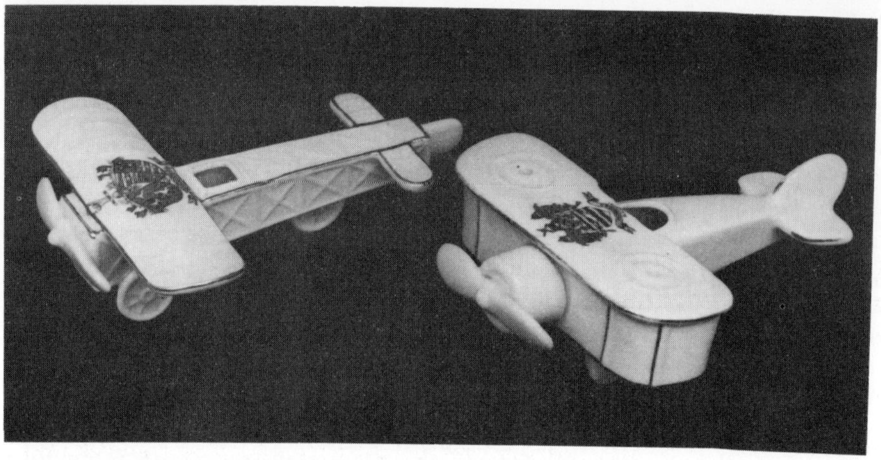

Shelley china. l. 155mm ins. 'Model of Bleriot warplane' No. 311. r. 145mm No. 344 model of biplane, resembling a Sopwith Camel.

The Pilots of No. 203 Squadron RAF pose in front of their Sopwith Camels at Izel le Hameau in July 1918.

Those who did survive enjoyed a life style which in comparison with the Tommy in the trenches was nothing short of luxurious. On airfields behind the lines, away from the mud and horror of the trenches, many of these 'high-spirited youngsters' were slow to realise the true meaning of war. Nevertheless reality was never far away, as so poignantly described by Sir Gordon Taylor in his book 'Sopwith Scout 7309'*....'We had casualties right from the very beginning which made one conscious of the serious purpose which lay behind the apparently lighthearted life of the squadron. Captain Lata, C Flight Commander was shot down on one of the first patrols and later we lost Lucas, a happy, good natured fellow in B Flight, in particularly wretched circumstances. Lucas was wounded in a flight and had managed to get back and land at Bellevue, where there was a field hospital. He had been shot in the leg and it didn't seem to be serious. Some of us planned to go over to see him. Then we heard he was dead. Apparently the wound had not been structurally serious, but some infection had set in and his leg was amputated to prevent the infection spreading. But it was already too late, and in those days nothing could be done to save him. His burial... the first I had witnessed at the squadron... horrified me. There was something so distressing about the sight of the still thing sewn up in sackcloth and carried to the grave. It hadn't the frightful trimmings with which ordinary funeral is invested, but it wasn't Lucas. It was some strange rite with a visible sacrifice; so unnecessary, such an indictment of the great glory of our cause. All the high-spirited adventure collapsed like a pricked balloon. The madness of the killing was exposed as the quiet words of the padre accompanied Lucas to the grave.'

In April 1918 the RFC and the RNAS joined forces to form the Royal Air Force. In the four years of the war the Air Arm grew from the tiny, unknown force of 860 men and 113 machines into a tried and tested fighting organisation with nearly 300,000 men and 20,000 machines. The tactics and strategies that had been learnt at great cost by trial and error provided the foundation blocks for aerial warfare of the future.

*Published Cassell 1968

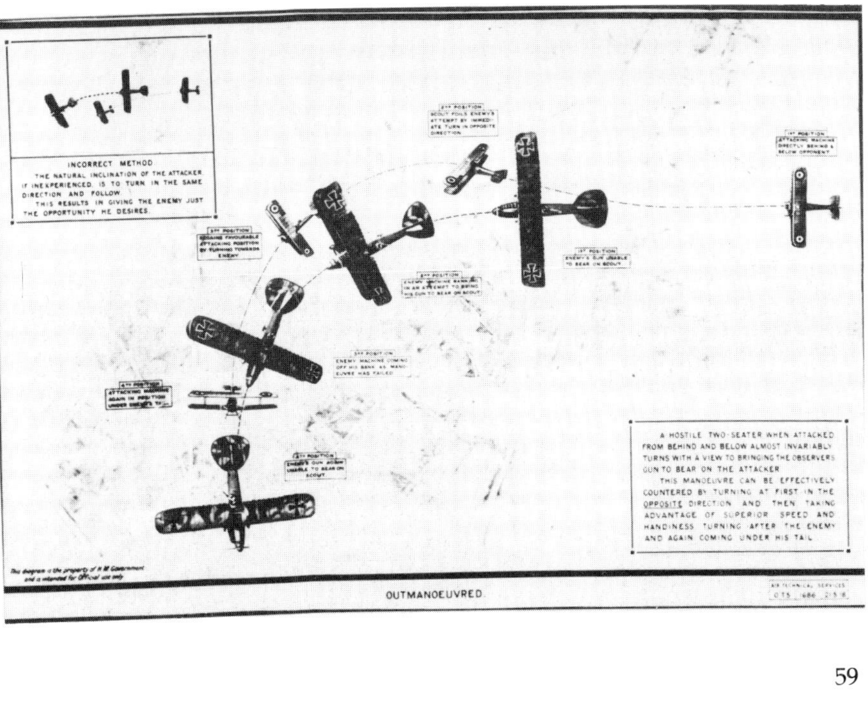

In 1914 tactical instruction for pilots was minimal. This 1918 instructional leaflet produced by the RAF was entitled 'Out manoeuvered'.

Arcadian china 120mm Reg. No. 607828 ins. 'Model of aeroplane'. This model was registered in 1912, the circular portion being added to accommodate the crest. The unglazed model (left), which has one propeller blade missing, may have been a factory reject. Also found in a two bladed version.

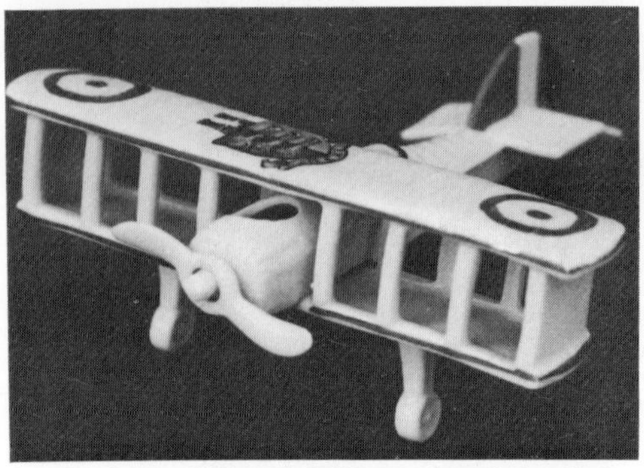

Savoy china. 135mm. A fine and well detailed model of a biplane with coloured roundels.

The China

The complexity in design and structure of the early aircraft do not lend themselves easily to reproduction in china. Nevertheless the designers managed to circumvent these inherent problems and produced some very fine models that were not too fragile and yet retained some characteristics of the original.

Of the fifteen different models of aircraft recorded, most with some accuracy, can be placed in the war years. Only one model has definitely been traced as being pre-war and two, post war. Models are found of biplanes and monoplanes although the latter are the more common and were made by a greater number of manufacturers. They are found with either fixed or moveable propellers and some carry the RFC roundels and colours which were introduced in 1915 as an aid to identification.

With few exceptions the models of monoplanes have characteristics derived from the Bleriot monoplanes that were flown before and during the war. It is possible that they were produced in response to Louis Bleriot's cross channel flight in 1909. Casting aside design and manufacturing problems this would explain their popularity for although Bleriot's flew in the war they were not common. Only the Shelley 'Model of Bleriot warplane' (Shelley 311), which was made in 1916, and the Willow monoplane, which first appeared in 1914, soon after hostilities commenced, can with certainty be placed in the war years. The latter is also found with RFC roundels which were no doubt added to post-1915 models.

The Arcadian model (Reg. No. 607828) which has a large circular disc on the fuselage, presumably to accommodate the crest, was registered in 1912 and despite artistic licence, has, like the Savoy model, characteristics of the Bleriot XI. These models may have been inspired by the success of Andree Beaumont flying such a plane in the Daily Mail circuit of Great Britain in 1911. The Arcadian model is found in 2 sizes with either a two or three bladed fixed propeller and the Savoy has a two bladed movable propeller.

Models of biplanes, although fewer in number, are somewhat more varied in origin than the monoplane. Most of the manufacturers solved the extra difficulty of modelling two wings by making models with the wing spaces filled in. The Carlton and Savoy designers as if to show their potting prowess, made models of biplanes with separate wings. Two different models are found in Carlton china: one (Reg. No. 657607) was registered in September 1916 and may have been based on the Sopwith 1½ Strutter, the other which probably followed at a later date is found

Foreign. l. 102mm.: r. 97mm. Models marked 'Foreign' are invariably of German origin and were made in the 1920s.

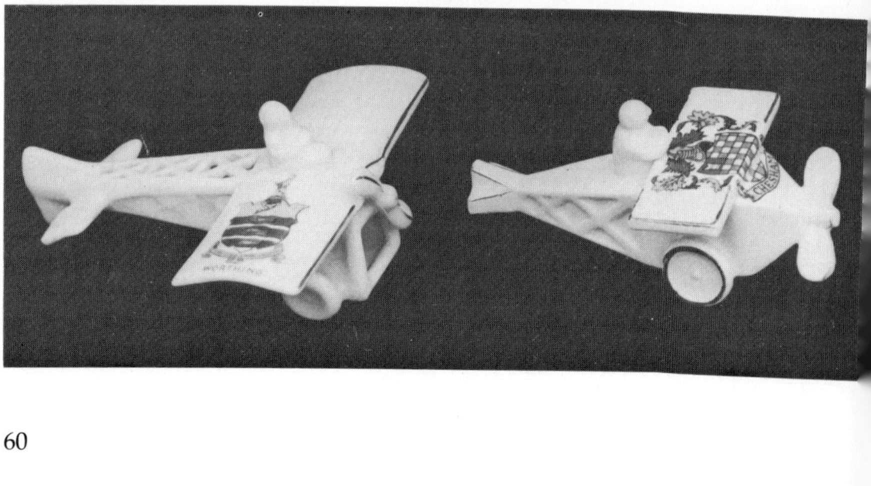

with the "Victory of Justice..." inscription. Both carry coloured roundels and have red, white and blue tail rudders.

The Arcadian 'Model of a new aeroplane' (Reg. No. 768683) dates from December 1916 and is almost certainly based on the Sopwith Pup. The fine Grafton biplane (Grafton 450) resembles a BE2c and the Shelley model (Shelley 344), dating from early 1918, a Sopwith Camel.

Models marked "Foreign" or "Made in Saxony" were made in Germany in the post-war years.

Models of aeroplane propellers are found in Willow and Wilton china. Some carry the crest of the RAF, RFC and RNAS. The Willow model first appeared in early summer 1916.

A model of a Cooper bomb, usually inscribed "Model of a British Aerial Bomb" (Reg. No. 657694) appears in Arcadian china.

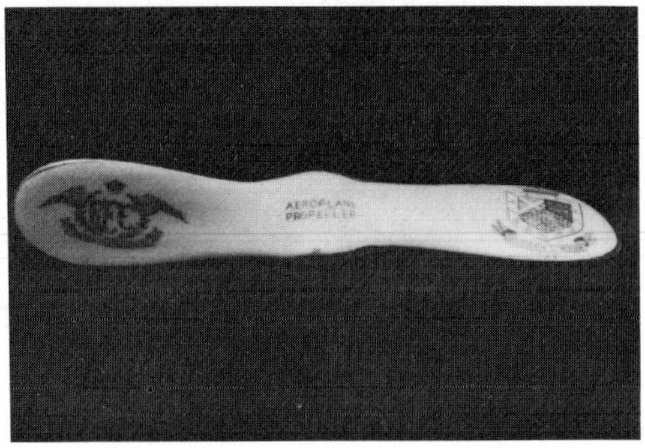

Unmarked. 150mm. ins. 'Aeroplane propeller' with RFC crest. Also found with RNAS and RAF crests.

Men of the newly formed RAF priming Cooper bombs. They are still wearing their RNAS caps.

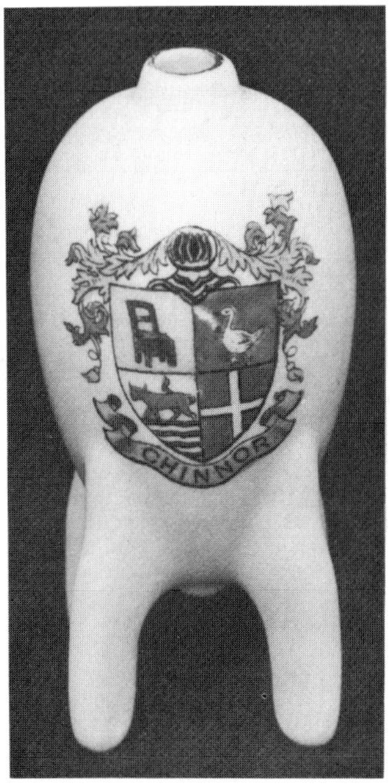

Arcadian China 78mm. Reg. No. 657694 ins. 'British Aerial Bomb'

6 Airships and Zeppelins

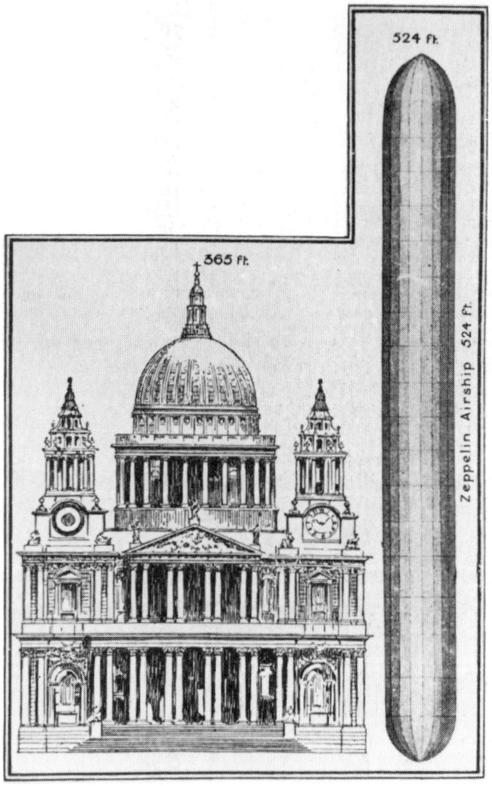

Zeppelin compared with St. Pauls. The latest 'Super Zeppelins' contained 2 million cu. ft. of highly inflammable hydrogen.

In the early days of aviation there was much interest in the exploration of the possibilities of using balloons filled with a lighter than air gas as a means of transport. The very first balloon to ascend, some two hundred years ago, had been filled with hot air but this was subsequently replaced by light but inflammable hydrogen. By the twentieth century this was still the main form of lift in airships which by then had evolved into three types. The non-rigid simply consisted of an envelope filled with gas; the semi-rigid was similar, but with the addition of a fixed keel; and the rigid variety which had a framework of aluminium or wood supporting the surrounding envelope. It was this latter type that was to enable airship construction and aviation to be taken to its fullest.

When war broke out Germany was in the forefront of airship design and technology, due mainly to the efforts of a retired military engineer Count Ferdinand von Zeppelin. After leaving the army at the age of 52 the Count was able to devote his time to what had been almost a life-long passion, namely the design and structure of heavier than air airships and their application in warfare. His first ship the LZ1 (Luftschill Zeppelin) a 420ft. rigid airship containing 400,000 cu. ft. of hydrogen, gingerly emerged from its hangar at Friedrichschafen on Lake Constance on 2nd July 1900. After only two flights the ship was dismantled. The Count, undaunted, continued and with the help of economist and journalist, Hugo Eckener, established the world's first passenger airline, DELAG (The German Airship Transport Company) in 1909. The airline prospered and up until the beginning of the war kept up regular passenger flights to and from the continent.

In the early months of hostilities the German Zeppelins were used to bomb various cities in Belgium and northern France. It was only a matter of time before they turned their attention to England. Initially the Kaiser, a relative of our own King George V, would not authorise bombing raids on London although acceptance was given to attacking dockyards and military installations on the east coast. On the afternoon of 19th January 1915 three army Zeppelins, L3, 4 and 6 left their hangars in northern Europe on what was the first bombing raid on English soil. Setting their sights for Norfolk and Grimsby they were to cross the North Sea in daylight, drop their bombs at or after dusk and to return to their

Poster advertising the 'Daily Chronicle'

AIRSHIP RAIDS, JANUARY 19th, 1915, TO APRIL 13th, 1918.

Date and Locality.	Civilian Casualties. Killed.	Civilian Casualties. Injured.	Sailors and Soldiers. Killed.	Sailors and Soldiers. Injured.
1915.—Jan. 19-20, Norfolk	4	15	—	1
April 14-15, Northumberland	—	2	—	—
April 15-16, Essex and Suffolk	—	—	—	—
April 29-30, Suffolk	—	—	—	—
May 9-10, Southend	1	1	—	1
May 16-17, Ramsgate	2	1	—	—
May 26-27, Southend	3	3	—	—
May 31st-June 1st, East London	7	33	—	2
June 4-5, Kent, Essex, and East Riding ..	—	8	—	—
June 6-7, Hull, Grimsby, and East Riding..	24	38	—	2
June 15-16, Northumberland and Durham ..	18	72	—	—
Aug. 9-10, Goole, East Riding, Suffolk, & Dover	17	18	—	3
Aug. 12-13, East Suffolk and Essex ..	6	24	—	—
Aug. 17-18, Kent, Essex, and London ..	10	48	—	—
Sept. 7-8, East Suffolk and London ..	18	37	—	1
Sept. 8-9, North Riding, Norfolk, and London	24	92	2	2
Sept. 11-12, Essex	—	—	—	—
Sept. 12-13, Essex and East Suffolk.. ..	—	—	—	—
Sept. 13-14, East Suffolk	—	—	—	—
Oct. 13-14, Norfolk, Suffolk, Home Counties, and London	54	107	17	21
1916.—Jan. 31-Feb. 1, West Suffolk and Midland Counties	70	112	—	1
March 5-6, Hull and East Riding, Lincolnshire, Leicestershire, Rutland, and Kent ..	18	52	—	—
March 31-April 1, Lincs, Essex, and Suffolk..	17	9	31	55
April 1-2, Co. Durham and North Riding*..	22	128	—	2
April 2-3, E. Suffolk, Northumberland, London, and Scotland	13	24	—	—
April 3-4, Norfolk	—	—	—	—
April 5-6, Yorkshire and Co. Durham ..	1	9	—	—
April 24-25, Norfolk, Lincs, Cambs, and Suffolk	1	1	—	—
April 25-26, E. Suffolk, Essex, Kent, & London	—	1	—	—
April 26-27, Kent	—	—	—	—
May 2-3, Yorks, Northumberland, & Scotland	7	25	2	5
July 28-29, Lincolnshire and Norfolk ..	—	—	—	—
July 31-Aug. 1, Norfolk, Suffolk, Cambs, Lincs, Notts, and Kent	—	—	—	—
Aug. 2-3, Norfolk, East Suffolk, and Kent..	—	—	—	—
Aug. 8-9, Northumberland, Durham, East Riding, North Riding, Hull, and Norfolk	10	15	—	1
Aug. 23-24, East Suffolk	—	—	—	—
Aug. 24-25, E. Suffolk, Essex, Kent, & London	9	25	—	15
Sept. 2-3, East Riding, Lincolnshire, Nottinghamshire, Norfolk, Suffolk, Cambridgeshire, Huntingdonshire, Essex, Hertfordshire, Beds, Kent, and London	4	12	—	—
Sept. 23-24, Lincs, Notts, Norf., Kent, & London	40	126	—	4
Sept. 25-26, Lancs, Yorks, and Lincolnshire..	43	31	—	—
Oct. 1-2, Lincs, Norfolk, Cambs, Northants, Herts, and London	—	1	1	—
Nov. 27-28, Durham, Yorks, Staffs, & Cheshire	4	37	—	—
1917.—March 16-17, Kent and Sussex ..	—	—	—	—
May 23-24, Essex, Norfolk, and Suffolk ..	1	—	—	—
June 16-17, Kent and Suffolk	3	14	—	2
Aug. 21-22, East Riding	—	1	—	—
Sept. 24-25, Lincolnshire and Yorkshire ..	—	3	—	—
Oct. 19-20, Midlands, E. Counties, and London	31	52	5	3
1918.—March 12-13, East Riding	1	—	—	—
March 13-14, Durham	8	39	—	—
April 12-13, Lincs, Lancs, & Warwickshire..	7	20	—	—
Totals for airship raids	498	1,236	58	121

Airship raids 1915-1918.

base under cover of darkness. The L6 developed engine trouble over the North Sea and returned to its base. The L3 and L4 commanded respectively by Kapitanleutnants Hans Fritz and Magnus Graf von Laten Hallermund, reached the coast of Norfolk where they separated. Fritz found the town of Great Yarmouth where he dropped six 110 pound explosive bombs and six incendiaries, none of which did much damage. Hallermund in the L4, thinking himself to be over Grimsby when in fact he was over the little village of Sheringham in Norfolk, dropped two bombs. More bombs were dropped in the area during the rest of the night but most fell in open country and caused minimal damage. Four people were killed and sixteen injured in the raid.

Although the immediate effects had been small this raid had set a precedent and opened the way for further attacks on English soil. In the remaining years of the war there were a further fifty airship raids (forty-two of which took place in the years 1915-16) on British soil which accounted for 566 deaths, 1,357 injured and an estimated £1.5 millions worth of damage. In the light of the bombing raids on London, some twenty five years later they were insignificant but to a naive populace they caused a great deal of alarm and scaremongering. In one instance after an attack on Hull in June 1915, troops had to be called in to quell rioters who ransacked shops owned by Germans, and for some time after the raid thousands of the city's inhabitants left their homes each night and slept in the fields. It was even officially suggested, and for some time considered, that any crew members captured should be made a special class of prisoner and shot!

Despite their apparent vulnerability it was not until the autumn of 1916 that one of these aerial raiders was shot down over England. On 2nd September sixteen airships from both army and navy set a course for various points on the east coast. During the night some 621 high explosive and 202 incendiary bombs were dropped. Four people were killed, 12 injured and an estimated £21,000 worth of damage was done.

Number 39 squadron based at Sutton Farm was charged with the defence of an area in the north east of London. At 11.08pm. Lt. William Leefe-Robinson with two other planes, took off on his regular patrol. At 1.10am. after a fruitless two hour search he encountered and then lost the

Diagrammatic representation of a Zeppelin dropping a bomb on the ill-fated city of Antwerp.

RAF recruitment poster. In April 1918 the RFC and RNAS amalgamated to form the Royal Air Force.

1 Top: 'RMS Lusitania' 168mm. Carlton Reg. No. 662104; also ins. 'Remember the Lusitania' and 'The Lusitania was sunk by a German submarine May 1915; Lives lost 1,198' or 'Sunk by German submarine off the Irish coast May 7th 1915; Lives lost 1,275, saved 703'.
Bottom. 'Lusitania' 165mm Victoria.

2 Savoy bust of a Sailor 'HMS Lion'.

3 Carlton vase with transfer of torpedo victim RMS Lusitania.

4 Biplane 165mm. Carlton; with coloured roundels and 'Victory of Justice' inscription. This model has the crest of La Boiselle, a small village on the Western Front which saw heavy fighting during the Somme offensive of 1916.

5 Monoplane 145mm. Willow Art.
Biplane 135mm. Carlton.
Both have the Air Force roundels introduced in 1915 as aids to identification.

6 Grafton China 70mm. Squatting sailor holding submarine in hands and with the words 'We've got 'U' well in hand' on his cap. The pipe in his mouth is turned downwards in characteristic naval fashion.

1

2

3

4

5

6

AIRSHIP SCHUTTE-LANZ

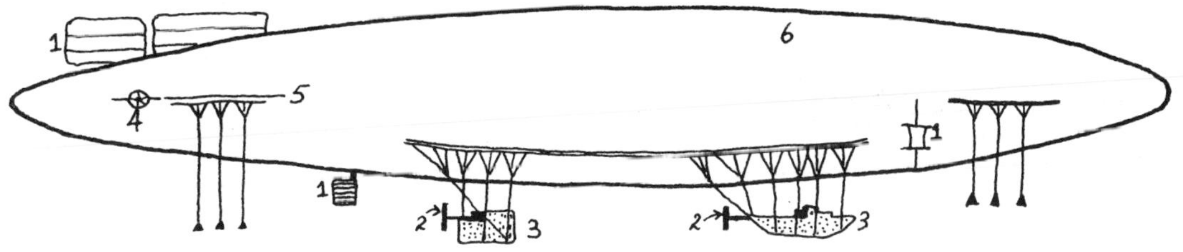

1. Rudder
2. Propellor
3. Gondola
4. Elevator
5. Stabilising Plane
6. Envelope (stretched) over plywood frame)

THE LAST FLIGHT OF THE SL11
September 3rd 1916

HISTORY
Commissioned - August 2nd 1916
Length - 570ft. 10ins.
Height - 81ft.
Diameter - 65ft. 11ins.
Lift - 46,200 lbs.
Max. Altitude - 12,000 ft.
Max. Speed - 57mph
Crew - 16
Volume - 1,369,300 cu. ft.

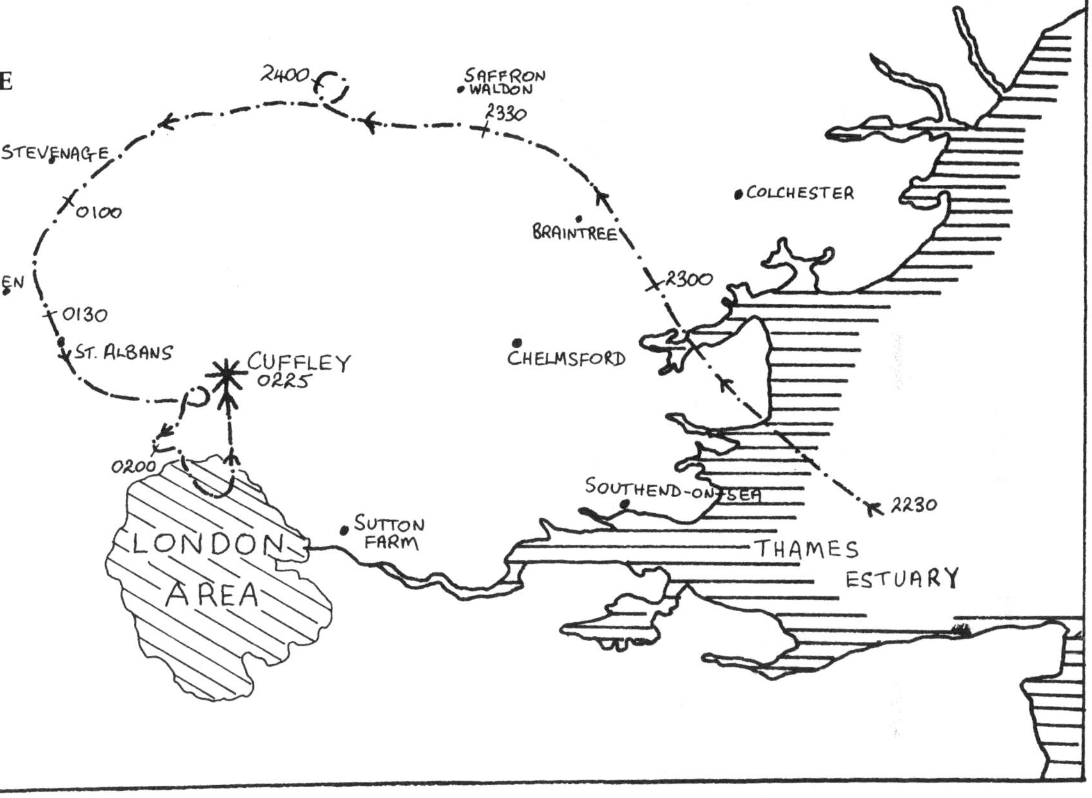

Memorial to Captain Robinson at Cuffley.

The morning after - remains of the SL11. The wooden frame burned and little was left. Thousands of Londoners flocked to the village to get a glimpse of the ship.

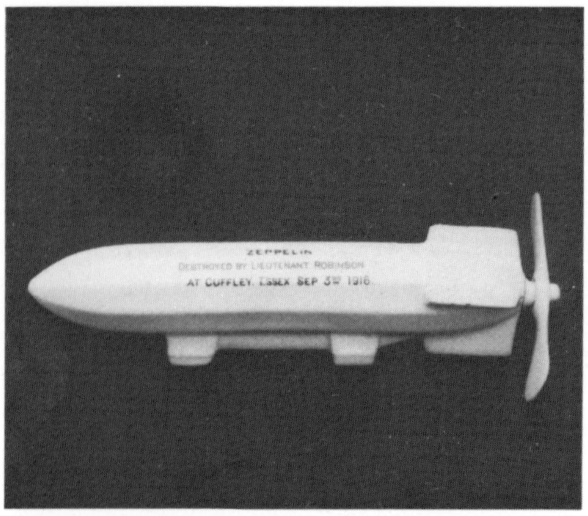

Savoy china 170mm. Reg. No. 659483 ins. 'Zeppelin destroyed by Lieutenant Robinson VC at Cuffley, Essex. September 3rd 1916'. Registered in Feb. 1917, two weeks after photographs of SL11 and LZ33 appeared together in the Great War magazine. The designers seem to have confused the two. Cuffley is in Essex, Robinson's airship was a wooden framed Schutte Lanz.

One of the gondola propellers of the L33. Did this photograph confuse the Savoy designers into thinking that their model of the SL11 should have one enormous rear propeller?

Areas bombed by Zeppelins 1915-1918

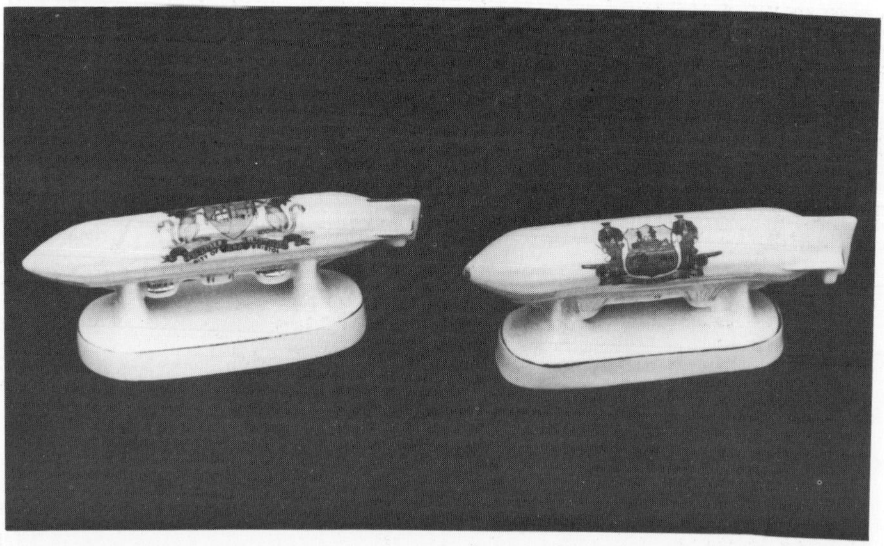

l. Alexandra china 132mm. Arcadian china 132mm. Reg. No. 652241. Registered in October 1915 one week after the worst Zeppelin raid to date. Surprisingly a very popular model.

Hero of the hour, Lieutenant William Leefe Robinson destroyer of the SL11. Seven months later he fell foul of von Richtofens flying circus.

army airship, L98. His report, written on landing carries on the account... "I managed to pick up and distinguish my flares again. At about 1.50am. I noticed a red glow in the north east of London. Taking it to be an outbreak of fire I went in that direction. At about 2.05am. a Zeppelin was picked up over NNE London (as far as I could judge). Remembering my last failure I sacrificed height (I was still at 12,000ft.) for speed and made nose down for the Zeppelin. I saw shells bursting and night tracers flying around it. When I drew closer I noticed that the anti-aircraft fire was too high or too low, also a good many rose 800ft. behind and a few tracers went right over. I could hear the bursts when about 3000ft. from the Zeppelin.

I flew to about 800ft. below it from bow to stern and distributed one drum along it (alternate new Brock and Pomeroy). It seemed to have no effect. I therefore moved to one side and gave it another drum along its side .... without much apparent effect. I then got behind it (by this time I was very close, 500ft. or less below) and concentrated one drum on one part underneath. I was then at a height of 11,500ft. when attacking the Zeppelin. I had hardly finished the drum when I saw the part fired at glow. In a few seconds the whole of the rear part was blazing. When the third drum was fired there were no searchlights on the Zeppelin and no A.A. was firing. I quickly got out of the way of the falling Zeppelin and being very excited fired off a few red Very lights and dropped a parachute flare.

Having little oil or petrol left, I returned to Sutton Farm landing at 2.45am. On landing I found that I had shot away my machine gun wire guard, the rear part of the centre section and had pierced the main spar several times..."

The airship that Lt. Leefe-Robinson shot down was not a Zeppelin as thought, but a (wooden framed) Schutte-Lanz; the SL11 commanded by Haptmann Wilheim Schramm. It fluttered to the ground and landed near the Hertfordshire village of Cuffley where its framework continued to burn for some time. The next day all roads to the small village were blocked as thousands of sightseers clamoured to catch a glimpse of the wrecked ship. Three days later Robinson was awarded the Victoria Cross and immediately became a popular national hero. Various businessmen had contributed to a reward for the first airman to shoot down a Zeppelin on British soil and much to the annoyance of the War Office Robinson

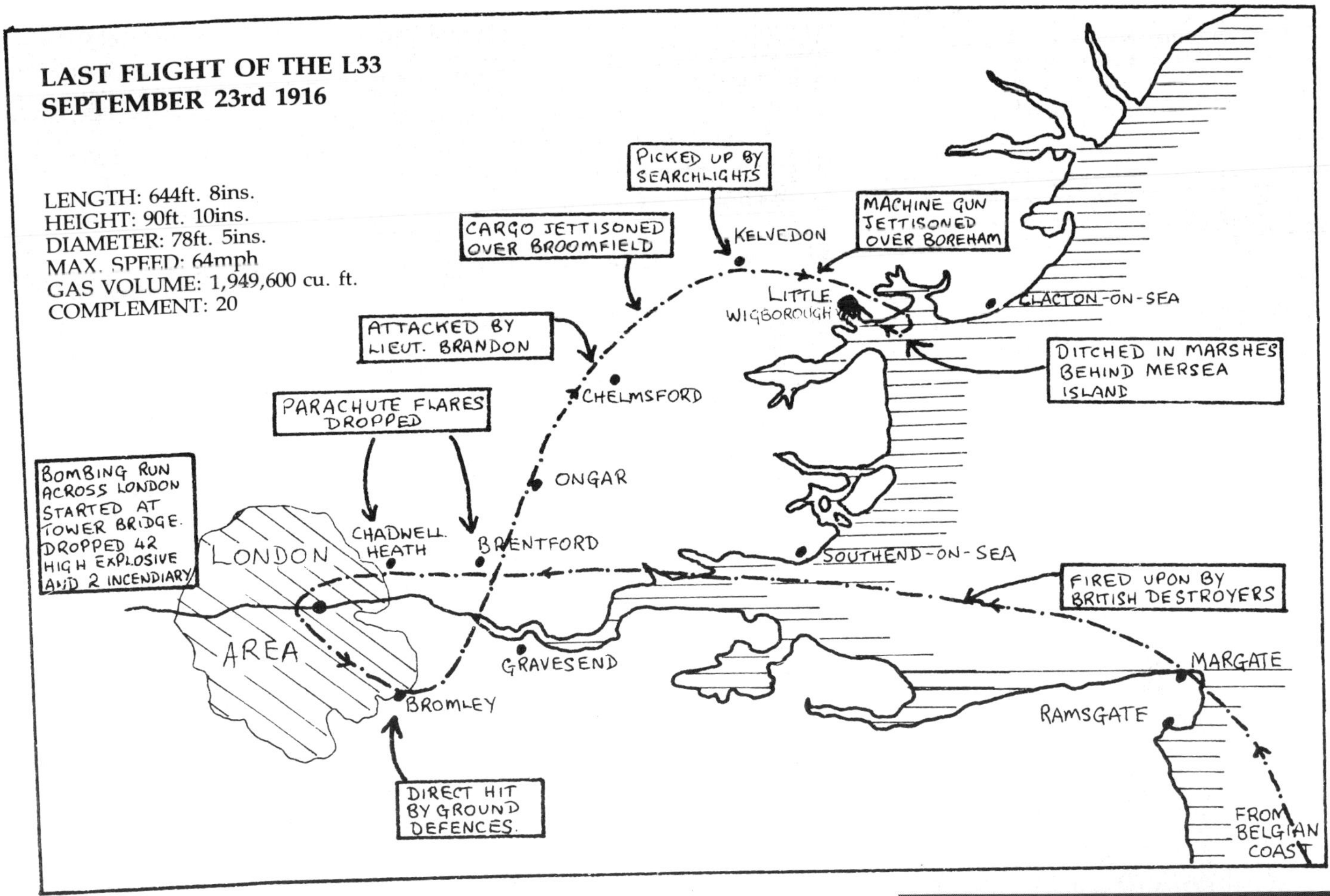

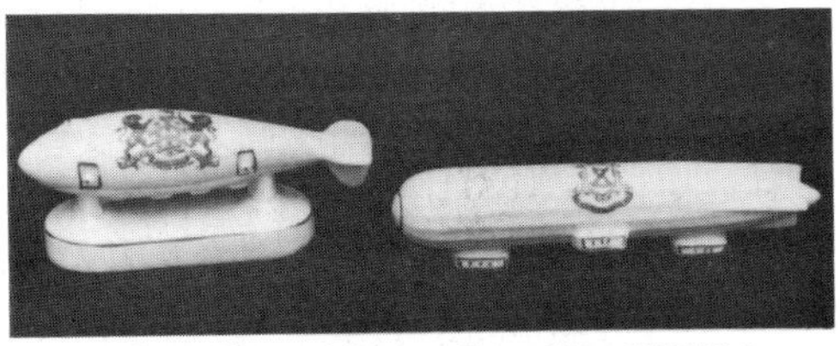

l. Arcadian China 117mm. Reg. No. 657735 ins. 'Model of Super Zeppelin' r. Shelley China 154mm impressed 'L33'. The totally inaccurate Arcadian design was registered four days after the L33 crashed. The more accurate Shelley design dates from early 1917.

Remains of the LZ33 brought down at Little Wigborough. Enough remained of this ship for experts to glean information on Zeppelin technology.

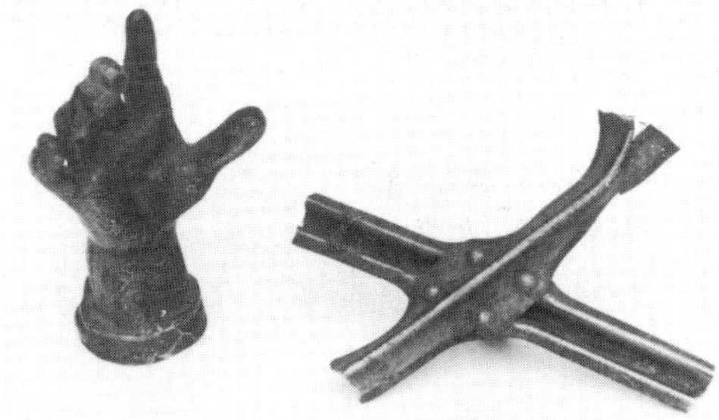

Zeppelin artefacts - l. hand moulded from aluminium alloy of a Zeppelin, r. part of the framework of a Zeppelin.

Willow Art China 82mm. ins. 'Beta'

Airship 'Beta'. Built in 1909, by 1914 she had been superceded by Gamma and Delta although she was used in the early part of the war for training pilots.

was presented with a cheque for £3,500. Steps were soon taken to see that it did not happen again! Robinson stayed with the flight for only a few more months and was then posted to the Western Front. On April 8th 1917 his flight encountered von Richtofen's flying circus and he was shot down and captured. He spent the rest of the war in various prison camps, returning to Britain on December 31st 1918. His health had suffered during his confinement and he died during the dreaded influenza epidemic on 17th January 1919. After his death a memorial was erected on the site of the crash and can be seen today bearing the inscription "Erected by the readers of the Daily Express to the memory of Captain William Leefe-Robinson, V.C., Worcs. Reg. and R.F.C. who on September 3rd 1916 above this spot brought down SL11, the first German airship destroyed over British soil".

That same autumn saw the appearance of some of the most awesome airships ever to fly... the 'Super Zeppelins'. These ships, all of the L30 class, (L30, L31 etc.) were over six hundred feet long and carried two million cubic feet of gas, five times as much as Von Zeppelin's original airship. They had a crew of twenty housed in three gondolas slung under the belly of the ship and were able to carry five tons of bombs.

The fate of the Zeppelin raids was sealed in the disasterous raid of 23rd September when four of these new Super Zeppelins and eight older types

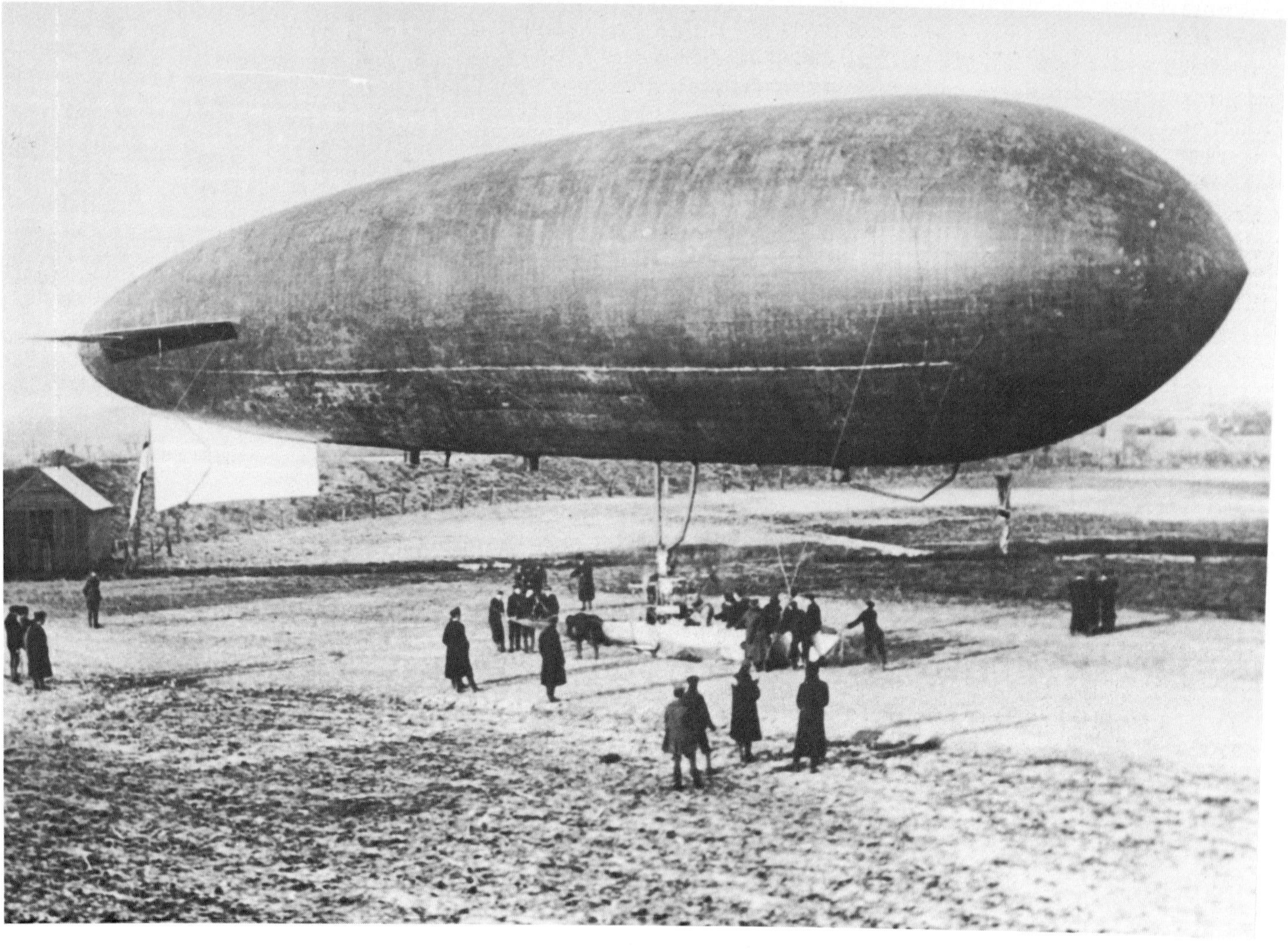

set course for London. Two, the L32 and L33, were brought down. The L33 falling at Little Wigborough in Essex in an almost intact state. Although it was set alight by the crew, who were later captured, enough remained to enable British scientists to learn a great deal about Zeppelin design and technology.

Britain, in contrast, was well behind in the field of rigid airships. After an abortive attempt with a rigid design in 1911 when 'His Majesty's Airship No. 1' (nicknamed 'Mayfly') broke in two as she was being hauled from her shed all plans for such an airship were shelved. It was not until the closing months of the war that the British 'R' series airships made their appearance and even then much of their technology had been gleaned from crashed Zeppelins.

Most of the British airships at the outbreak of war were of the non-rigid type. In 1907 the Army balloon factory produced a non-rigid airship called 'Nilli-Secundus' (second to none) which was later used to make the semi-rigid 'Nilli-Secundus II'. This airship completed a few short flights in 1908 and was then dismantled. In the same year work began on a 21,000 cu. ft., 84ft long airship called 'Baby', an enlarged version of which, called 'Beta', appeared in 1909. Beta had a capacity of 35,000 cu. ft. and was powered by a single 35hp engine. Amongst her exploits she flew from Farnborough to London and back on 3rd June 1910 in the then record time of four hours and four minutes. In February 1911 she was the first aircraft to have radio equipment fitted. By 1914 she had been superceded by 'Gamma' (75,000 cu. ft.) and 'Delta' (175,000 cu. ft.) although she was used in the early part of the war for training pilots.

British Sea-Scout Airships (Blimps) were developed in 1915 as small, low powered, semi-rigid airships for use in coastal defence and convoy escort. They were powered by a variety of engines, the type with a 70hp engine was capable of an airspeed of forty miles per hour and could remain on patrol for eight hours. By the end of that year they were making daily patrols over the English Channel and Irish Sea from RNAS bases in Kent, Sussex and Anglesey and from the Pas de Calais in France. Although their success in submarine destruction was limited, by demonstrating their presence, they most certainly made the job of the U-boat commanders more difficult and helped to save a great deal of Merchant shipping.

Arcadian 119mm. Reg. No. 658679 ins. 'Model of British Airship'.

British Sea-Scout airship, nicknamed 'Blimps', were developed in 1915 as convoy escorts in an attempt to counter the submarine blockade that was gradually strangling Britain.

British Caquot observation balloon being hauled down near Fricourt, France in 1916. The motor winch vehicle is in the bottom right of the picture. The basis for the design for the British 'sausage' balloons came from a captured German balloon.

Another important service provided by aircrew was that of artillery spotting. This was carried out, not only by aircraft but also by air balloons. The British Kite Balloon service grew out of the need to range artillery. Floating above the trenches, their lifeline a thin steel hawser, the men in these hydrogen filled sacks provided an invaluable service to the gunners below. Although protected heavily by ground gun crews they were easy prey for marauding enemy planes for with no inboard defence, their only means of escape was to be wound to earth by the ground crew. It is not surprising that when parachutes were first available they were given to the spotters in these balloons.

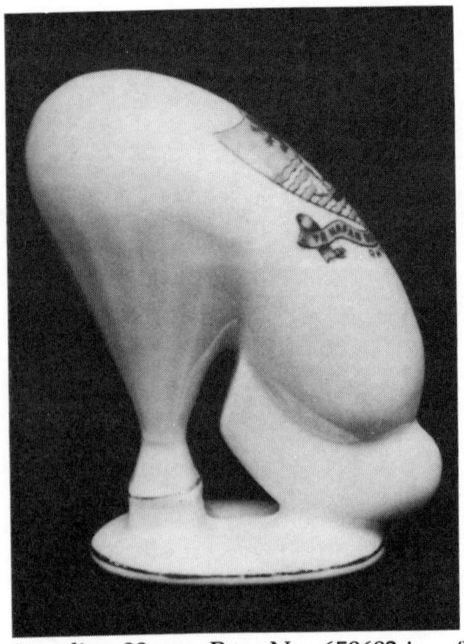

Arcadian 90mm. Reg. No. 658682 ins. 'Model of Observer Sausage Balloon'.

The China

Several models of British airships are found in china although more surprising is that models of Zeppelins exist as well. One would think that with the fear and consternation that they brought to the people of Britain there would be little desire to buy them as mantelpiece objects.

The earliest model is most probably that of the non-rigid airship 'Beta' which is found in Willow Art china and may have been inspired by the ship's flight from Farnborough to London in 1910. The shape of the original is somewhat deviated from although the gondola suspension wires are rather cleverly shown, gathered into a narrow base. Models are found both with and without the ship's name printed on the base.

Designs for a model of a British Sea Scout (Blimp) and a Drachen Kite Balloon were registered on 6th December 1916 by H.T. Robinson and are found in Arcadian china with the inscriptions, 'Model of British Airship' (Reg. No. 658679) and 'Model of Observer sausage balloon' (Reg. No. 658672) respectively. Both are remarkably accurate in shape and appearance although for some reason the latter is shown in a semi-inflated state.

The remaining models are of rigid airships and perforce must be based on German airships. The model of an airship on a plinth (Reg. No. 652241) was registered by J.A. Robinson on 20th October 1915, a mere six days after what was up to then the worst raid on England. It was subsequently copied by other manufacturers and is the most common model of an airship found. A similar model, with three gondolas is found in Alexandra china.

A splendid model of the ill-fated SL11 appears in Savoy china (Reg. No. 659483) and carries the erroneous inscription, 'Zeppelin destroyed by Lieutenant Robinson VC at Cuffley, Essex. Sept. 3rd 1916'. Two weeks before this design was registered on 16th February 1917 photographs of the wrecked L33 appeared in the 'Great War' magazine, with the subtitles, 'Skeleton of Zeppelin brought down on the Essex coast Sept. 24th 1916'. For some reason the designers seem to have confused this with the SL11, brought down in Cuffley, Hertfordshire, three weeks earlier. A close up photograph of one of the gondola propellers, giving a completely wrong impression of size, probably inspired the large and totally impractical rear propeller found on the model.

An accurate model of the L33 was made by the Shelley works (Shelley 332) although the Arcadian 'Model of a Super Zeppelin' (Reg. No. 657735) which was registered one week after the L33's crash, would seem to have been derived from it as well. So inaccurate is the shape of the latter (it is even described in the Patent Office Register as a 'Torpedo'!) that I consider it to be a combination of written press reports and the designers imagination. The Carlton model that appears with a black Maltese Cross in addition to the crest is also Zeppelin based although no information as to its date of origin has been found. Some models are found with the cross unpainted but with the addition of an RFC roundel, no doubt added to later models which appeared when the British 'R' series were flying.

Models of bombs dropped from Zeppelins were made by a variety of manufacturers. Arcadian china commemorated the first Zeppelin raid on Britain with, 'Model of bomb dropped from Zeppelin upon Sheringham during the first raid on England: 8.30pm. Jany 9th 1915'. This model is like the Carbonite incendiary bombs that were used in these first raids. They were made from a blunt-nosed, cylindrical sheet steel

Carlton China 122mm. Originally based on a German Zeppelin this model has the Maltese Cross impressed. On post 1918 models the cross was left unpainted and a colour transfer of the RAF roundels added.

Sheringham bomb disguised as the Loftus bomb. An alternative, very rare, inscription found on the bomb.

Arcadian China 110mm. Reg. No. 664837 ins. 'Model of bomb dropped from Zeppelin upon Sheringham during the first raid on England 8.30pm. Jan. 19th 1915 and 'Made for Bertram A. Watts Sheringham'. The model resembles a carbonite incendiary bomb. The propeller revolved as it fell and activated the fuse. For some reason a registration certificate was not given for this model nevertheless the number of the refused certificate invariably appears on the model.

Goldschmidt bomb. An early German incendiary bomb. The detonator was at the bottom and the rope prevented leakage of chemicals.

container fitted with a tail fuse and stabilising fin. The propeller like tail fuse rotated during its downward path and activated the bomb which contained three and a half kilograms of a highly inflammable mixture of benzole, kerosene and tar. The stabilising fin, which surrounded the propeller, is missing from the model. No doubt the original photograph, which has not been traced, was of a 'dud' which had lost its tail fin as it plunged into the ground. For some reason the model was not registered at the Patent Office until August 1918 and then the design was refused. Nevertheless all models still carry the Registration Number 664837, that for the refused certificate. Unfortunately the representations of refused designs are not available to the public and so we have no way of knowing whether or not this was Robinson's original design or a modified version to which he added the registration number for good measure. Models are found with the added inscription 'Made for Bertram A. Watts, Sheringham',... which leads me to surmise that they were made in a small quantity at the request of the said Mr. Watts who also provided the photograph. Very rarely the model is found with the inscription, 'Model of first bomb dropped from Zeppelin at Loftus Sept 8 1915'.

W.H. Goss commemorated two raids with a 'Model of German bomb dropped on Bury St. Edmunds from a Zeppelin, 30th April 1915' and a 'Model of a German Incendiary Bomb dropped at Maldon 16 April 1915 from a German Zeppelin'. Both these appeared in the War Edition of the Goss Record (1917) without the above inscription and in its place a rather secretive, 'Models of bombs dropped in the Eastern counties'. Similar models were made by Arcadian, Grafton (405) and Shelley (177) which are often found inscribed, 'Model of German Incendiary Bomb' or 'Model of Zeppelin Bomb'. All are copies of the Goldschmidt incendiary bombs used at the time. These consisted of an iron cylinder filled with thermite which was surrounded by a thin sheet metal container filled with three and a half litres of benzol which were wrapped in a tarred rope which prevented dispersal of the benzol. A percussion cap on the base exploded on contact and ignited the contents which burnt vigorously at the very high temperature of 3000 degrees Centigrade. Remains

Which way did it go? Bemused inhabitants of the Norfolk village of Sheringham examine a bomb crater made near their village during the first Zeppelin raid. The soldier was stationed nearby.

of some of these bombs can be seen in the Imperial War Museum, London.

Carlton China modelled a 'Model of British Searchlight' which is also found with the inscription, 'The Zeppelin Finder', while Savoy, forever finding the unusual, chose a 'British Motor Searchlight' for their model. No firm identification has been made of the latter although it closely resembles such a vehicle that was used in South Africa and was featured in the 'Great War' Magazine.

l. to r. Arcadian china 79mm., Swan China 79mm., ins. 'Model of bomb which killed a chicken at Southend' (What will they think of next!), Goss China 76mm. ins. 'Model of German incendiary bomb dropped at Malden 16th April 1915 from a German Zeppelin', Shelley China 84mm. ins. 'Model of Zeppelin bomb', Goss 75mm. ins. 'Model of German bomb dropped on Bury St. Edmunds from a Zeppelin 30th April 1915'.

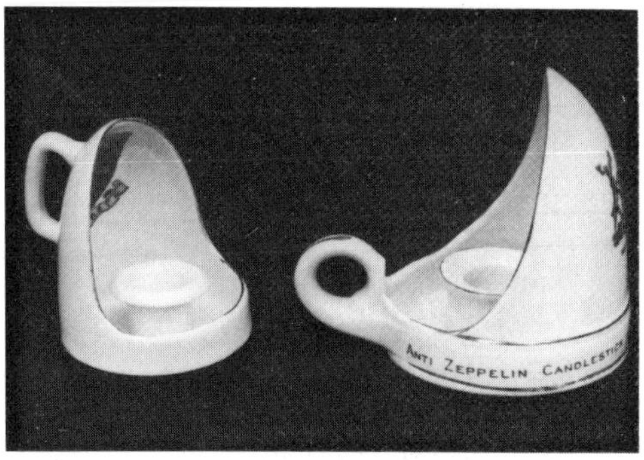

l. Arcadian China 64mm. r. Shelley China 83mm No. 348. ins. 'Anti-Zeppelin candlestick as used in the Great War - Souvenir'. The Arcadian model has the handle in the wrong position.

l. Savoy China 110mm. ins. 'Model of British Motor Searchlight' r. Carlton China 74mm. ins. 'Model of British Searchlight - The Zeppelin Finder'.

'British Motor Searchlight'

7 Ships and Submarines

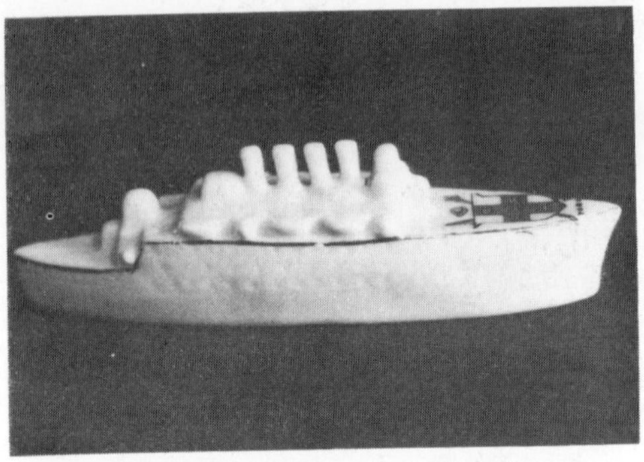

Willow Art china 135mm. Liner converted to troop carrier. One of this factory's 1914 models. Probably based on one of the transports that carried troops across the channel.

In the years leading up to 1914 Admiral Sir John Fisher, then First Sea Lord, initiated the reorganisation of the British Navy. Like the other powerful nations the tendency was to concentrate on the all-big-gun battleships of the Dreadnought class. So great was the firepower of these ships (they were capable of firing a broadside of 5 tons over ten miles) that the strength of a country's navy was gauged on the number of Dreadnoughts it had. In August 1914 the British Navy had forty-four of these Capital ships and the German Navy twenty-eight.

Such was the optimism of the British that a great sea battle was anticipated that would leave the enemy fleet in tatters and Britannia still ruling the waves. In reality there was to be only one instance when the Grand Fleets were to meet each other - at the Battle of Jutland - where they were destined not to come to a head on confrontation but, as one historian put it, 'to hail each other in passing'. For the war at sea the focal point was the new and growing threat that came from under the waves. This was to be the first war in which submarines played an important part.

In the first month of hostilities British cruisers, destroyers and submarines raided German patrols off Heligoland with the intention of enticing the German High Seas Fleet out of its base at Wilhelmshaven. The German Fleet did not oblige and in reply sent a force of battlecruisers and cruisers across the North Sea to bombard various towns on the east coast. On the morning of December 16th 1914 the inhabitants of Scarborough, Whitby and Hartlepool were rudely awakened by the sound of the heavy guns of the warships. Two hours later, having caused much chaos, the ships departed leaving behind seventy-eight dead and two hundred and twenty-eight injured in the three towns.

The first true sea battle of the war was fought off the coast of South America on November 1st. The British ships The Good Hope, Monmouth, Glasgow and Otranto sought to engage what their commander, Sir Christopher Craddock, thought to be a lone German cruiser, the Leipzig. As the British ships spread out in battle formation the German cruisers Scharnhorst and Gneisenau appeared on the horizon. The anticipation of an easy kill now turned sour. Within the hour the Good Hope went to the bottom, followed shortly by the Monmouth. The Glasgow and Otranto managed to escape and the German ships steamed on, virtually unscathed.

Provisions for a warship with a complement in excess of 1000. To this had to be added coal for the engines and ammmunition for the guns.

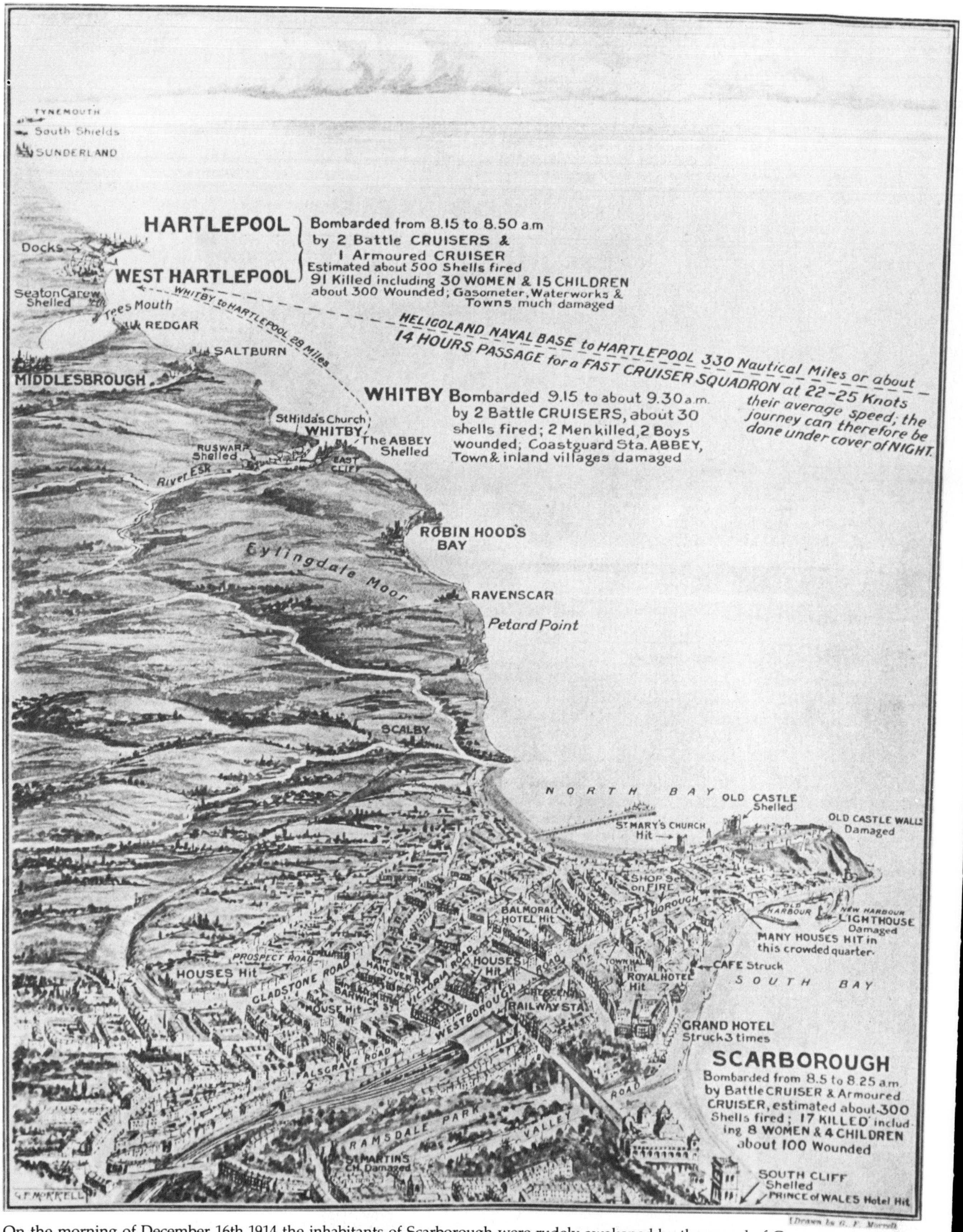

On the morning of December 16th 1914 the inhabitants of Scarborough were rudely awakened by the sound of German heavy shells falling on their town.

Scarborough lighthouse received a direct hit from a German gun.

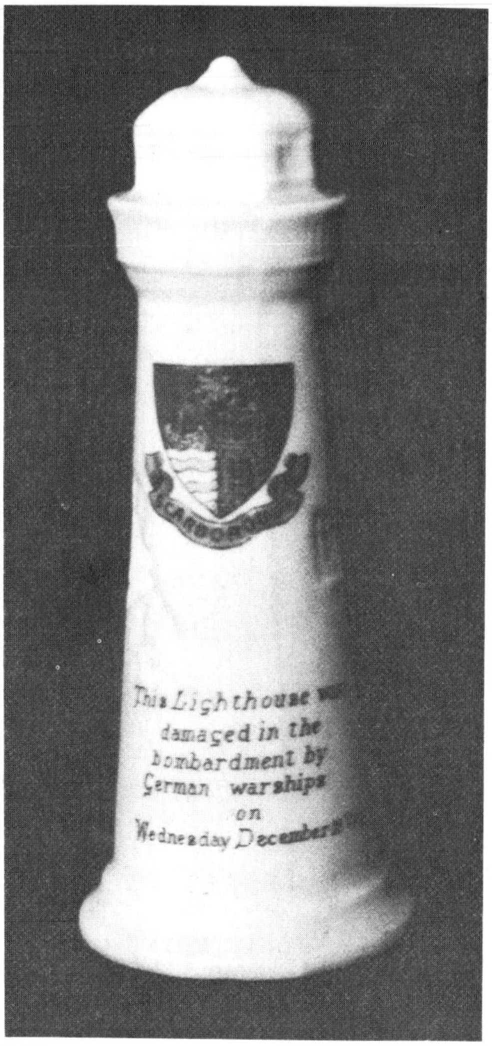

Willow Art China 133mm. ins. 'This lighthouse was damaged in the bombardment by German warships on Wednesday December 16th 1914'. Shell hole at side.

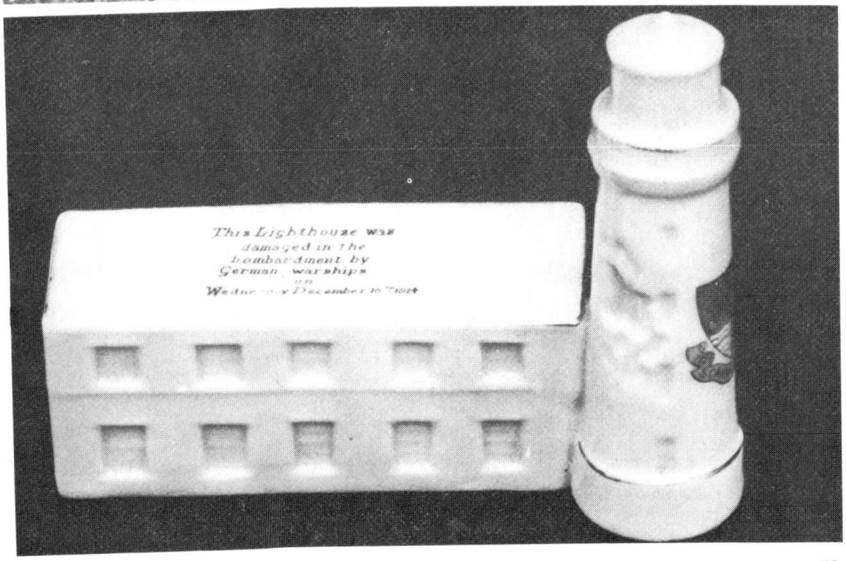

Scarborough lighthouse and coastguard station. Willow 110mm.

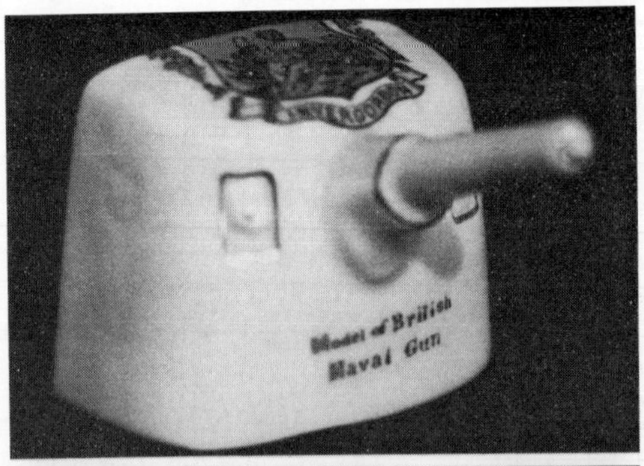

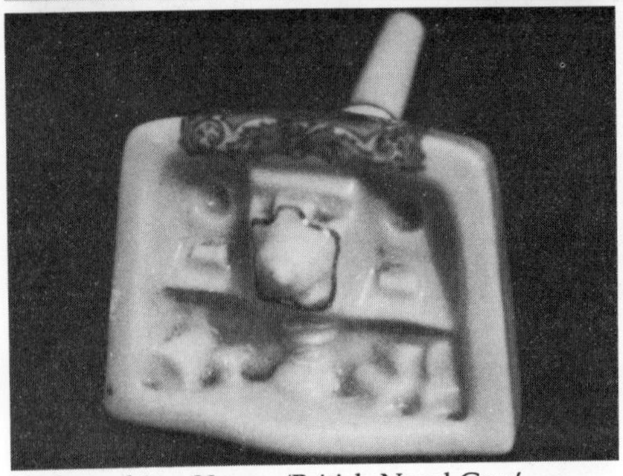

Carlton china 88mm. 'British Naval Gun'.

HMS Queen Elizabeth - the first of the 'Super Dreadnoughts', armed with eight 15 inch guns. Acted as support ships for troops in the Dardanelles campaign in 1915. Surrender of the German Fleet signed on board 21st November 1918. Found in Arcadian, Carlton and Savoy china.

The victory was short-lived for within the month the fleets came to grips again off the Falkland Islands. As if to put the record straight this was a sound British victory. Of the German ships only one, the Dresden, escaped. The Scharnhorst went down under the blazing guns of the Inflexible and Invincible, the Nurnberg under the Kent and the Leipzig to the Cornwall and Glasgow. The Gneisenau went down with flags flying and sailors cheering the Kaiser.

After a disasterous encounter off the Dogger Bank in January 1915, when the German Navy lost the Blucher, the two fleets settled down to a game of cat and mouse. The British fleet looking for a favourable opportunity of engaging the enemy, but at the same time fearful of being drawn into a trap, and the German Fleet looking for opportunities of drawing the British into a trap. At last, on May 31st 1916, the two fleets, numbering some sixty Dreadnoughts (37 British and 23 German) backed up by a large fleet of destroyers and cruisers found themselves in close proximity on the open sea.

Earlier in the year Germany had laid plans for a bombardment of Sunderland hoping this would entice the British squadrons out of port where they would be easy meat for U-boats waiting offshore. Due to bad weather an alternative plan was implemented. Admiral Franz von Hipper was to sail his battlecruiser force north from Heligoland Bight and demonstrate his presence off the Norwegian coast with the intention of luring the British Battlecruiser Fleet, under Vice-Admiral Sir David Beatty, out of its base at Rosyth. The German High Seas Fleet was to follow at a distance and provide the hook on which the British Fleet would be caught.

The British, however, unknown to the Germans, were able to intercept and decode German Naval Radio messages. Since the sinking of the German cruiser, the Magdeburg, in August 1914 when the German Navy cipher and signal books had been found on the body of a dead German, British Intelligence had been able to monitor German Navy signals. Thus the plan was known and a counter attempted. On May 30th the British Grand Fleet was ordered to sea. Admiral Sir John Jellicoe, commanding the main section, sailed eastwards from Scapa Flow for a rendezvous with Beatty's battlecruisers off the Norwegian coast. Beatty sailed from Rosyth with orders to be at a point sixty-nine miles SSE of the main rendezvous point by 2pm on 31st May. Vice-Admiral Sir T.H. Martyn Jerram's squadron left Invergordon and joined the main fleet on the way.

HMS Lion - the leader of Beatty's famous 'Cats'. Completed in 1912 with a speed of 27 knots she was the fastest of the Dreadnoughts. Severely damaged at Jutland and nearly sank. Her sister ship, the Queen Mary, blew up with the loss of all but seven of the crew, a total of 1276. Found in Willow, Carlton and Savoy China.

1

1. Aynsley china regimental crests.
Top: l. to r. Pith helmet 42mm. Reg. No. 442812; King's Own Scottish Borderers 25th Foot; Colonial Hat 106mm.; Royal Army Medical Corps. Pith helmet 42mm. Reg. No. 442812; Royal Horse Guards.
Bottom: l. to r. Shell 106mm. Reg. No. 444369; Black Watch 42nd & 73rd Foot. Pot 46mm. 2nd Dragoons The Royal Scots Greys. Bomb with flames coming out of top 95mm. Reg. No. 444522 1st Middlesex, Victoria & St. Georges Rifles.
All Aynsley military models were registered in 1904 and relate to the Boer War. They are invariably found bearing the crests of regiments, many of which disappeared with the Haldane Reforms of 1908.

2. l. to r. 'Royal Sussex Regiment' : 'Manchester Regiment' : Oxon & Bucks L.I: 'RGA'.

3. War Memorials: l. to r. RAF Memorial 170mm Alexandra; the original stands on London's Embankment, the golden eagle atop looking out over the Thames.
Cumberland and Westmoreland Memorial 152mm Leadbeater Art; Erected to commemorate the 10,000 men and women of the two counties who lost their lives in the war.
Llandudno War Memorial 180mm Unmarked.

4. Battleship crests: HMS Belerophon; HMS Ceres; HMS Thunderer.

5. The Highland Light Infantry.

2

3

4

5

1. Savoy foreign crests with informative inscriptions on reverse. l. to r. Servia, Ypres, Malines, Arras.
This factory produced a total of twenty-three recorded foreign crests with inscriptions.

2. Goss 'Flags of the Allies' designs. l. Seven flag designs - Great Britain, France, Belgium, Servia, Russia, Japan and Italy. Alternatively found with the wording: 'L'Union Fait La Force - Eendracht Maakt Macht' in the place of the country names.
r. Four flag design - Great Britain, France, Belgium, Russia.
Flags designs were produced soon after the commencement of hostilities. As more countries joined in the design was changed. Originally the Russian Naval Flag (Blue cross on white background) was incorrectly used.

3. L. to r. Pair of candlesticks 90mm Corona china; Flags of Russia, France, Great Britain and Belgium. Top hat 46mm. Corona china; Royal Standard with portrait of General French inset. Collar stud 34mm. Unmarked; Portrait of Lord Kitchener surrounded by flags of France, Belgium, Great Britain and Russia.

4. L. to r. '12th Lancers'; 'The Man in Khaki'; '1st Life Guards' Corona china.

5. Bulldog looking out of kennel: l. Arcadian 97mm. r. Carlton 85mm. Both inscribed: 'The Black Watch'.

6. Fireplaces: top l. Arcadian 93mm. ins. 'We've kept the home fires burning'. r. Carlton 86mm. long. ins. 'Keep the home fires burning'. Bottom: l. Unmarked 73mm. long ins. as Carlton r. Shelley 71mm. ins. as Carlton & 'Till the boys come home'.

1

2

3

4

5

6

On reaching his turning point Beatty sailed northwards to meet Jellicoe One of his light cruisers, the Galatea, sighted a lone merchant steamer and bore off to examine. As luck would have it one of Hipper's cruisers sighted the steamer from the other side and turned to investigate. As they steamed closer they sighted each other and the message, 'Enemy in sight' was passed to their commanders. Throughout the afternoon and night flanks of the two great fleets engaged each other and under cover of darkness the German fleet was able to slip through and sail to safety. Had this chance encounter been missed then the fleets would have met further north and closer to the British main fleet.

The total loss for the British was three battleships, three armoured cruisers and eight destroyers and for the Germans one battleship, one battlecruiser and four light cruisers. The British had lost over 6,000 men compared to the German 2,545, The Indefatigable, Queen Mary, Nester, Defence, Invincible and the armoured cruiser, Black Prince had gone to the bottom. The Barham, Warspite and Beatty's flagship, the Lion, had been damaged. The survival of the latter being due to the heroism of a dying Major of Marines, Major Harvey, who, with both legs shattered and mortally wounded, managed to shout down the voice tube the order to flood the magazines and thus save the ship.

Although the British press boldly announced that 'German losses are heavier than the British' and that a 'New Admiralty statement shows Jutland was a British victory', Beatty's famous 'Cats' had taken a pounding. His legendary remark, made to his Flag-Captain after seeing the Queen Mary blow up with the loss of all but twenty of her crew, 'There seems to be something wrong with our bloody ships today' had more than a grain of truth to it. It became all too evident that British ships had inadequate flash protection for the magazines.

While the battle went on spasmodically on the surface the submarines provided an ever constant threat under the waves. Submarine development had progressed in leaps and bounds in the closing years of the nineteenth century and by 1914 the British Navy had ninety-six submarines in commission.

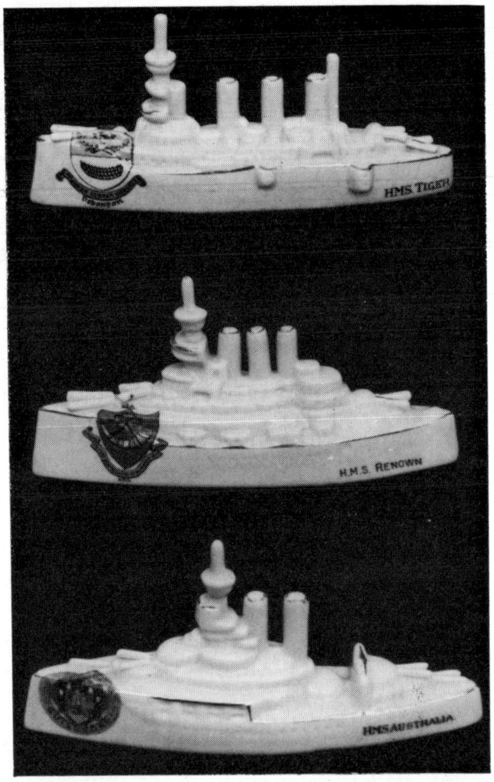

Carlton China Warships: top, 160mm. ins. 'HMS Tiger'. This model resembles a cruiser of the Cressy class. The casemates at the side housed the six-pounder guns. Middle, 160mm. ins. 'HMS Renown'. Bottom, 160mm. ins. 'HMS Australia'.

Carlton China 160mm. inscribed 'HMS Canada'. This factory seems to have had a nautical bent - the names of no fewer than 14 Dreadnoughts were used on one or more of their warship models.

Savoy 167mm. Reg. No. 659327 ins. 'HMS Lion'. Bottom: 163mm. ins. 'HMS Iron Duke'.

Grafton China: top HMS Iron Duke, No. 431. 152mm. Bottom: 'Dreadnought' 141mm. No. 408. Also found with 'Victory'.

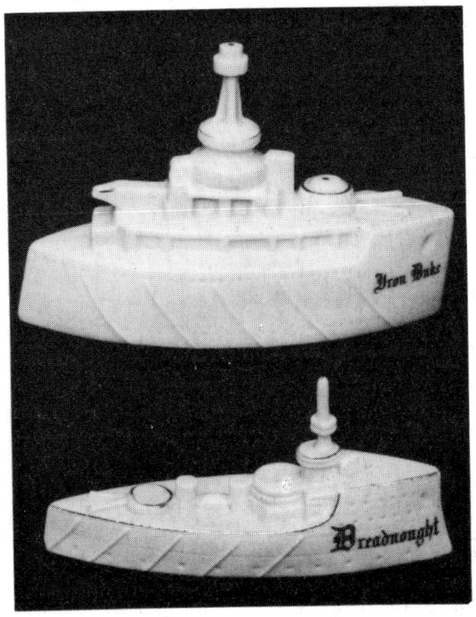

Willow Art China 140mm. 'HMS Lion' impressed on bow.

Warships: top Shelley china 120mm. : Bottom l. Milton china 117mm. r. Carlton china 112mm.

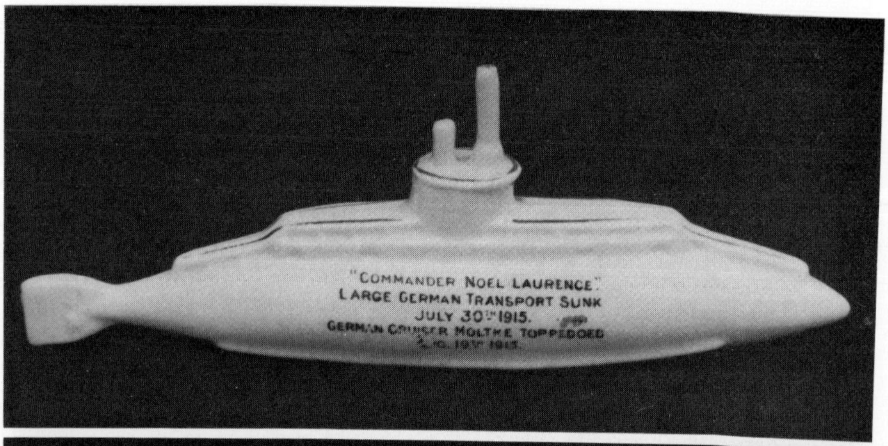

Savoy china 143mm. Reg. No. 651546 with inscription. The E1 and E9 spent the war in the Baltic. In 1918 they were scuttled by their crews at Helsingfors.

Arcadian china: top 120mm., bottom: 163mm. ins. 'Queen Elizabeth'.

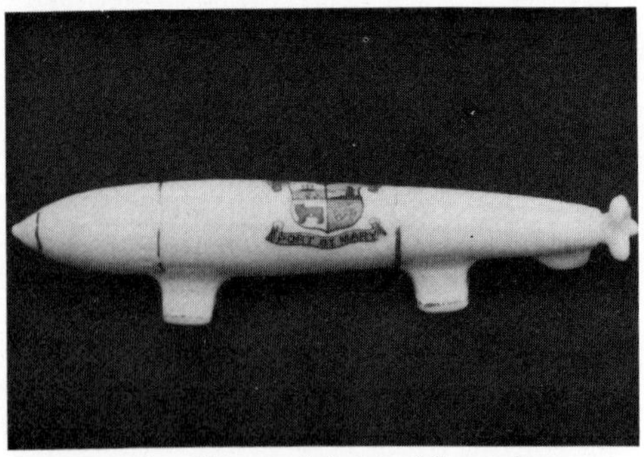

Corona china 154mm. Model of Torpedo.

The seven classes of British submarine were: Holland 1-5; A class, B, C, D and E, progressing in size and development. The first of the E class submarines were completed in 1912 and were four times as big as the A class. Nine of these were in commission in 1914 with a further fifty-six being built. They had a surface displacement of 700 tons and carried four 18ins. torpedo tubes, two fore and two aft. Their 800hp diesel engines gave them a surface speed of 16 knots while electric motors made 10 knots under water. They had a useful range of 1500 miles.

The torpedo of 1914 was an improved version of the original invented by an Austrian Naval Officer, Captain Lupis, aided by an Englishman by the name of Mr. Whitehead. In 1871 the British government paid £15,000 for the patent and rights to manufacture a fourteen foot torpedo that was able to carry sixty-seven pounds of gun-cotton a distance of 600 yards at a speed of seven and a half knots. Subsequent developments and modifications resulted in the 1914 torpedo which was seventeen feet in length and able to carry 330 pounds of TNT up to 7,000 yards. The modern torpedo made the submarine a force to be reckoned with.

The first British submarine to draw blood was the E9, commanded by Lieutenant Max Horton, which sank the German cruiser Hela off the coast of Heligoland on 13th September 1914. On his next patrol Horton sank a German torpedo boat destroyer in the mouth of the Ems River. It is said that while submerged in the enemy harbour he kept his crew amused with a gramophone concert and bridge playing! A reminder that in those early days, when submarine detection was in its infancy, the submarine was a relatively safe, albeit claustrophobic war machine.

In October the E9 and the E1, commanded by Captain Noel Laurence, were despatched to the Baltic. Operating from Russian bases they, and other submarines that joined them later, spent the rest of the war sinking and harassing enemy shipping. With the Treaty of Brest-Litovsk in March 1918, when the Russians made their peace with Germany, the ships surrendered. Without hope of escape they were scuttled to prevent them getting into enemy hands and the crews made their way home overland.

The Germans with their technically advanced Untersee-boats, pursued the offensive role of the submarine to its fullest. Realising that the surest way of bringing an island to its knees was to cut off its supply routes, the Kaiser instigated a submarine blockade around the coast of Britain. When it became apparent that this was having little effect Germany took the unprecedented step of declaring the waters around Britain a war zone. From 4th February 1915 all British ships were to be sunk on sight and the safety of neutral ships was not guaranteed because of the difficulty of identifying flags at a distance and because of the ... 'unscrupulous (British) practice of running up neutral flags when the occasion requires'!

Throughout the war the U-boats maintained this blockade, accounting for a large tonnage of shipping and supplies. It was the sinking of neutral shipping that caused much anti-Germanic feeling and played a large part in America's entry into the war.

The incident that became reknowned for its infamy took place on the 7th May 1915. On that morning the U20 was starting for home after a successful patrol off the south west coast of Ireland. At 1.20pm off the Old Head of Kinsale a very large steamer was sighted sailing eastwards. At 2.09 at a range of 200 yards Lieutenant Commander Walter Schweiger ordered one torpedo to be fired. The torpedo hit the Lusitania amidships. Moments later there was a second terrific explosion and within twenty minutes the great liner and more than 1,200 souls were lying at the bottom of the sea.

The Lusitania, the pride of the Cunard Line, had left New York on May 1st bound for Liverpool. Since her maiden voyage she had crossed the Atlantic some two hundred times during which she established a new record for the crossing (4 days, 19 hours and 52 minutes). She was described as, and well merited the description, a 'floating palace'.

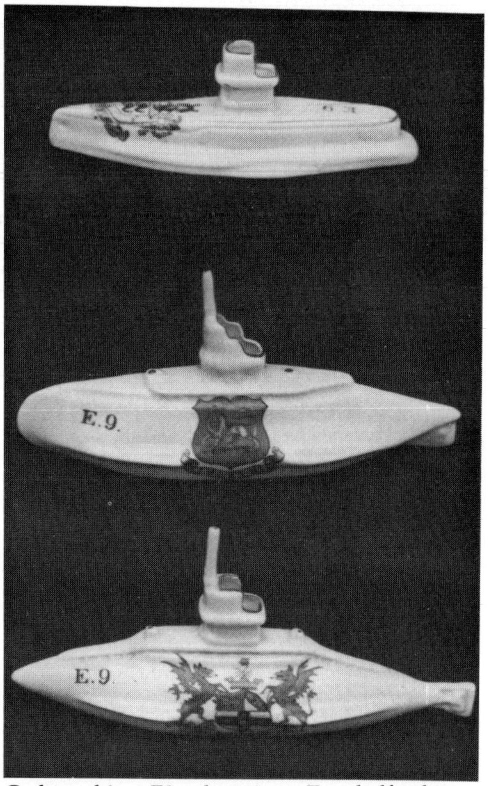

Carlton china. E9 submarines. Top: half submerged 122mm. Middle: 144mm. Bottom: 145mm.

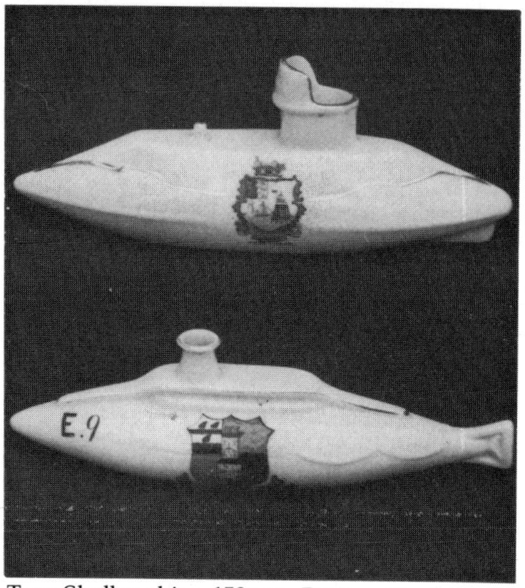

Top: Shelley china 150mm. Bottom: Grafton china 150mm. ins. 'E9'.

Lusitania postcard

BRITISH SUBMARINES IN THE BALTIC

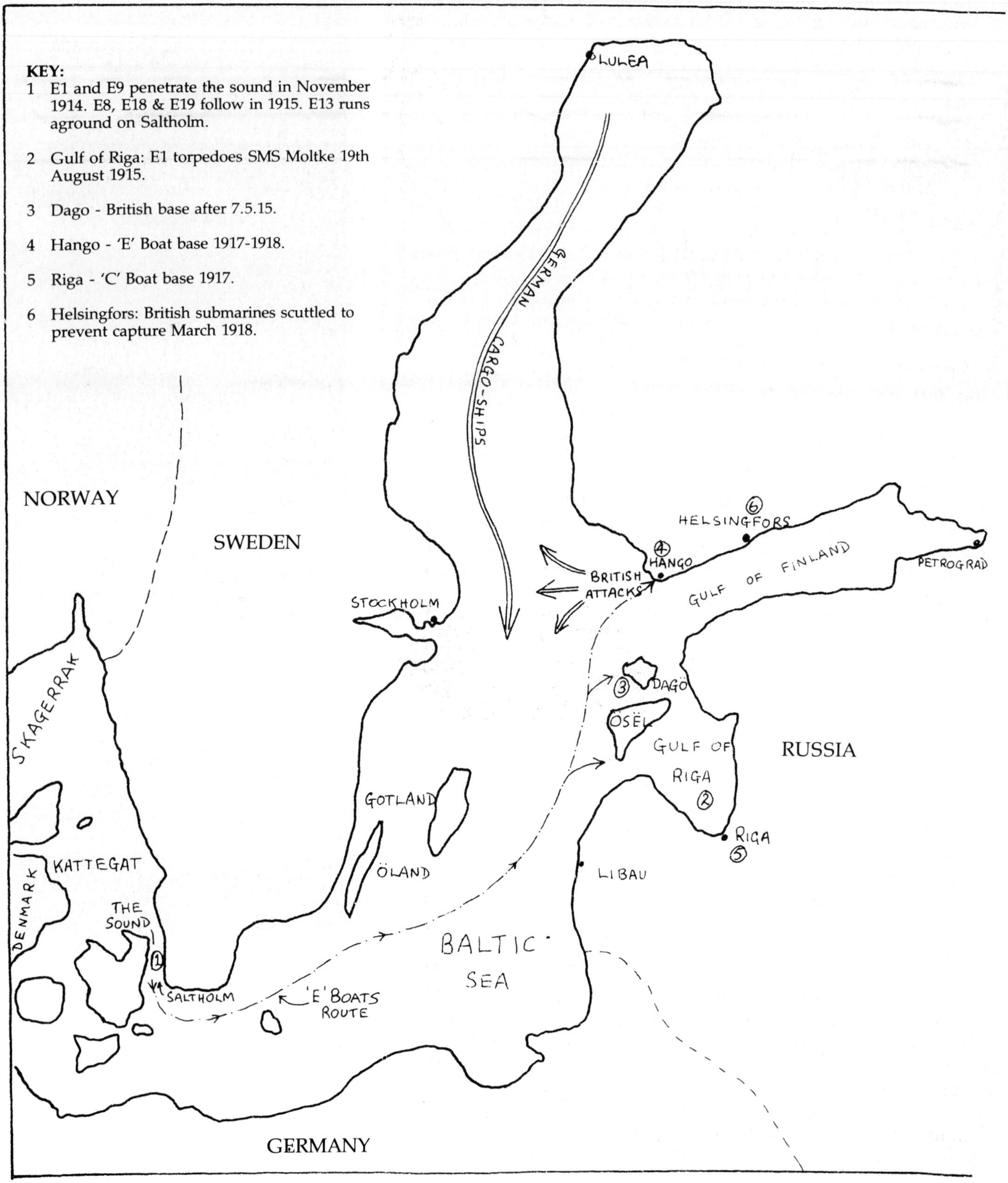

Lusitania map

How a small fish sank a big whale.
The Lusitania was hit by one torpedo. The second explosion that survivors reported hearing was probably caused by munitions the ship was carrying.

According to an agreement with the British government which dated back to her conception in 1902, the ship could be requisitioned by the Military should hostilities ever break out. Although never used in her entirety by the Navy, certain modifications were carried out when war was imminent. Gun mountings were placed in readiness on the decks and parts of the cargo holds were sealed off from the rest of the ship. The intention being to use these for 'unknown cargoes'... cargoes that did not appear on the ships manifest. It transpires that at the time of sinking the Lusitania carried, amongst other things, a cargo of munitions. It may have been this that caused the second explosion that many survivors reported and which did most damage to the ship.

Of the 1,964 passengers, the majority of whom were non-combatants, 764 were saved. When the news of the disaster reached the press the protests flooded in. The initial shock and horror was followed by a wave of anti-German feeling that did much harm to the German people in general and the Kaiser in particular. The German reaction was singularly self-assertive, negating their responsibilities by pointing out that a notice had been clearly displayed in the German Embassy in New York stating that all passengers travelled in British waters at their own risk.

A Munich silversmith struck a commemorative medal which on one side has a picture of death selling tickets to passengers of the Lusitania and on the other a picture of the Lusitania sinking, its decks piled high with guns and munitions. It was soon copied by British smiths and sold in a suitably anti-Germanic box.

Lusitania medallion struck by Munich silversmith and copied by British Naval Intelligence and sold in an Anti-Germanic box. On one side is 'Death' selling tickets to intending passengers with the wording 'Business above everything Cunard line - booking office - submarine danger' and on the other side, showing the ship sinking with its decks covered in munitions, 'No contraband, the great liner Lusitania sunk by German submarine 5th May 1915'.

A third danger that faced Merchant and Navy shipping alike as they sailed through hostile waters was the ever constant threat of mines. Laid singly or more often in groups, they accounted for a large tonnage of shipping. There were two main types in use: contact mines and observation mines. The contact mines were anchored by long cables enabling them to float a few feet below the surface. Another cable connected the first mine with a second. When a ship struck this line the two mines

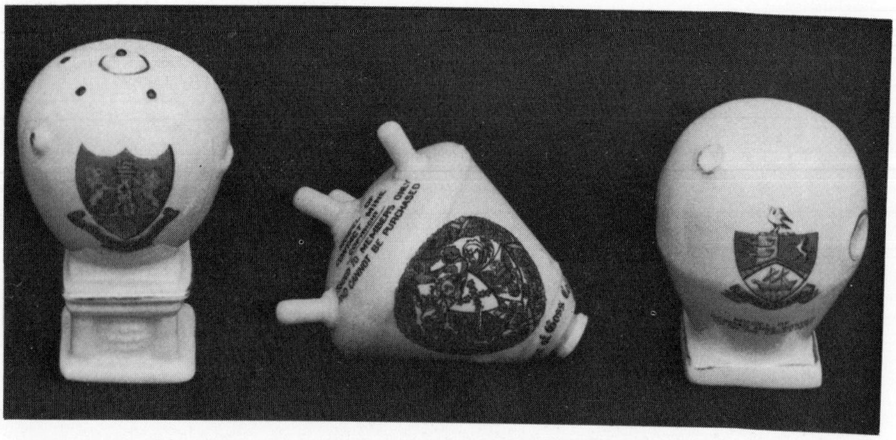

l. to r. Carlton china 79mm. Reg. No. 662100 ins. 'Model of Floating mine'. Goss china 79mm. ins. 'Model of Contact mine' - a League of Goss Collectors piece. Shelley china 69mm. ins. 'Model of mine washed up on the East coast'.

were pulled together, striking either side of the ship's hull. The projections or whiskers on top, when pushed in, detonated the explosive charge which varied between 76 and 200 pounds. Observation mines were used mainly for harbour and coastal protection. They were much larger than the contact type, containing 500-2,000 pounds of explosive, and were activated by an observer on the shore. Both types of mines were used by the waring nations although the British government took steps to restrict the use of unanchored mines and anchored mines that remained armed when broken free of their moorings.

On the advice of Lord Charles Beresford ordinary steam fishing trawlers were adapted for mine-sweeping duties. In 1909 the British Admiralty started to purchase trawlers for such work. Shortly after a trawler section of the Royal Naval Reserve was formed from the Captains and men of fishing fleets who had volunteered for training in this highly dangerous work of minesweeping. The mine-sweepers worked in pairs dragging a weighted hawser between them. When this caught on the anchor ropes of the mines it dragged them along until they exploded by contact with each other or came to the surface whereupon they were exploded by small arms fire. From early in 1915 many of the ships of the trawler fleet were used for blockading the Otranto Straits thus preventing the Austrian Fleet from leaving the Adriatic. The barrage was maintained successfully until the end of the war.

Under the terms of the Armistice the German Fleet, consisting of seven battleships, five battlecruisers, eight light cruisers, fifty torpedo boats and one hundred and thirty U-boats were handed over to the Allies. After seven months internment at Scapa Flow and with their fate still not settled, Admiral von Reuter, commander of the internal ships, gave orders for the fleet to be scuttled. On 21st June 1919 the entire fleet of warships slowly sank into the waters of Scapa Flow. Attempts by the British to rescue some of the ships were unsuccessful and while some were salvaged later at considerable cost, the remainder still lie where they settled.

The war ended without the full scale sea battle that everyone had anticipated. There was never again the potential for such an impressive sight for post war trends were away from the all big-gun warships towards smaller, lighter craft. Nevertheless while the war waved out the old it unveiled the new. Submarines, the novelty of this war had been provided with an ideal testing ground to formulate and establish tactics which were used in later wars.

Map 1

THE OTRANTO BARRAGE

Map 1

The Austrio-Hungarian surface fleet was trapped in the Adriatic by Allied control of the Straits of Otranto although U-boats were able to penetrate the barrage and sink shipping. Early in 1915 British fishing vessels with 30ft. wire drift nets were used to block the submarine's path. In April 1918 a 150ft. deep fixed barrage was started which was completed in September.

Map 2

On the night of May 14/15 1915 the Austrians mounted an operation against the Allied trawler line. Among the many scenes of gallantry as the Austrian cruisers picked their targets from the line of poorly armed trawlers and drifters was that demonstrated by Capt. J. Watt of the Gowan Lea. Ignoring orders from the Austrian cruiser - The Novara - to abandon ship, he turned his ship's one 57mm. gun on the foe. The gun was hit and put out of action and the crew set about repairing it. The Novara passed on confident that the drifter could not have survived such a pounding, however the men continued to try to right the damage.

Many mines broke their moorings and added to the danger of sailing in hostile waters.

HMHS Anglia: Carlton China. 166mm. Reg. No. 662104 ins. 'Model of British Hospital ship whose voyage was disregarded on three occasions by German submarines'. Although registered in October 1917 it bears no reference to this ship's actual fate.

The China

Many manufacturers included one or more models of warships in their range of Heraldic china. Most are fanciful in design, however, some have retained characteristics of the original which make identification possible. Models are found in named and unnamed versions. A complete list of the named ships and details of the originals will be found in Appendix iv.

Whether or not anyone in the Carlton factory had a nautical bent is not known but they certainly were in the forefront with their nautical mementoes, making no fewer than ten different models of ships and using on these the names of fifteen real life ships. It is evident that they were not consistent in naming their models, no doubt a name was put on any model at hand, and the names listed with models below are those that have been seen by the author.

The models are as follows:

1. A three funnelled warship with eight guns found with the names: 'HMS Canada', 'HMS Queen Elizabeth', 'HMS Lion' and 'HMS Tiger' (this model is very similar to the Savoy model found with 'HMS Queen Elizabeth' or 'HMS Iron Duke'.
2. A two funnelled warship with eight guns found with the names: 'HMS Marlborough', 'HMS Queen Elizabeth' and 'HMS Canada'. This model resembles the ships of the Iron Duke class.
3. A four funnelled warship with six guns and found named with 'HMS Lion' and 'HMS Tiger' although more usually found with the peace inscription (see below). These names, used here, appear to be a complete error for this model is based on an armoured cruiser of the Cressy class.
4. A three funnelled warship with six guns which is distinguished by its high decks. It is found named as 'HMS Warspite', 'HMS Inflexible' and 'HMS Iron Duke'.
5. A high bowed 'Monitor' ship with two guns which is found named with 'HMS Humber' and has the same general appearance as the Grafton model that is found with 'Dreadnought' or 'Victory' inscribed on it. Monitor ships were flat-bottomed river boats that were armed with a heavy gun or howitzer and used for inshore shelling from shallow waters.

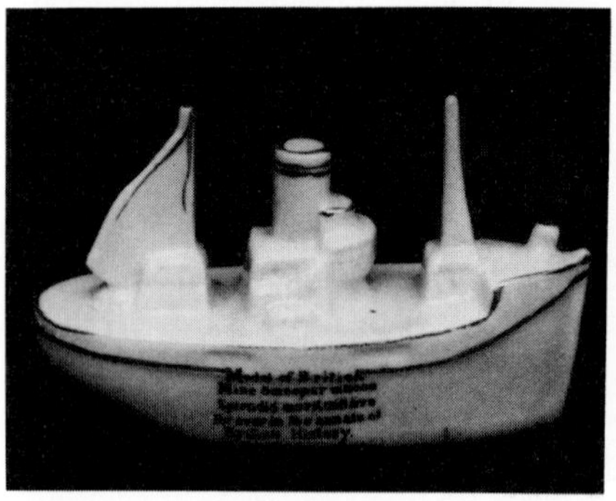

Top: Carlton china 113mm. Reg. No. 661565 ins. 'HMMS Gowan Lea. Model of British Mine-sweeper whose splendid work will live forever in the annals of history'. Registered in September 1917, four days after her Skipper's award of the Victoria Cross was gazetted. Also found named as 'HMMS Peggy'. Bottom: Arcadian China 122mm.

Top: Arcadian 115mm. Reg. No. 658677 ins. 'Model of Torpedo Boat Destroyer'. Bottom: Savoy 140mm. ins. 'Model of Torpedo Boat Destroyer'.

All these models are found with the inscription: 'Great War 1914-18. The German Fleet surrendered 74 warships Nov. 21st 1918', instead of or in addition to the ship's name.

6. A warship measuring 120mm with three funnels and three guns.
7. A warship, similar to the above, but measuring 112mm.
8. A model of a trawler (Reg. No. 661565) which is usually found with the inscription: 'Model of British Minesweeper whose splendid work will live forever in the annals of history'. Less frequently it appears with the name 'HMMS Gowan Lea' or 'HMMS Peggy'.
9. A model of the Cunard liner 'Lusitania' which is inscribed: 'Remember the Lusitania; the Lusitania was sunk by German submarine May 1915; lives lost 1,198'.
10. A model of the hospital ship, 'HMHS Anglia' (Reg. No. 662104) which is found inscribed: 'British Hospital Ship whose voyage was disregarded on three occasions by German submarines'.

Although it was registered in 1917 there is no reference to the ships actual fate. She was sunk by a mine in the Channel on November 17th 1915.

The Grafton designers modelled a fine, albeit totally inaccurate model which is found inscribed: 'HMS Iron Duke' or simply 'Dreadnought' as well as their high bowed model referred to earlier. Willow china was offering a 'Liner converted to troop carrier' in the early months of the war and some time later made a model of a six gun warship with 'HMS Lion' impressed on the bows. Arcadian china, uncharacteristically, made only five models. Three of which are warships differing only in size. The larger two are often found named 'HMS Queen Elizabeth'. They also made a 'Model of Torpedo boat destroyer' (Reg. No. 658677) and a larger version of the Carlton minesweeper which appeared in their catalogue as a model of a trawler. Savoy registered a design for a three funnelled warship (Reg. No. 659327) which is very similar to the Carlton model (1) It is found inscribed 'HMS Lion', 'HMS Iron Duke' or 'HMS Queen Elizabeth'. In addition this factory made models which are inscribed: 'Model of Torpedo Boat Destroyer' and 'Model of British Minesweeper'.

HMHS Anglia: sunk by mine in the English Channel in 1915.

Carlton China 141mm. ins. 'HMS Humber' and 'Model of British Monitor'. Monitors were flat bottomed river boats that were used for inshore shelling. They usually carried one heavy gun or howitzer and were very much floating gun platforms.

Top: Arcadian china 125mm. Reg. No. 658687 ins. 'E5, model of New Submarine'. Registered in 1916 but with no reference to the fact that the ship was lost with all hands in March of that year. Middle: Unmarked 121mm. E4. impressed on conning tower. Bottom: Arcadian 98mm. Reg. No. 652242 ins. 'E4'.

Of the named warships, six are Dreadnought Battleship and five Dreadnought Battlecruisers. As there does not seem to be any apparent connection between the ships it would seem that they were chosen at random.

Some of the ships were well known amongst the general public and it is not surprising that they are more common than the lesser known ships. HMS Lion, Beatty's flagship at Jutland, is found with no fewer than nine factory marks while HMS Iron Duke, Jellicoe's flagship, surprisingly in only three. HMS Queen Elizabeth, then a new class of ship and described as the finest battleship ever built, was Beatty's flagship but was under refit at the time of Jutland, is found with five different marks. HMS Humber, a relatively unknown Monitor, came to the attention of the public on October 19th 1914 when she, together with her sister ships, Mersey and Severn, bombarded German positions along the Belgium coast between Ostend and Nieuport.

The model of the trawler was inspired by the action in which the skipper of the Gowan Lea distinguished himself and was awarded the Victoria Cross. The award was gazetted on 29th August, a mere five days before the design was registered and read as follows: 'Joseph Watt, Skipper, Royal Naval Reserve, 1206 W.S.A. For most conspicuous gallantry when the allied drifter line in the Straits of Otranto was attacked by Austrian light cruisers on the morning of 15th May 1917. When hailed by an Austrian cruiser at about 100 yards range and ordered to stop and abandon his drifter the Gowan Lea, Skipper Watt ordered full speed ahead and called upon his crew to give three cheers and fight to the finish. The cruiser was then engaged, but after one round had been fired, a shot from the enemy disabled the breech of the drifters gun. The gun's crew, however, stuck to the gun, endeavouring to make it work, being under heavy fire all the time. After the cruiser had passed on, Skipper Watt took the Gowan Lea alongside the badly damaged drifter Floandi and assisted to remove the dead and wounded'. Like any 'David and Goliath' story this attracted public attention and was widely reported in the press. The skipper was even awarded a 'purse of Treasury notes' by the people of Fraserburgh (the ship's home port) and was given a gold hunting watch and chain by the ship's owner.

HMS Peggy has posed something of an enigma as to why it should be commemorated. Up to 1917 it patrolled from its home port of Peterhead but after that date it became commissioned officers quarters. Did one of the visiting officers want a memento of his stay on the ship and ask the china manufacturers to transfer 'HMMS Peggy' on to some of their models of the trawler?

Models of submarines are fewer in number and, almost invariably, are named. All are members of the E class. The E1 is found in Savoy china with the inscription, 'E1, Commander Noel Laurence; Large German transport sunk July 30 1915; German cruiser Moltke, torpedoed August 19 1915' (Reg. No. 651546). It was designed soon after the event it commemorates and was registered on 18th September 1915. Similar models are found in Bow and Porcelle china. The E4 is found in two sizes (95mm & 120mm) both of which seem to have been based on the original patent given to H.T. Robinson in October 1915 (Reg. No. 652242). At least ten different marks are found on this model. It achieved prominence

In October 1914 HMS Humber and her sister ships Severn and Mersey bombarded the German lines between Ostend and Middlekerke.

Inset: A.L. Snagge, Commander of HMS Humber.

HMS Humber in Mudros Harbour. Originally built for Brazil in 1914 but taken over by the Royal Navy. Served in the English Channel, Gallipoli and the Eastern Mediterranean.

when, on August 28th 1914, during the Battle of Heligoland Bight, the British cruiser, the Defender, sunk the German destroyer V187. Having lowered a boat to pick up survivors, the German cruiser SMS Stettin came up and chased the Defender away, leaving her boat and crew adrift, 250 miles from friendly shores. In true Jules Verne fashion the E4 popped up out of nowhere and took the stranded sailors ashore. The E5, also patented by Robinson (Reg. No. 658687) was made by three manufacturers and is frequently inscribed: 'Model of New Submarine'. The model was registered in December 1916 and it seems to have escaped the designer's notice that it had been posted missing in early March that year, having failed to return from patrol off Heligoland and assumed sunk by a mine.

The E9, made famous by the exploits of its commander, Max Horton is found in five different models, three of which were from the Carlton factory, the others by Shelley (328) and Grafton (405). One of the Carlton models shows the submarine half submerged and is inscribed 'Model of British submarine'.

Two models of torpedoes are known. One, found in Corona, Alexandra, Victoria and Grosvenor china (the latter inscribed 'Model of Sea Torpedo) is accurate and well detailed, while the other, made by Arcadian does require the inscription 'Model of Aerial Torpedo' (Reg. No. 657210) to enable identification.

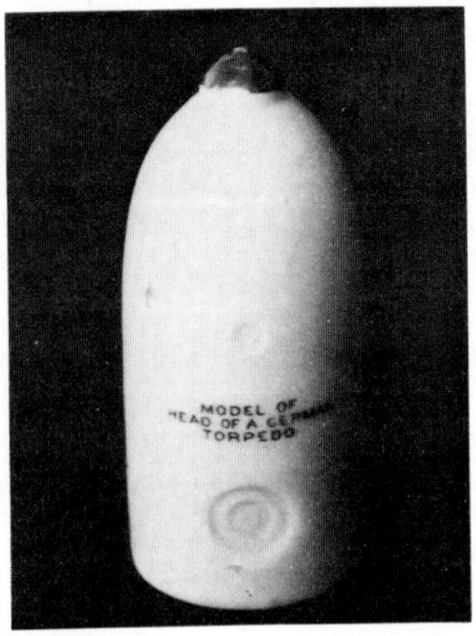

Shelley china 70mm. ins. 'Model of head of German torpedo'.

Dramatic rescue of sailors by the E4.

Carlton, Arcadian, Shelley and Goss all made models of mines. The Carlton model is inscribed 'Model of Floating Mine' and the Shelley 'Model of German Mine washed up on the East Coast' (Shelley 188) The Goss model of a contact mine was a League of Goss Collectors piece, made in 1917, and available to members of the League only.

Several models were made commemorating the German bombardment of east coast towns in December 1914. One, made by Willow, is of Scarborough Lighthouse which was damaged by shellfire. The model even shows the hole made by the shell and the model is inscribed 'This lighthouse was damaged by bombardment by German warships on Wed 16th Dec 1914'. Another is of the 'Scarborough coastguard station shelled by Germans'.

The Goss factory produced a very colourful three quarter shaped plate carrying seven flags of the Allies and the inscription, 'Up, ye Sons of England, and Wreak Vengeance on The Baby-Killers of Scarborough' and 'We Follow You In Our Daily Thoughts On Your Certain Road To Victory. George R.I. Dec. 5th 1914'.

Models of a ship's capstan are found in Arcadian and Carlton china.

Models of Capstans. l. Carlton china 70mm. r. Arcadian 58mm.

THE E4 AT HELIGOLAND BIGHT

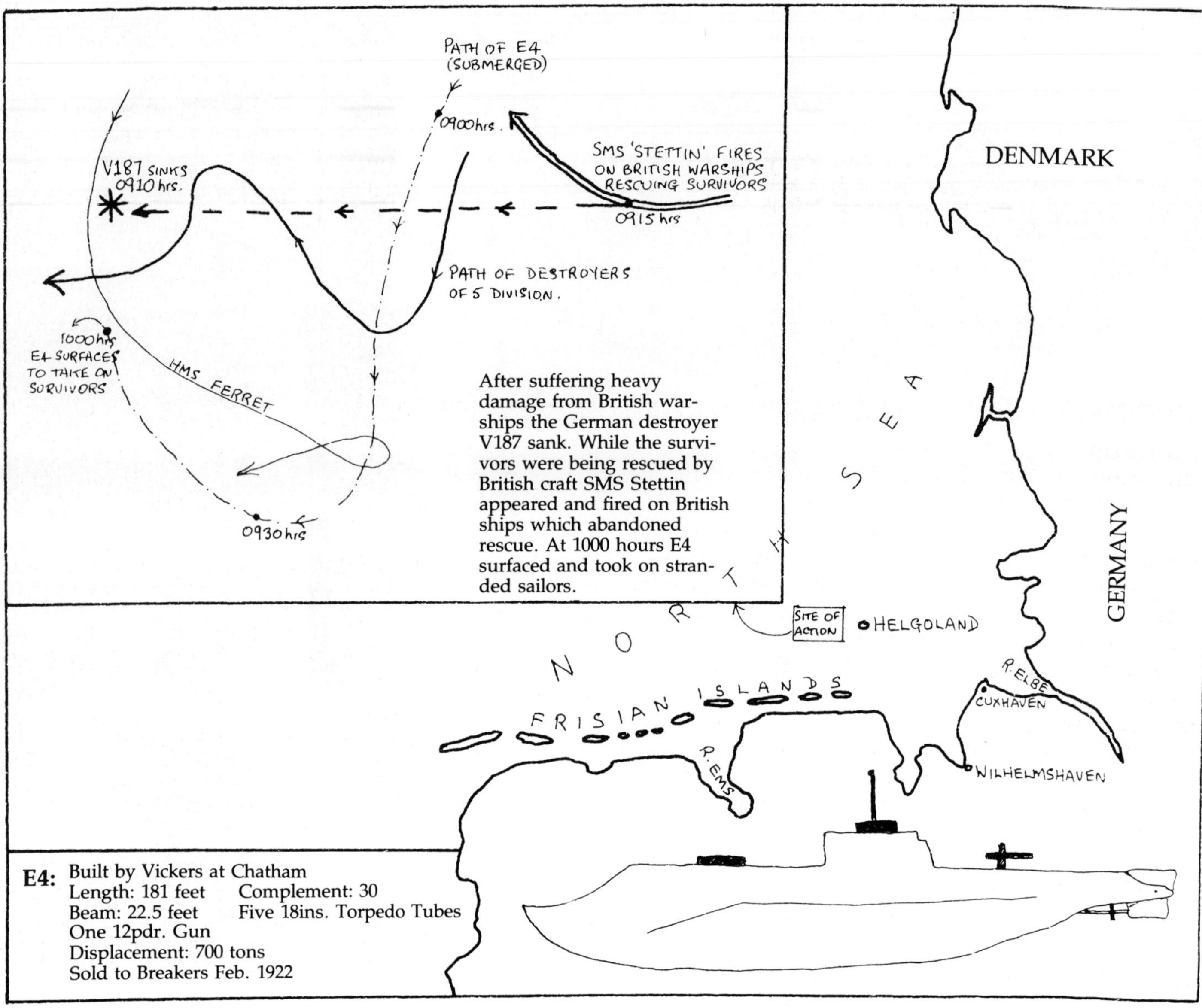

8
Memorials

At 4.04am on 11th November 1918 the Armistice was signed. At 11.00am that morning: the 11th hour of the 11th day of the 11th month, a general cease fire was sounded along the Western Front. The Great War, which had lingered on for four long years and had brought with it carnage on a scale never before experienced, had come to an end.

The year had dawned with no sign of a break in the deadlock and the tired armies had settled down to what they thought would be another year in the trenches. In March, Russia, torn apart by revolution, made her peace with Germany and immediately thousands of German troops were released from the Eastern Front and transported across Europe to supplement the dwindling forces in the West. Only the timely arrival of America helped to redress the balance. The German Spring Offensive on the Somme had succeeded in breaking the British Front Line for the first time in four years, but at tremendous cost. The following Battles of Lys and the Allied counter offensive in the summer which included the Second Battle of the Marne and the Battle of Amiens were the straws that broke the camel's back; the German army was near disintegration.

Grandfather clock. Corona china 125mm. ins. 'Peace signed 3.25 June 25th 1919' - with hands stopped at 3.25.

The French Peace celebrations were held on 14th July 1919.

London's Cenotaph at its unveiling on November 11th 1920. The temporary structure erected for Armistice Day 1919 was replaced by the permanent structure that we see today.

RUMNEY PARISH.

PEACE CELEBRATIONS
July 19th, 1919.

Order of Service ::

To be held on THE GREEN

CONDUCTED BY

REV. D. J. DAVIES
(VICAR), ASSISTED BY

REV. THOS. SMITH
(WESLEYAN).

To Commence at 1 o'clock.

R. GUY, CARDIFF.

Peace commemoratives. The Armistice was technically only a ceasefire. Peace was not finally settled until the signing of the Treaty of Versailles on June 25th 1919.

At home the effects of the Allied food blockades were taking their toll and there was starvation, famine and rioting in the streets of Berlin. In November, when ordered to sea as a last resort, the German Navy mutinied. The end had arrived. Germany called for Armistice.

On the evening of 10th November the German Secretary of State, Matthais Erzberger, accompanied by Count von Oberndorff, Major General von Winterfeldt and Captain Vanselow of the German Navy arrived at Marshall Foch's headquarters in the Forest of Compeigne. With Foch, and representing the Allies, were Admiral Sir Rosslyn Wemyss and General Weyland. After a meeting that carried on well into the early hours the Germans finally accepted the terms laid down. The cease fire was to take effect from 11.00am the same morning and was to be effective for thirty-six days.

l. to r. Margate War Memorial Arcadian 160mm.
Romsey War Memorial Corona 155mm.
Llàndudno War Memorial Unmarked 180mm.

The Cenotaph was very popular in crested china.
Top row: l. to r. Grafton china 155mm. Willow china 180mm. Shelley china 153mm.
Second row: Victoria 140mm. Carlton 140mm. Foreign 140mm.
Third row: Goss china 145mm. (unglazed), Arcadian china 145mm. Royal Val china 145mm.
Fourth row: Arcadian, Foreign 108mm. Arcadian china 80mm.
The Arcadian and Goss models are probably from the same mould.

Great Yarmouth War Memorial: l. to r. Arcadian china 146mm. Willow Art china 168mm. Foreign 132mm.

Southsea Naval Memorial: l. Foreign china 117mm. r. Unmarked 160mm. The design for this memorial by Sir Robert Lorimer was also used for the Chatham and Plymouth Naval Memorials. Unveiled in 1924.

Newhaven Transport Memorial Arcadian china 154mm.

After the smoke cleared from the battlefields for the last time, after the excitement peace had brought had abated and as the remnants of the once glorious armies returned home, the final toll was counted. By any standards the sacrifice had been colossal. The loss of military life has since been estimated at 8 million. Germany had lost 2 million, France 1.4 million, Austria-Hungary 1.2 million, Russia 1.7 million and Great Britain 760,000. If prisoners and wounded are included the total is a staggering 37.5 million, more than half the present population of Great Britain. Hidden in these statistics is the heartbreak and anguish suffered by thousands of individuals, families, villages and towns, many of which lost an entire generation of their menfolk. It was not a war that could be forgotten in a hurry, and in all parts of the Empire committees were formed to look into the question of erecting memorials to those who had died 'For King and Country'.

The one memorial that is known and respected by all is the Cenotaph that stands in London's Whitehall. For some sixty years it has received the wreaths and salutes from those that have fought and survived in what is now two world wars. Originally conceived as a saluting point for the Victory celebrations of 1919, the Cenotaph captured the hearts and imaginations of thousands of people, standing, as it does, for ...'the sacrifice of a generation for King and Country' and a reminder of the indebtedness of the living for the dead'.

Early in 1919 the Cabinet, feeling that there was a need for some organised Peace celebrations after the signing of the Treaty of Versailles, anticipated in late summer, charged the Foreign Secretary, Lord Curzon, with responsibility for their organisation. The Peace Committee first met on May 9th 1919 and plans were laid for a date early in August. With the signing of the Treaty in June the date was brought forward to July 19th. Lloyd George, who had learned that the centre piece for the French celebrations on July 14th was to be a 'great catafalque', suggested to Curzon that a similar model should be included in his plans.

For the design of such a monument the eminent architect, Sir Edwin Lutyens, was approached. Summoned to 10 Downing Street in early July, he was asked to design a non-denominational shrine which was to be erected by July 19th, some two weeks away. The following day plans for a 'Cenotaph' were handed to the contractors and work began. By the 19th a temporary structure was ready.

Next of kin medallion: designed by a Mr. E. Carter Preston and selected from the many entered in an open competition in 1918. Given to the next-of-kin of those killed in the war.

Commemorative plate

Commemorative plate

l. to r. Black Watch Memorial, Willow Art china 126mm., Tunbridge Wells War Memorial Carlton china 168mm., unveiled on 11th February 1923 by Viscount Harding of Penshurst with a guard of honour provided by the 4th Battalion Royal West Kent Regiment: Dartford War Memorial Coronet china 163mm., unveiled on 7th May 1922 by Air Vice-Marshal Sir H.G. Salmond KCMG CB DSC· Killin Memorial Arcadian china 145mm.

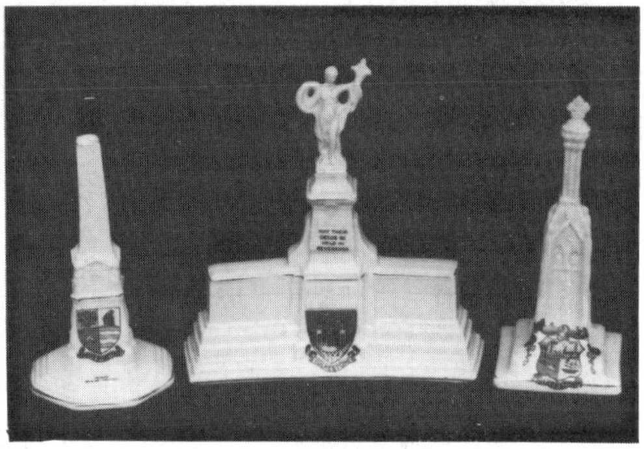

l. to r. Bishops Stortford War Memorial Arcadian china 130mm. unveiled in 1921 and dedicated to the 200 local men who died.
Folkestone War Memorial Arcadian 156mm. unveiled 2nd December 1922, comprising an angel holding a cross surmounting a stone plinth. Ulverstone War Memorial Carlton china 142mm.

Nearly 15,000 troops took part in the Victory Parade. The King received the troops at Buckingham Palace and soldiers and leaders such as Haig, Beatty, Pershing and Foch saluted their dead comrades at the newly erected Cenotaph. This moment, captured by the lenses of photographers, caught the public imagination in the days and years that were to come. Celebrations were held, with few exceptions, throughout the country. Services, parades and parties in churches, homes, streets and village halls served to mark the day. Many authorities presented their schoolchildren with a peace commemorative, almost invariably a mug carrying a suitable transfer or inscription.

The unanimous acceptance of the Cenotaph soon resulted in the erection of a more permanent structure. For Armistice Day 1920, as the body of the Unknown Warrior was laid to rest in Westminster Abbey, the Cenotaph as we know it today was unveiled. In the three days that followed it was visited by some 400,000 people. Soon it was followed by memorials in other parts of the country, erected to commemorate the local men and women who had died in the war. Designed by a local committee or well known artist and often built out of local stone, these memorials appeared in the early years of the twenties and each unveiled with due pomp and ceremony accorded such an event.

Of the many memorials erected one in particular is worthy of note: the memorial to Nurse Edith Cavell that stands in London's St. Martins Lane, overlooking the statue of Lord Nelson in Tragalgar Square.

Born on December 4th 1865 at Swandestone, Norfolk, Edith Cavell entered her nursing career when she was thirty-nine. After nursing in Britain she went to Belgium on the invitation of a Dr. Antoine Depage as a child nurse. She became Directresse of the Ecole d'Infirmeries Diplomees in 1907 and by 1914 was responsible for the training and staffing of the hospitals around Belgium. When Belgium fell she stayed on and soon became involved in the underground organisation led by Prince Reginald de Croy and his sister, Princess Marie, which helped stranded Allied soldiers to the Dutch Border. Through the information of spies, informers and infiltrators, suspicions came to rest on her. On August 4th

Dover War Memorial. Arcadian china 142mm. Comprises a bronze figure of youth holding a fiery cross and with feet surmounted with thorns and standing on a stone base. Unveiled 5th November 1924.

Loughborough War Memorial Arcadian china 152mm. unveiled by Field Marshal Sir William Robertson on 22nd July 1925. The tower houses a carillon of 47 bells.

Edith Cavell's birthplace.

Edith Cavell Memorial Postcard. On the back are the words: 'Condemned by a military tribunal in Belgium under the charge of having favoured the evacuation of British soldiers, Miss Edith Cavell of Norwich, a voluntary nurse, is taken to the execution ground on 12th October at daybreak. She faints, the German officer gives his soldiers the order to fire, they hesitate to fire on the prostrate body of a woman. The fiend takes out his revolver and leaning on his victim, blows her brains out. Whatever the reality, her death did much for recruitment.

Savoy china 168mm. ins. 'Edith Cavell'

The only complete version of the London Memorial that stands outside St. Martins-in-the-Fields, London. Leadbeater Art 200mm.

Edith Cavell Memorials l. to r. Alexandra 117mm., Willow Art 172mm. ins. 'Memorial Statue Norwich', Carlton 163mm., Arcadian china 160mm.

l. to r. Clacton War Memorial Carlton china 149mm. with top unglazed. Plymouth War Memorial Arcadian china 115mm. Worthing War Memorial Willow Art china 160mm.

1915 she and the organisation's financier, Phillipe Baucq, were arrested. She was tried before a German Military Court on October 7th 1915, and was sentenced to death. Despite appeals by friends and politicians she was led from her cell in the early hours of October 12th and without emotion faced the firing squad.

Immediately the anti-German propaganda machine was wheeled into action. Stories and rumours of her death abounded. Of how the soldier who refused to fire was summarily shot; of how, when faced with the firing squad… 'she faints; the German officer gives his soldiers the order to fire: they hesitate to fire on the prostrate body of a woman. The fiend takes his revolver out and, leaning on his victim, blows her brains out'. Whatever the facts her death did much to aid recruitment. In the month following her death the numbers of volunteers for the Forces doubled.

In 1919 her body was brought back to England and laid to rest in Norwich Cathedral. Her memorial in London's St. Martin's Lane, was unveiled on 17th March 1920 by HRH Queen Alexandra and comprises a life-sized figure in white marble backing onto a tall block of granite surmounted by a cross and a half figure of mother and child. The words on the memorial, taken from one of her last letters, read: 'Edith Cavell; Dawn October 12 1915; Patriotism is not enough; I must have no hatred or bitterness for anyone'. Around the base are the words: 'Humanity'; 'Sacrifice'; 'Fortitude'; and 'Devotion'.

In France the Imperial War Graves Committee was set the almost impossible task of finding and listing the names of those that had fallen. Shortly after the war memorials appeared all along the front line listing those that had died in the vicinity, and who had no known grave. It is these, with their seemingly endless lists of names that bring home to us the true pathos of war; the 54,896 on the Menin Gate, the 73,412 on the Thiepval Memorial; the 35,928 on the Arras Memorial and the 34,888 on the Tyne Cot Memorial. So large are these numbers that they lose all sense of meaning, it is only when we see one such as the Delville Wood Memorial to the men of the South African Brigade of the 9th Scottish Division who in six days in July 1916 were reduced from 3,153 to a meagre 104 all ranks, that we can grasp the enormity of the carnage that literally brought about the death of the first generation of this century.

Ilkestone War Memorial Willow Art china 130mm. March War Memorial, Arcadian china 160mm.

Brighton War Memorial Carlton china 107mm.

HERALDIC CHINA WAR MEMORIALS IN GREAT BRITAIN

The China

Bearing in mind their raison d'etre it is surprising that the china manufacturers saw fit to copy war memorials in china. Nevertheless many models do exist and represent some of the best examples of the potters' craft. All models were made in the twenties, probably shortly after the original was unveiled, and include some of the rarest models found in Heraldic china.

The most popular was, not surprisingly, that of the Cenotaph, which is found bearing no fewer than fourteen different makers' marks. The various models differ little in shape and design although there is great variation in size. Four models are found in Arcadian china, ranging from a giant 183mm model down to a miniature 70mm model. Goss made two models, the smaller of which is found glazed and unglazed. The Grafton and Shelley models have flags in relief on their sides. Many carry an inscription 'Model of Cenotaph' to which may be added 'Erected in Whitehall, London, in Memory of the fallen in the Great War 1914-19'.

A total of fifty-seven models of war memorials from around the country have been recorded (see map). Most are from English towns and villages and are true to the original in design, obviously being copied from a photograph. Many are quite intricate pieces of chinaware and serve well to illustrate the skill of the potter... like the Dover memorial with its delicate 'figure of youth with arms upstretched' or the Killin Memorial with its detailed figure of a Highland Soldier or the fragile wings of the angel on the Clacton-on-Sea memorial. These, and others, must have taxed even the most accomplished designer.

Details of the memorials will be found in Appendix v but some are especially worthy of note. Surprisingly only one model of a French memorial has been recorded, that to the 36th Ulster Division found in Leadbeater Art China. The Ulster Tower stands in a small park near Thiepval in Northern France, near the spot where over 5,000 men of the Division fell on the first day of the Somme in 1916. The memorial itself is a copy of the one that stands in the Dufferin family park in Clanboye, Co. Down where the Division trained before embarking for France, and is dedicated to Helen, the mother of the Marquis of Dufferin. At the other end of the scale is the figure of the Kilted Scotsman on the Killin Memorial that was erected by the five hundred inhabitants of this small Perthshire village to commemorate the twenty-eight local men who died.

One of the finest, and rarest, is the Alexandra model of the Royal Air Force Memorial that stands on the Victoria Embankment in London. The base, built of the same stone and in the same form as the nearby Cenotaph, supports a gilt effigy of the Air Force Eagle, with wings outstretched, overlooking the Thames. It was erected in 1923 by the RAF Benevolent Fund in commemoration of the officers and airmen who died in the war.

Of the few memorials that were erected to single people, those dedicated to Edith Cavell and Charles Fryatt are reproduced in china. Captain Charles Fryatt commanded the Great Eastern Steamship 'Brussels' and at the beginning of the war ran between Holland and England. On 28th May 1915, having been attacked by a U-boat, he turned the tables on his predator and succeeded in ramming and sinking it. Bound for Tilbury on June 23rd of the next year, he was captured by a German destroyer and taken to Bruges where he was court-martialled as a franc-tireur for his action against the U-boat, his log-book being used

l. Folkestone 'Road to Remembrance 1914-1918'. Wilton china 75mm.
r. Dover Patrol Memorial Arcadian 131mm.

Lloyd George statue. Carlton 155mm.

The 36th Ulster Division Memorial, Thiepval, stands amongst the trenches of the Schwaben Redoubt, still clearly visible after sixty years of ploughing, where 5,500 of their ranks became casualties on the first day of the Somme in July 1916. Unveiled on Armistice Day 1921, the tower houses, a chapel, visitor's room, apartment and rooftop lookout from which the surrounding battlefields can be seen. Inset: Leadbeater Art china 136mm. with the crest of Belfast and Thiepval.

in evidence. He was condemmed and shot the same evening. There was tremendous public outcry although the German Commission of Enquiry which considered the sentence after the war, upheld the action taken but expressed regret for the haste with which it had been executed. His body was returned to England and after a service at St. Paul's, London was buried at Dovercourt on July 9th 1919. A wing was added to the Cottage Hospital at Dovercourt in his memory and a Memorial Tablet in marble with a bronze medallion portrait of Captain Fryatt was installed in the booking hall of Liverpool Street Station on July 27th 1917. The tablet is inscribed: 'To the memory of Captain Charles Fryatt, July 17th 1916; From the neutral admirers of his brave conduct and heroic death. The Netherlands Section of the League of Neutral States July 27th 1917'. The model in Arcadian China, is a copy of the memorial that stands in Dovercourt Churchyard which was 'erected by the Company as an expression of their admiration of his gallantry'.

Edith Cavell memorials are found with a number of factory marks. Most, with slight variation are models of the gowned figure standing on a plinth, taken from the front portion of the original London Memorial. Only one manufacturer, Leadbeater Art, made a model of the complete statue which, at 200mm, is the largest of the models. Most carry part of the inscription found on the original. A model of the Norwich memorial of Edith Cavell was made for a R. Townsend, Tomb Land House, Norwich, by the Arcadian works and comprises an embossed figure of a soldier on a cenotaph holding up a wreath. On top is a bust of Nurse Cavell. According to the telephone directory of the time this Mr. Townsend is listed as an Antique Furniture Dealer ...no doubt he had an eye for antiques of the future!

The Arcadian works made the greatest number of different models, totalling twenty-three recorded memorials of provincial towns. Willow, Carlton and Leadbeater Art came not so close runners-up with eight, seven and six respectively. It is interesting to note that we find a number of manufacturers listed in this section that do not appear elsewhere, e.g. Leadbeater Art, Saxony, Foreign. New factories did appear in the twenties, when the memorials were made, although few lasted for more than a decade. The German pottery industry returned when trade embargoes were lifted and provided cheap, poor quality models for the English market. It is a wry twist of fate that German hands modelled the design for an English war memorial.

Rushden War Memorial unmarked 158mm. ins. 'To keep in mind those from the town who gave their lives in the Great War 1914-1918: their name liveth forever'.

Matlock Bath Memorial Podmore china 197mm. Erected late 1920 and dedicated to the 22 local men who died. The figure of the soldier and sailor holding the flag are in white marble and the pedestal of Cornish granite.

'Illegally executed by the Germans on 27th July 1916'. So said the propaganda notices that followed his death. Capt. Charles Algernon Fryatt of the Steamship Brussels lived at 55 Oakland Road, Dovercourt and left a widow and seven children. After the war a memorial was erected by the company in Upper Dovercourt Churchyard. Model in Arcadian china.

9
Miscellany

Military looking gentleman in lifebelt. Grafton china 68mm. No. 214. Sometimes referred to as a rather distasteful commemorative of Lord Kitchener's death in the sinking of HMS Hampshire, however the factory number places it well before the war.

Bear. Arcadian china 125mm. Sometimes found with the inscription 'War Edition 1914-15'. Said to represent the Russian Bear.

There are a large number of pieces of Heraldic Chinaware which by virtue of their crest or inscription, show a relationship to the Great War. Such pieces include: models bearing 'Flags of the Allies' transfers, models bearing Regimental Crests, models bearing foreign crests and an inscription relating to the war and lastly models that are not directly connected with the war but for some reason can be linked to it.

1. Flags of the Allies

Non-military models, and less frequently military models, are found bearing the 'Flags of the Allies' instead of a crest. At the outset of the war it was such a design that first struck the mind of at least one of the manufacturers. The Pottery Gazette records, when writing about W.H. Goss, that ...'The flags of the Allies badge was prepared with remarkable celerity immediately after the outbreak of war, being in fact upon the market within a fortnight of the commencement of hostilities and taking the place of the seaside souvenir trade which naturally experienced a somewhat severe check'.

As time progressed and more countries became involved so the badge design was revised. In all twenty countries entered the hostilities on the side of the Allies. In alphabetical order they were: Australia, Belgium, Canada, China, France, Great Britain, Greece, India, Italy, Luxembourg, Japan, Montenegro, New Zealand, Poland, Portugal, Rumania, Russia, Serbia, South Africa and the United States. Given that some of these countries had more than one flag then the total number of possible flags becomes twenty-six. In reality only about half of these were used on china crests, the largest number appearing on any one model being eight, in the case of a Goss design which has the flags of France, Russia, Italy, Serbia, Japan, Montenegro, Great Britain and Belgium.

The Goss factory produced the greatest number of variations in flags' designs, including two (GB and USA), four, six and seven, as well as the eight flag design above. The Goss plate which has either six or seven flags around the perimeter (GB, France, Russia, Japan, Serbia and Belgium) has in its centre the patriotic verse...

Regimental crests.

Egg cup. Unmarked. Ins. 'I have no hesitation in saying that economy in consumption and use of food in this country is a matter of the greatest possible importance to the Empire at the present time. D. Lloyd George' and 'Made by the girls of Staffordshire during the winter of 1917 while their boys were in the trenches fighting for liberty and civilization'.

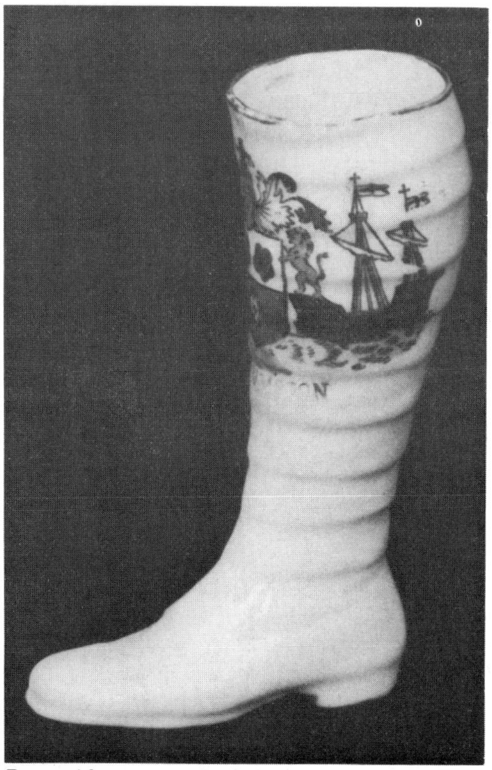
Boot with puttees. Grafton china 75mm. No. 389.

TO COOK A GERMAN
Cook on a British Kitchener,
Use a Japaned enamelled saucepan,
Grease well with Russian tallow,
Flavour with a little Jellicoe,
Servia! up with French capers and Brussels Sprouts.

The Goss factory's design for a Peace Plaque (see back cover) must rank amongst the finest produced. The central figure of an angel is surrounded by the flags of eleven countries which are in turn bordered by laurel leaves carrying the names of famous leaders. Below the angel are the words 'Peace 1919' and a list of Britain's Dominions and Allies.

Aynsley china:
Cartridge case 60mm. Reg. No. 444366. Crest: 2nd UB Manchester Regiment.
High Boot 110mm. Reg. No. 444523. Crest: 1st Essex Volunteer Artillery, Eastern Division RA.
Drum 57mm. Reg. No. 444367. Crest: 4th Dragoon Guards.

Other manufacturers made flag designs but they lack the perfection of Goss's work. Most consist of a number of flags, usually four, five or six, and the inscription: 'The Triple Entente; United we stand; The Allied Armies', or some variation of the same.

The flags most frequently used were as follows:
GREAT BRITAIN: Union Jack or Royal Standard or White Ensign.
FRANCE: Blue, white and red vertical stripes.
BELGIUM: Black, yellow and red vertical stripes.
RUSSIA: Double headed eagle on yellow background or white, blue and red horizontal stripes (civil flag) or blue cross on white background (Naval flag).
LUXEMBOURG: Red, white and blue horizontal stripes.
ITALY: Green, white and red vertical stripes. (Naval flag the same with cross on white stripes).
JAPAN: Rising sun with sixteen radiating rays (red on white) or red circle on white background.
POLAND: White and red horizontal stripes.
MONTENEGRO: Red, blue and white horizontal stripes with crown on the blue.
SERVIA: Red, blue and white horizontal stripes.
USA: Stars and stripes.

2. Regimental Crests (see Appendix iii)
Together with the Flags of the Allies, the Regimental crests were amongst the first ideas that the Goss firm had for models relating to the war. The War Edition of the Goss Record (1917) states that... 'With the coming of war the collection of Goss Heraldic porcelain was threatened with a serious setback. But instead of this fear being realised there has been a decided impetus in new directions. The first idea was that of reproducing the Army Regimental badges in the beautifully illuminated heraldry, and the soldiers themselves have taken the greatest delight in obtaining the charming little models bearing their regimental arms and sending them to relatives and friends as keepsakes'. They advertised a total of one hundred and twenty-nine Regimental, eleven overseas and forty-seven Battleship crests.

Postcard with the verse used on the Goss 'To Cook a German' plate. Note how the last word has been changed from 'scouts' to 'sprouts'.
(see colour section)

Unfortunately, Goss was the only manufacturer to list his range of Regimental arms and while other firms used regimental crests, their lists (see Appendix iii) are almost certainly incomplete. Aynsley china, dating from 1904, designed twenty-five recorded crests, all of units that disappeared with the Haldane reforms of 1908. Almost invariably they are found on one of a small range of military models that they made. Arcadian, Carlton and a handful of other manufacturers appear to have had some regimental crest designs which they used on a variety of models.

3. Foreign Crests and Inscriptions (see Appendix ii)

The Pottery Gazette of 3rd April 1917 records the following... 'It is interesting to learn that there is a strong demand from our troops in France for Heraldic ware with the arms of various places in which they are billetted; so that, if the Military Censor permits, they, with later on the arms of the Belgian and even German towns, may tell a story of the 'Big Push' '. Whether this is just journalistic exaggeration or the Military Censor did intercede is supposition but certainly Goss used over thirty foreign crests which could have originated from the war. Whichever the case, no doubt the "strong demand" waned somewhat when it became obvious that the war would not "be over by Christmas".

It was left to another manufacturer to take up this original idea and follow it through. Birks, Rawlins & Co, the manufacturer of Savoy China designed an extensive range of foreign crests to which they added an inscription detailing the events concerned with it. Twenty-one such crests have been traced and range from the crest of Armentieres with the inscription... 'Desperate battle between British and Germans Nov. 1914; June 1915' to the crest of Ypres with the inscription, 'German rush stemmed by the valour of the British troops; Oct 27 1914; Canadians gallantry saved the situation April 24 1915'. The only British crest found with such an inscription is Sheringham which has, 'German Air Raid on Sheringham Jan 19 1915'. (See Appendix i)

Arcadian and Carlton china also used foreign crests at one time or another although there is very little information regarding them. Arcadian used the crests of various countries (New Zealand, Belgium, India, Russia and Canada have been traced) to which they added the wording: 'War Edition 1914'.

4. Models that do not have any apparent connection with the War

Wiltshaw and Robinson (Carlton) designed a 'Map of Blighty' which they registered on June 14th 1917 (Reg. No. 660695). It is found with the inscription: 'Blighty' and the verse:

Take me back to dear old Blighty,
Put me on a train for London town,
Drop me anywhere,
Liverpool, Leeds or Manchester,
I don't care.

Presumably because of design problems Scotland was left out - no doubt the piece was not well received by our fighting forces from north of the border.

Various models of homely looking fireplaces are found. Some inscribed with a verse such as 'Keep the home fires burning'; 'East or West, Home is best. The kettle on the fire is singing, the old clock ticks, and the teapot is on the hob. Sure it's a good old home, sweet home'. Only the Carlton model (Reg. No. 659332) registered on 6th February 1917 can definitely be placed in the war years.

Several models of animals appear with a Great War inscription. Savoy made a model of a Lion which has the word: 'Dreadnought' on its side. Was it conceived directly from HMS Lion or was it just a play on words? The Lion being the king of the jungle, the Dreadnoughts the 'Queens' of the seas. Arcadian models of a Bear and Bulldog have been found with the wording 'War Edition 1914-15', but was this accidental or do they represent the Russian Bear and the British Bulldog... if so might we not expect to find the French Cockerel? Grafton added the word Dreadnought to their model of a charabanc, although judging from the factory number (975) it was made well after the war. Several models of a Bulldog peering out of his kennel are found with the wording 'The Black Watch'.

10
In Conclusion What if.....?

It is unfortunate that the china manufacturers failed to document their designs and sales lists in a manner that has survived the passage of time. Catalogues and lists of such therefore have to be compiled indirectly by studying the models that appear in collections and sales lists now. In many ways this can prove to be a 'block' for any intending researcher as there is little 'original' printed material available. However to the collector this might be seen as an endearing feature for there is always the possibility of the unrecorded, the unusual or the unexpected being discovered. Even at this moment there may be models, perhaps of a failed line and now ones of a handful that have survived, languishing under layers of dust in some attic or back room of a shop, forgotten for many years and now just 'waiting' to be discovered.

As to what these models may be we can only speculate but a quick search through the preceding chapters reveals many apparent omissions. Where, for instance, is Sir Douglas Haig who took over from Sir John French in 1916? Where is the model of an Indian Soldier, one of many who fought so gallantly in the hostile environment of Northern Europe? Where is the soldier's Lee-Enfield rifle, the lifeblood of the infantry? Where are the models of the smaller classes of submarines and indeed the others of the E class? Where are the other twenty or so Dreadnoughts that fought alongside the ships that are named in china? These only represent some of the factual possibilities, we know that the designers were not averse to comic, gruesome or fantastic, what of these?

If we speculate further then the list of possibilities becomes endless. As a gourmet might anticipate the flavours of an untried dish so the collector may savour the reports and possibilities of what may have or might exist.

What becomes apparent when this collection of models is studied are the omissions. It is evident, albeit unfortunate, that no china manufacturer consciously set out to provide a 'potted' history of the war. The result of the potters' inspirations is simply an assortment of models linked together by the single greatest event of the century. The fascination that they have is not so much in what they represent but in the fact that they exist at all. They were chosen at random from the thousands of pictures, photographs and descriptions that were seen in the press

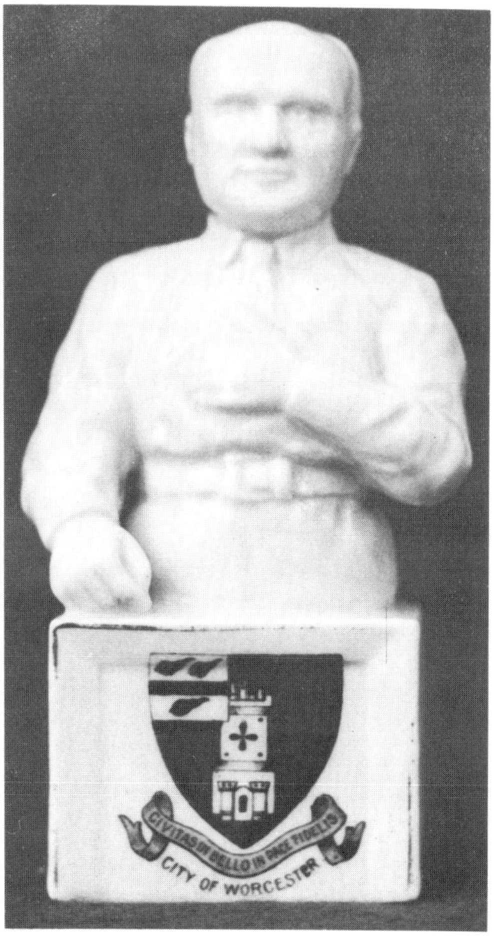

A sign of things to come. An unmarked model, although with distinctly Foreign manufacturer's characteristics, of what appears to be Mussolini. Probably dates from the late twenties when he first came to power. 130mm.

simply because they were thought to have some appeal to the china collectors as models. The successes were those that caught on and were produced for many years; the failures or 'flops' are those that were soon withdrawn when a ready market was not found. The appeal that they had, or were thought to have had, must seem to us now to have been singularly inapt.

When the war ended so did a way of life and with it went the demand for these novelties. Some of the manufacturers struggled on until the 1930s when the depression finally squeezed out their last breath of life. People no longer had money to fritter away on the luxuries of life, all they had was needed to keep body and soul together. Those firms that could not adapt to making the more necessary items of chinaware: cups and saucers, jugs and teapots or plates and dishes, went to the wall.

Had production and demand continued into the thirties and forties I have no doubt that the far-sighted collector of Heraldic Chinaware would be adding to his collection... a 'Model of Spitfire' inscribed: 'Battle of Britain 1939-40', or a 'Model of Doodlebug, as fired on London by the Germans' or a bust of Montgomery or De Gaulle or even a 'Model of Tommy driving a steamroller over Hitler!' Perhaps they would have drawn the line at a 'Model of A-bomb: dropped on Hiroshima and Nagasaki - 6th and 9th August 1945' .....or would they? If we inwardly recoil at this then it is because we are part of a generation that are all too aware of the horrors of twentieth century warfare. Our predecessors of 60 years ago, in their naivety, sought to commemorate what we would now choose to forget.

World War Two's equivalent to Crested China? Hitler potties - 'Gest-a-Po' with Hitler's face painted inside looking suitably concerned. Unfortunately the Crested china industry died in the thirties, had they continued I am sure they would have had a field day in World War Two.

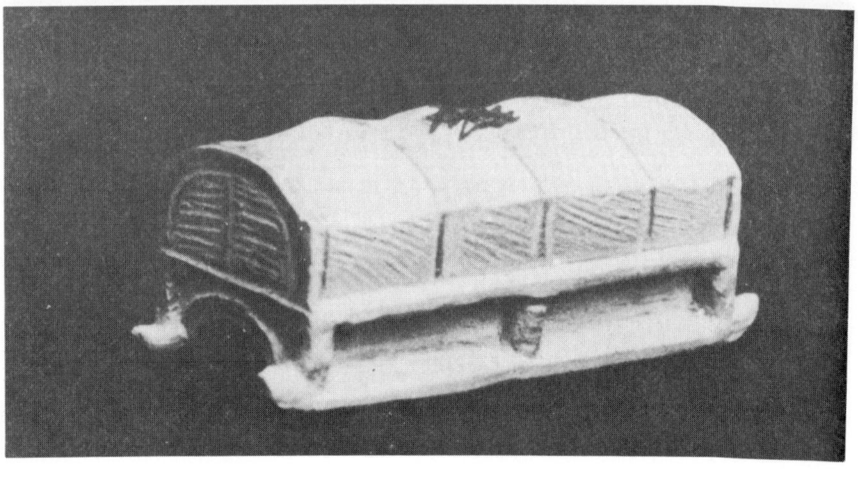

Where is it? The manufacturers did not always produce models they had registered in any quantity. This model of a Red Cross Desert sledge was registered by the Carlton factory in September 1917 (Reg. No. 661566) but no model has been traced.

APPENDIX

i
Patents and Registration Numbers

Under the Patents and Designs Act of 1907 registered designs of ceramics were protected for five years. Photographs or drawings of designs were submitted to the Patent Office and, if acceptable, a certificate and registration number was issued. This number was displayed on the article which could not be copied without the consent of the holder of the certificate.

Many models carry a registration number and this has proved useful in dating and identifying the origins of their design. The numbers by themselves do not give any indication of when, for how long or how many of the actual models were made, although viewed collectively they provide us with an insight into the workings of some of the factories.

In the period 1914-18 H.T. Robinson of the Arcadian works made greatest use of the Patent Office, registering designs for a total of 49 models with a military connection. (Others were registered before and during the war but are outside the scope of this book.) Most of these were registered in the second half of 1916 when the Somme offensive was in full swing. No doubt the increased national interest in the 'Big Push' inspired their manufacture. Robinson was also first off the mark to patent models of some of the new and historic weapons of war. The model of a Zeppelin, patented one week after an historic bombing raid; the model of an armoured car which preceded the first pictures of the tanks; the model of a tank designed within one week of their appearance in British newspapers and the model of a 'Super Zeppelin' made within days of the crash of the L33. It is not surprising that in his haste he sacrificed accuracy... the fictitious "armoured car", the one-wheeled tank, the incorrect 'torpedo' shaped Zeppelin. Nevertheless he exploited the possibilities the war gave to their fullest and made some of the most interesting models that are found in china. After this burst of activity in 1916 there were no further registrations for the Arcadian factory for almost two years. Their last registration appears on August 6th 1918 when a design was submitted for an 'Aerial bomb' (the Sheringham bomb). For some reason the design was not approved and a certificate refused. Nevertheless models are always found carrying the registration number for the refused certificate. Unfortunately, since the design photographs of refused certificates are not available to the public we have no way of knowing whether the bomb that appears in china is the same as the refused design or whether it was modified.

Messrs. Wiltshaw & Robinson of the Carlton works registered twelve models in the war years. Their earliest model, dating from September 1915, was the Scots soldier. It is rather surprising that they did not register either of their models of British soldiers, both of which may pre-date the Scottish soldier. After registering only one model in 1916 (aeroplane) they warmed up in 1917 and submitted designs for a further ten models in the course of the year. Their model of "Tommy in dugout" (or as it is described in the register... "boy in hut") appeared in June 1917 and the Map of Blighty one week later, although this may have been on sale before the design was registered. In September they registered designs for a "steam ship" (minesweeper), a canvas sled, which is a copy of a desert Red Cross sledge and is the only design that has not been traced in china, and a model of a 'minehead' which was refused. Finally in October they registered models of a naval gun, steam ship (HMS Anglia and Lusitania), a munitions girl and, trying again with the mine, had a model of a floating mine accepted.

Messrs. Birks, Rawlins & Co. of Savoy china registered a total of eight models. Their first, a model of the E1 submarine was designed in September 1915, four weeks after the action that is commemorated on the model and this was followed in November by a design for a Red Cross van (based on an Argyll ambulance) and an armoured car (based on a Talbot). In February 1917 they registered models of a warship and an airship (the SL11) that was shot down by Leefe Robinson in September 1916. The latter appearing two weeks after photographs of the crashed (L33) ship appeared in the press. Later on in the year they designed a two-piece model of a Vickers machine gun, a German trench mortar (which is found with the inscription "British trench Mortar") and a Scots Bonnet.

It is interesting that the two factories that made most use of their own stock numbers did not register many pieces. A.B. Jones & Sons Ltd. (Grafton) tried to register designs for a hand grenade and tank in December 1916 but they had been beaten to the post by H.T. Robinson by some two months and their designs were refused. Their only other registered model, that of a bust of Lloyd George, was submitted in February 1917. Wileman & Co. (Shelley), like Grafton, numbered their models and in the years 1914-20, registered only one piece, a model of a soldier playing a concertina while sitting at the entrance to his tent. They did register a batch of their models in 1903 which includes a bandman's drum and peaked cap.

This section on patents cannot be concluded without reference to Aynsley China. Although pre-war their military china precedes all others (except the Shelley drum and cap). They were the first china factory to make a number of such models and would appear to have some connection with the Boer War. All models are found with regimental crests. In between October 29th and November 9th 1904 they registered a total of eleven military pieces, ranging from a hand bomb with flames coming out of the top, to a cavalry high boot.

All these factories (except Aynsley) made other military models which merited patenting, but were not. Why should Carlton china register their model of Tommy's dugout but not their model of "Old Bill"? Both are from Bruce Bairnsfather's cartoons and probably date from the same time. Why should Arcadian china register a model of a drummer boy, but not the model of its pair, the Bugler? Was the latter an afterthought? Why should Shelley china only register one of their thirty-three models ...and so the questions go on, unfortunately unanswered and largely unanswerable.

Before listing the registrations that were made it is necessary to point out two things. Firstly manufacturers were none too careful when putting registration numbers on to their models and frequently models turn up carrying the wrong number. The following numbers are extracted from the Patent Office register and are correct for the models listed. Secondly, designs for models were frequently exchanged, and along with them the registration number. Thus it is quite possible to find a model registered by, for example, H.T. Robinson, appearing in Willow China with the same number. The registration number for the tank (658588) is a prime example of this - being used by no fewer than four manufacturers on their models of Mark I and Mark IV tanks.

PATENTS ISSUED FOR MILITARY HERALDIC CHINA

1. Issued to: H.T. Robinsons & Sons Ltd., Wolfe St., Stoke-on-Trent. (Arcadian China)

Date	*Registration number*	*Design*
19.9.12	607828	Aeroplane
20.10.15	652241	Airship on plinth
	652242	Submarine (E4)
	652243	Model of Sailor
	652244	Bust of Sailor
	652245	Field gun
16.8.16	657210	British Aerial Torpedo
	657211	Mills bomb
	657212	Mortar
	657213	Soldier in Sentry box
	657214	Soldier with machine gun
	657215	Soldiers hut
21.9.16	657648	Clip of bullets
	657649	Trench dagger
	657650	Steel helmet
	657651	Spigott Mortar bomb
	657652	Soldier wearing gas mask
	657653	Pistol
26.9.16	657694	British Aerial bomb
	657695	Water bottle
	657696	Trench lamp
	657697	German stick grenade
	657698	Ghurkas knife (Kukri)
	657699	Plum Pudding bomb
	657700	Cannister bomb
	657701	Trench pig
	657702	Hairbrush grenade
27.9.16	657733	French soldier
	657734	Scottish soldier
	657735	Super Zeppelin
	657736	Armoured car
	657737	Soldier on motorbike
	657738	Australian hat
29.11.16	658588	Tank
6.12.16	658674	Nurse and wounded Tommy
	658675	Sailor winding capstan
	658676	Soldier in bayonet attack
	658677	Torpedo boat destroyer
	658678	Sandbag
	658679	British airship (Blimp)
	658680	Soldier on horseback
	658681	Soldier throwing grenade
	658682	Observer sausage balloon
	658683	Aeroplane
	658684	Mounted Cossack
	658685	Australian soldier
	658686	Field gun with screen
	658687	Submarine (E5)
12.12.16	658737	Drummer boy
2.8.18	664837	Aerial bomb (refused)

2. Issued to: Wiltshaw & Robinson Ltd., Carlton Works, Copeland St., Stoke-on-Trent. (Carlton China)

Date	*Registration number*	*Design*
1.9.15	651139	Scottish soldier
16.9.16	657607	Aeroplane
6.2.17	659332	Kitchen range
8.6.17	660613	Tommy in dugout
14.6.17	660695	Map of England and Wales
3.9.17	661565	Trawler
	661566	Red Cross sledge
	661567	Na.
	661568	Mine-head Refused
17.10.17	662103	Naval gun
	662104	Steam ship
	662105	Munitions girl
	662106	Floating mine

3. Issued to: Birks, Rawlins & Co., Vine Pottery, Summer St., Stoke. (Savoy China)

18.9.15	651546	Submarine (E1)
13.11.15	652655	Red Cross van
	652656	Armoured car
5.2.17	659327	Warship
16.2.17	659483	Airship (SL11)
20.8.17	661446	Machine gun
11.9.17	661740	German Trench Mortar
	661741	Scots bonnet

4. Issued to: A.B. Jones & Sons Ltd., Grafton China, Marlborough Rd., Longton. (Grafton China)

16.12.16	658803	Hand grenade (Refused)
	658804	Tank (Refused)
12.2.17	659418	Bust of Lloyd George

5. Issued to: Wileman & Co., King St., Fenton, Stoke-on-Trent. (Shelley China)

6.03	412407	Bandman's drum
1.18	664306	Bell tent with soldier

6. Issued to: Aynsley & Sons, Portland Potteries, Longton. (Aynsley)

Between 29.10 & 9.11.1904	442812	Pith helmet
	444365	Water bottle
	444366	Cartridge case
	444367	Drum
	444368	Tent
	444369	Loaded cartridge
	444521	Horses hoof
	444522	Hand grenade
	444523	Cavalry high boot
	444579	Military helmet
	444580	Forage cap
	445700	Glengarry
	446680	Boot

APPENDIX 1a. MANUFACTURERS NUMBERS

The Shelley and Grafton factories numbered their models. The following are lists of the military models made by these factories and their corresponding factory number.

Shelley China

Number	*Model*
54	Peaked cap
57	Bandman's drum (Reg. No. 412407)
170	Model of Greek vase: found in Jan. 1916
175	Shrapnell shell
176	Glengarry
177	Zeppelin bomb
179	Trench mortar
187	Head of German torpedo
188	German mine washed up on East Coast
191	Flash lamp
311	Bleriot warplane
316	Bulldog in kennel 'The Black Watch'
319	Warship
327	Trench mortar
328	Submarine E9
329	Armoured car
330	Red Cross van
331	German howitzer
332	Zeppelin L33
334	Mills grenade
338	Fireplace 'Keep the home fires burning'
340	Howitzer
341	Tommy in tent (Reg. No. 664306)
343	Binoculars
344	Biplane
348	Anti-Zeppelin candlestick
354	Bugle
362	Paddle steamer
368	Cenotaph
400	Tank, Mark I
400a	Tank, Mark II
402	Scottish soldier
403	Britannia
406	'Vive la France'
413	Tank bank

NOTE: On their own the factory numbers do not give any indication as to the date of origin of the model. However if we link up the number with other factors then we are able to estimate the date.

Shelley 54 (Drum) can be fixed accurately by the date of registration (June 1903). Shelley 170 (Greek vase... found by British troops entrenching in Jan 1916) would obviously post-date the find, probably by two or three months. Shelley 332 (L33) would have appeared at the earliest in September 1916 although it most likely came out some months later when accurate photographs were available, perhaps in early 1917. Shelley 341 (Tommy in tent) can be dated accurately from its registration date i.e. January 1918 and Shelley 368 (Cenotaph) could not have appeared earlier than July 1919 when the temporary structure was unveiled, but more probably dates from November 1920 when the permanent structure was erected.

Allowing for an error of a few months the above can be summarised as follows:

Shelley 54	June 1903
Shelley 170-332	Feb. 1916-Feb. 1917
Nos. 216-299 do not appear to have been used.	
Shelley 333-341	March 1917-Jan 1918
Shelley 342-368	Jan 1918-December 1920
Shelley 369+	Jan 1921 onwards

Interestingly, the models of the tanks did not appear until well after the war, possibly as late as 1921. Did they wait until Robinson's original patent had expired before issuing their own model? If this was the case then they would have appeared after November 1921.

Grafton China

Number	*Model*
85	American soldier
214	Military gentleman in life belt
234	Water bottle
238	Colonial hat
239	Tent (two models)
262	British Territorial Bulldog
389	Boot with puttees
394	Alpine gun
395	Bust of Kitchener
397	Motor ambulance
399	Shell
400	Shell
403	German gun and 'Over the top'
404	Howitzer
405	Zeppelin bomb
406	Submarine E9
408	Warship 'Dreadnought'
411	Mills bomb
412	French 75 on sled
413	Tank Mark I & IV
414	Monoplane
415	Bust of Lloyd George (Reg. No. 659418)
425	'The Bomb Thrower'
430	Desert gun
431	Warship: HMS Iron Duke
449	Whippet tank
450	Biplane
452	Squatting sailor
460/456	Motor tractor
568	Charabanc 'Dreadnought'

NOTES: The dating of the Grafton numbers is less accurate than those of the Shelley factory. Nevertheless some broad outlines are given below.

Grafton 262 (British Territorial Bulldog) could only have appeared after the Territorial force had been formed in 1908. Grafton 395 (Kitchener bust) carries an inscription to his death in 1916 and although it sometimes carries extra wording (including the year 1918) it is probable that this was designed as a piece to commemorate Kitchener's death and was brought out soon after the fatal accident, the extra wording being added to later models. The factory attempted to register a model for a Mills bomb and Tank in December 1916 but was refused. It would seem logical, as they presumably considered them to have a good sales potential, that they would hastily rather than leisurely approach Robinson for use of his copyright and thus 411 (Bomb) and 413 (Tank) probably arrived on the scene in early 1917. Grafton 415 lends weight to this as the model (Bust of Lloyd George) was registered on 12th February 1917. The model of the whippet tank (449) could not have appeared before April 1918 (they were first used in March) but probably came out even later. The charabanc (568), which is sometimes found with the word 'Dreadnought' on its side, must be a very late model as it just precedes their model of the Banbury Cross which was registered in 1922 or later.

To summarise:	262	earliest possible is 1908
	395	earliest possible is 1916
	411	probably January 1917
	415	registered February 1917
	449	middle of 1918
	568	1922 or later

The enigma in the Grafton pieces is the model which has been called, for want of anything else, 'an American soldier'. If the number given is correct and if the factory numbers are consecutive then it puts this model at a very early date... even as early as the turn of the century.

These photographs and the ones that follow are the design representations that were submitted to the Patent Office for approval. Most were sculpted in clay and are interesting for the detail they show which is often lost on the subsequent glazed models.

Mounted soldier. Reg. No. 658680. Registered in the name of H.T. Robinson on 6th December 1916. The same horse was used for the Russian Cossack Reg. No. 658684 registered on the same day.

Soldier in bayonet attack. Reg. No. 658676. Note the absence of a bayonet. No doubt it proved too fragile.

Soldier throwing hand grenade. Reg. No. 658681. Registered on the same day as the Mounted Soldier and Cossack.

Australian soldier Reg. No. 658680. Not a popular model, very few have been recorded in china. Perhaps visiting colonials bought up all the stocks and took them home?

Scottish soldier. Reg. No. 657734. Registered on 27th September 1916.

Drummer boy. Reg. No. 658737. The last model to be registered by the Arcadian works in 1916 - and the last for almost two years.

Nurse tending wounded soldier. Reg. No. 658674. Registered on 6th December 1916.

Armoured Car. Reg. No. 657736. Registered on 27th September 1916, ten days after the tanks were first used. Note the detail on the tracks (copied from Army tractors) and the totally ficticious top and gun. Described in the Patent Office Register as 'Motor Vehicle "Tank" '.

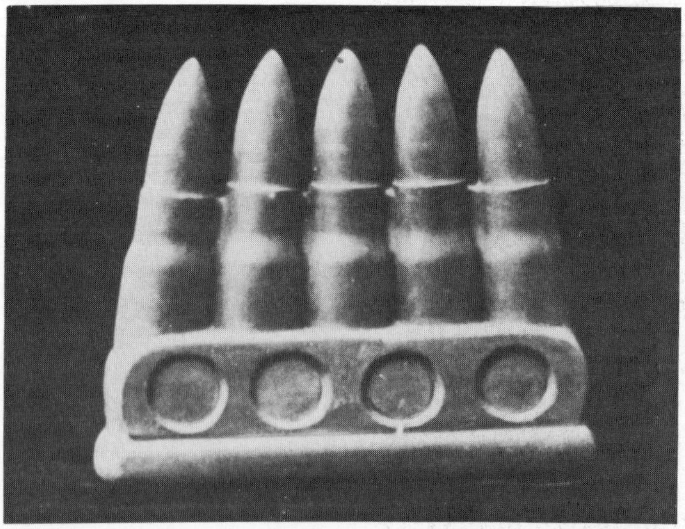

Clip of bullets. Reg. No. 657648.

Aeroplane. Reg. No. 658683. Registered on 6th December 1916.

Kitchen range. Reg. No. 659332. Registered on 6th February 1917 and one of thirteen models registered by the Carlton factory during the war.

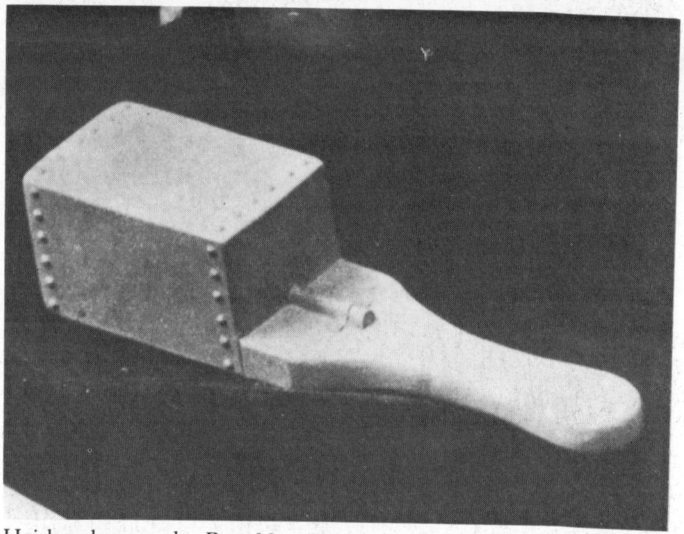

Hairbrush grenade. Reg. No. 657702. September 26th 1916 was bomb day for Robinson. This model was registered with the Aerial Bomb, German Stick Grenade, Plum Pudding Bomb, Cannister Bomb and Trench Pig.

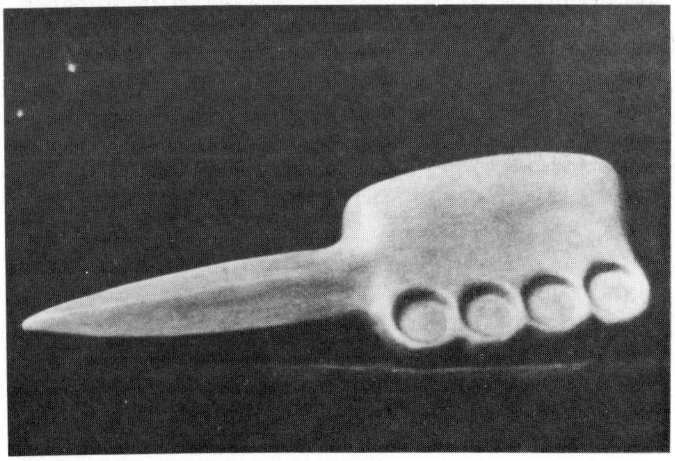

Trench dagger. Reg. No. 657649. Registered on 21st September 1916. Robinson registered a total of twenty-two models in this month.

Trench helmet. Reg. No. 657650.

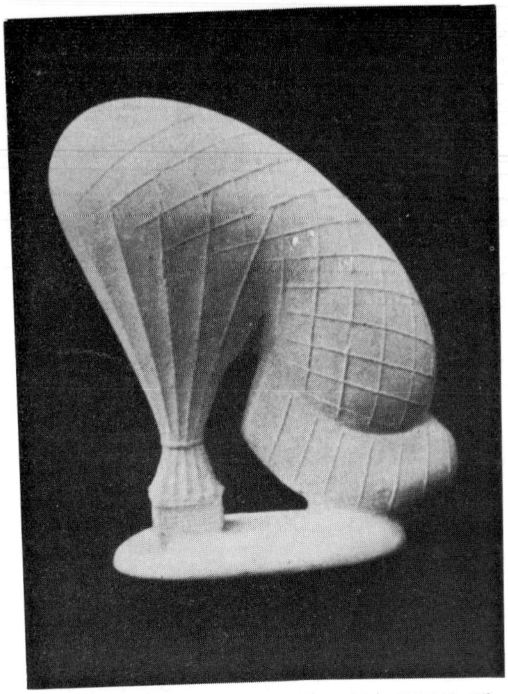

Observer sausage balloon. Reg. No. 658683. The basket and wires are clearly visible.

Soldier playing a concertina. Reg. No. 664306. Issued to Wileman & Co (Shelley) in January 1918. Surprisingly the only model registered by this factory in the war years.

One-wheeled tank. Reg. No. 658588. Registered on 29th November 1916 - six days after the Daily Mirror photograph on which it was based.

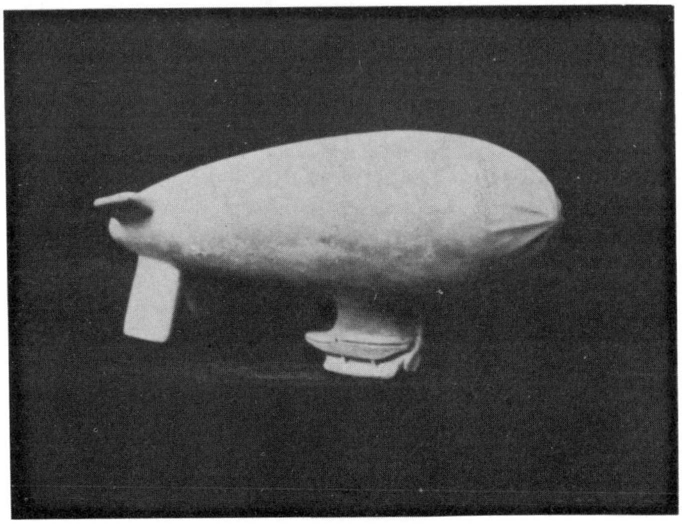

British Airship. Reg. No. 658679. One of the fourteen models registered on 6th December 1916.

ii
Inscriptions appearing on Military Heraldic China

The term 'inscription' is strictly incorrect when used to describe the writing that appears of Heraldic china since it was not 'inscribed' but 'transferred'. However for convention the term 'inscription' is used.

In addition to the standard, 'Model of...' many models carry extra wording. Birks, Rawlins & Co. (Savoy) and Wiltshaw & Robinson (Carlton) were the two factories that made most use of inscriptions although Arcadian, Grafton, Shelley, Goss and Willow made some models with additional words or verses.

The inscriptions do not necessarily appear on Military models although most of them do. They may appear on various parts of the model and are not always visible on the upper surface.

The following have not been included in this list: inscriptions stating what the model is (although where some extra wording appears the whole inscription is listed), inscriptions that read... 'Made for...' that are found on the bases of some models. Inscriptions that are found on memorials are listed separately.

1. ARCADIAN CHINA

Bust of 'Tommy Atkins':

'It's the soldiers of the king,
My lads,
Who fought for England's glory,
Lads,
And when they say we've always
Won
And when they ask us how
It's done
We'll proudly point to every
One of us
England's soldiers of the
King.'

Nurse: 'A Soldier's Friend'

Bust of Sailor: 'Queen Elizabeth'

Tommy on Steamroller: 'To Berlin'

Fireplace: 'We've kept the home fires burning'
or
'There's no place like home'

Shell: 'Hartlepool Bombardment Dec. 16th 1914'

Zeppelin Bomb: 'Model of bomb dropped from a Zeppelin upon Sheringham during the first raid on England 8.30pm Jany 19th 1915'

'Model of first bomb dropped from Zeppelin at Loftus September 8th 1915 at 9.30pm'

'Model of bomb that killed a chicken at Southend'

King George V: 'King George V: Born June 3rd 1865; ascended the throne May 6th 1910'

Queen Mary: 'Queen Mary: Born May 26th 1867'

Prince of Wales: 'HRH Prince of Wales: Born June 23rd 1894'

2. CARLTON CHINA

Figures:

British Soldier: on base: 'Are we downhearted? NO!'
on back: 'It's a long way to Tipperary,
It's a long way to go,
It's a long long way to Tipperary
To the sweetest girl I know,
Goodbye Piccadilly,
Farewell Leicester Square,
It's a long way to Tipperary,
For my heart is right there'.

Sailor: 'We've got 'U' well in hand'

Old Bill: 'Yours to a cinder Old Bill'

Tommy in dugout: 'Tommy's dugout somewhere in France' and 'Shrapnell Villa' or Peace inscription.

Munitions worker: 'Doing her bit: Shells and more shells'

Bust of Sailor: 'HMS Dreadnought' or 'Handy Man'

Ships

Trawler: 'Model of British Minesweeper whose splendid work will live forever in the annals of history' and 'HMMS Gowan Lea' or 'HMMS Peggy' or Peace inscription.

HMHS Anglia: 'Model of British Hospital ship whose voyage was disregarded on three occasions by German submarines'

Lusitania: 'Remember the Lusitania: The Lusitania was sunk by a German submarine May 1915. Lives lost 1,198' or 'Sunk by German submarine off the Irish coast May 7th 1915. Lives lost 1,275; saved 703'

Submarine E5: 'Great War 1914-18; 150 German U-boats surrendered Nov. 20th 1918'

Warships: 'Great War 1914-18; the German Fleet surrendered 74 warships Nov 21st 1918'

Map of Blighty: 'Blighty'
'Take me back to dear old Blighty
Put me on a train for London town,
Drop me anywhere,
Liverpool, Leeds or Manchester,
I don't care.'

Tanks: 'HMLS Creme-de-Menthe' the British tank successfully used against the Germans, Combles Sept 1916' or
'The British tank that gave them hell at the Marne 1918' or
'Buy War Bonds... The Tank Bank... War Bonds sold £3,423,234'

Caps: 'Anzacs forever'

Kit-bag: 'Pack up your troubles'

Searchlight: 'Model of British Searchlight: The Zeppelin Finder'

Tent: 'Tommies bungalow'

Shell: 'Jack Johnson'

Peace inscription: on a variety of models: 'The victory of Justice: Armistice of the Great War signed Nov 11th 1918'
or
'The Victory of Justice: Peace signed at Versailles June 28th 1919'

Fireplaces: 'We've kept the home fires burning'
or
'East or West Home is best. The kettle on the fire is singing, the old clock ticks, and the teapot is on the hob, sure it's a good old home, Sweet Home'

3. GOSS

Commemorative plate:
'To Cook a German'
Cook on a British Kitchener,
Use a Japaned enamelled saucepan,
Grease well with Russian tallow,
Flavour with a little Jellicoe,
Servia! up with French capers and Brussels Sprouts'.

Scarborough Bombardment Plate: 'Up ye sons of England and wreak vengeance on the baby-killers of Scarborough. We follow you in our daily thoughts on your certain road to victory. George RI Dec. 5th 1914'

Shell: 'Model of Russian Shrapnell shell; the original was captured by the Germans and fired by them at the British'

'British 6ins Incendiary Shell'

Bomb: 'Model of German bomb dropped on Bury St. Edmunds from a Zeppelin 30th April 1915'

Bomb: 'Model of German Incendiary bomb; dropped at Malden 16 April 1915 from a German Zeppelin'

Tank: 'Model of British Tank; every tank will do its damdest'

4. GRAFTON

Lord Kitchener of Khartoum; Creator of the British Army 1914-1916; born June 24th 1850; died serving his country June 5th 1916 by sinking of the HMS Hampshire off the Orkneys'

Motor Ambulance: 'Model of Motor Ambulance car given by the Staffs china operatives; British Red Cross and St. Johns Ambulance Association. Load not to exceed 1 driver, 1 attendant and patients'

Field Gun: 'German gun captured by the British'
'Alpine gun' : 'French 75' : 'Desert gun'

Tractor: 'Model of motor tractor used on the Western Front'

Soldiers: 'Over the top' and 'The Bomb Thrower'

Tanks: 'HMLS Creme-de-Menthe'

5. SAVOY

a. Inscriptions found with foreign crests, usually on non-military models.

Crest:	
ARMENTIERES	'Desperate battles between British and Germans Nov 1914 and June 1915'
ANTWERPEN	
ARRAS	'Great battle between French and Germans French gain trenches June 1915' or '13,000 German prisoners, 160 guns captured 1917'
AUSTRALIA	'Herbertshone German Pacific Island captured by Australian Navy September 11th 1914. The German cruiser Emden attacked and burnt by H.M.S. Sydney Nov. 8th 1914'
BELGIUM	'Belgium invaded by Germany August 4th 1914. Capital occupied August 20th 1914'
BRITISH EAST AFRICA	'South Togoland seized by Britain August 7th 1914'
BOULOGNE	'Hospital base for British wounded soldiers'
BRUGES/ BRUGGE	'Bruges occupied by the Germans Oct.16 1914'
BUCHAREST	
CALAIS	'German life and death advance'
COMBLES	
DUNKERQUE	'Dunkerque bombarded by long range German guns'
FRANCE	'France; French territory invaded by German troops August 2nd 1914; Battle of the Marne Sept 8th Sept 12th'
GAND	
GREECE	'Allies land at Salonika October 5 1915'
LIEGE	Invested and bombarded by the Germans August 9th 1914'
LILLE	'Lille captured by the Germans Sept 1914'
LOUVAIN	'Louvain burned and destroyed by the Germans August 25th 1914'
LUXEMBOURG	'Luxembourg invaded by Germans Aug. 1914'
MALINES	'Town and cathedral bombarded by Germans August 27th 1914'
MONS	'Battle of Mons, historic retreat begun August 23rd 1914'
NAMUR	'Namur forts destroyed by large German guns August 23rd 1914'
NEUVE CHAPELLE	'Neuve Chapelle, brilliant British victory over Germans at Neuve Chapelle, March 10th 1915'
OSTEND	'Occupied by the Germans October 16th 1914. British ships begin to take part in coast battle October 8th 1914'

PARIS	'German rush on Paris; reached 20 miles from Paris Sept 3rd 1914'
PERSIA	'Persia; British defeat Turks at Kut-el-Amara Sept 28th 1915'
RHEIMS	'Rheims bombarded by Germans Sept 2 1914; Cathedral destroyed Sept 19 1914'
SERVIA	'Austrians defeated by Serbians at Kolubra Dec 3-6 1914'
VERDUN	'German defeat before Fort Daumont Feb 26th 1916'
YPRES	'German rush stemmed by the valour of the British troops: Oct 27 1914; Canadian gallantry saved the situation April 24th 1915'
BRITISH CREST: SHERINGHAM	'German air raid on Sheringham: Jan 19 1915'

b. Inscriptions found on Military models.

Airship:	'Zeppelin destroyed by Lieutenant Robinson VC at Cuffley, Essex; Sept 3rd 1916'
Busts:	
Beatty:	'Admiral Sir David Beatty KCB: Soudan Campaign 1898; Naval Victory off Heligoland Bight August 28th 1914; Battle of Dogger Bank, Blucher sank Jan 24th 1915; Naval Victory off Jutland: 'We have only won the first round' May 31st 1916'
Cornwell:	'John Travers Cornwell, the boy aged 16, hero of Jutland Battle, Faithful unto death'
Joffre:	'General Joffre; Commander in charge of the French Army'
Kitchener:	'Lord Kitchener of Khartoum; Field Marshal K.G. K.P. Secretary of State for War. Born 1851. Drowned at sea off the Orkneys June 5th 1916'
Helmet:	'French helmet worn by the dauntless French Poilu'
Submarine:	'El: Commander Noel Laurence; Large German transport sunk July 30th 1915; German cruiser Moltke torpedoed August 19th 1915'
Shells:	'Iron rations for Fritz'
Tanks:	'HMS Donner Blitzen; Model of British tank as first used by the British troops at the Battle of the Ancre: Sept 1916'

c. Miscellaneous:

Lion and Bulldog:	'Another Dreadnought'

5. SHELLEY

Britannia:	'Rule Britannia'
Scottish soldier:	'Scotland forever'
Marianne:	'Vive la France'
Candlestick:	'Anti-Zeppelin candlestick as used in the Great War. Souvenir'
Fireplace:	'Keep the Home fires burning'
Fireplace:	'There's no place like home'

6. WILLOW

Model of Lighthouse:	'This lighthouse was damaged by bombardment by German Warships on Wed. 16th Dec 1914'
Soldier and Sailor:	'Our Brave Defender'
Nurse:	'A Friend in Need'

7. MISCELLANEOUS

Unmarked:	'Souvenir of the Imperial Bazaar, Albion Hill, Ramsgate. Twice wrecked by Zeppelins May 17th 1915 and July 17th 1917'

(This appears on a number of models and is a retailers mark)

Unmarked:	'Scarborough Coastguard station. Shelled by Germans'

INSCRIPTIONS APPEARING ON MEMORIALS

Alexandra:
RAF Memorial: *'Ad Astra: Unveiled by HRH Prince of Wales July 16th 1923'*

Arcadian:
Burford: *'In grateful memory of the men of Burford who fell in the War 1914-18'*

East Dereham: *'In honour of the men of East Dereham who fell in the Great War 1914-18'*

Folkestone: *'May their deeds be held in reverence'*

Fryatt: *'In Memory of Captain James Fryatt; Master of the Great Eastern Railway steamship 'Brussels'; illegally executed by the Germans at Bruges on Juy 27th 1916. Erected by the Company as an expression of their admiration of his gallantry'*

Great Yarmouth: *'For God and King and Right. These nobly played their part. They heard the country's call. They gave their all'.*

Kitchener Memorial Tower, Orkneys: *'This tower was raised by the people of Orkney in memory of Field Marshal Earl Kitchener of Khartoum on the corner of his country, which he served so faithfully, nearest the place where he died on duty. He and his staff perished along with the officers and nearly all the men of HMS Hampshire 5th June 1916'*

Newhaven Transport: *'This Memorial is erected to the memory of the Captains, Officers and seamen of HM Transports who lost their lives whilst sailing from this port during the Great War 1914-18 and also in commemoration of the valuable services rendered by the Mercantile Marines of the United Kingdom in the War'*

Sheringham: *'To keep in remembrance of those men from the parishes of Sheringham and Beeston Regis who gave their lives in the course of right and justice in the Great War 1914-18. Their name liveth forever. Greater love hath no man than this'* HH Palmer, Sculptor, Sheringham.

Woodhouse Eaves: *'Their name liveth forever'*

Carlton:
Tunbridge Wells: *'Our Glorious Dead 1914-1918; Honour, Gratitude, Praise'*

Devonia Art:
Cheddar: *'Praise God and remember the men of Cheddar who died for their country in the Great War 1914-1919'*

Podmore:
Blackpool: *'1914; In memory of our glorious dead: 1918'*

Regis:
Weymouth: *'To our glorious dead'*

Willow Art:
Great Yarmouth: *'They gave their all. They nobly played their part. They heard their country's call. For God and King and Right'*

Ilkestone: *'To the glory and to the memory of the men of Ilkestone who gave their lives in the Great War 1914-1918'*

Wilton:
Folkestone: *'Road to Remembrance'*

Foreign:
Clacton-on-Sea: *'1914-1918; To the glorious memory of those brave men of Clacton who sacrificed their lives in the Great War'*

CENOTAPHS:
Cenotaphs are usually found with all or part of the following:
'Erected in Whitehall, London, in memory of the fallen in the Great War 1914-18; The Glorious Dead MCMXIV-MCMXIX; The blood of heroes is the seed of freedom'

Edith Cavell: usually with a variation on the following:
'Brussels Dawn October 12 1915; Edith Cavell; Nurse; Patriot and Martyr; Sacrifice : Humanity'

iii
Regimental Crests on Heraldic China

The firm of W.H. Goss made up for its paucity of Military models by offering an extensive range of Regimental Crests on their china. In the 1917 edition of the Goss Record a total of 129 Regimental, 11 Overseas and 47 Battleship crests were listed. Other factories, notably the Arcadian, Aynsley and Carlton works, made models with regimental and other military crests but none seem to have surpassed Goss in numbers. Aynsley china, dating from 1904, carries the badge of regiments that disappeared when the British Army was reorganised following the Haldane reforms of 1908.

HERALDIC PORCELAIN: Regimental Badges

W.H. Goss
1st Life Guards
2nd Life Guards
2nd Dragoon Guards
4th Dragoon Guards (Royal Irish)
5th Dragoon Guards
6th Dragoon Guards
Coldstream Guards
Irish Guards
Scots Guards
Welsh Guards
2nd Dragoon (Royal Scots Greys)
3rd Hussars (Kings Own)
8th Hussars (Kings Royal Irish)
10th Hussars
11th Hussars (Prince Alberts Own)
14th Hussars
15th Hussars
18th Hussars
19th Hussars (Q.A.O.R.)
20th Hussars
12th Lancers
17th Lancers
Argyll & Sutherland Highlanders
Army Ordnance Corps
Army Service Corps
Bedfordshire Regiment
Berkshire Reg. (Royal)
Black Watch
Border Regiment
Cambridgeshire Regiment
Cameron Highlanders (The Queens Own)
Cameronians (Scottish Rifles)
Cheshire Regiment
Connaught Regiment

Devonshire Regiment
Devonshire (1st Yeomanry)
Dorsetshire Regiment
Dorsetshire (1st Yeomanry)
Duke of Cornwall's Light Infantry
The Durham Light Infantry
2nd Volunteer Battalion, Durham Light Infantry
Essex Regiment
Glamorgan Yeomanry
Gloucestershire Regiment
Gloucestershire Hussars
Gordon Highlanders
Hampshire Regiment
Hants RGA
Herefordshire Regiment
Hertfordshire Regiment
Highland Light Infantry
Honourable Artillery Company
Huntingdonshire Regiment
Huntingdonshire Cyclist Corps
Inniskilling Fusiliers (Royal)
Irish Rifles (Royal)
Kent Regiment (East) 'The Buffs'
Kent Regiment (Royal West)
Kent Regiment (VAD)
King Edward's Horse
King's Own Scottish Borderers
King's Own Light Infantry
King's Royal Rifles
Lanarkshire Yeomanry
Lancashire Fusiliers
Lancashire Regiment (East)
Lancashire Regiment (West) Howitzer Brigade
Lancashire Regiment (South) Prince of Wales Volunteers
Lancashire Regiment Loyal North
Lancaster Regiment (Royal)
Leicestershire Regiment
Lincolnshire Regiment
Liverpool Regiment 5th Battalion (King's)
Liverpool Regiment 6th (King's)
Liverpool Regiment 8th (Irish)
Liverpool Regiment 10th (Scottish)
Liverpool Regiment Comrades Battalion
London Electrical Engineers
London Regiment 4th Battalion (Royal Fusiliers)
London Regiment 8th Battalion (PO Rifles)
London Regiment 9th Battalion (Queen Victoria's Rifles)
London Regiment 14th Battalion (London Scottish)
London Regiment 15th Battalion Civil Service Rifles
London Regiment 16th Battalion (Queen's Westminsters)
London Regiment 18th Battalion (Irish Rifles)
London Regiment 21st (1st Surrey Regiment)
London Regiment 25th (Cyclists)
London Regiment 27th (Inns of Court O.T.C.)
London Regiment 28th (Artists Rifles)
London Rifle Brigade
Manchester Regiment
Middlesex Regiment (Duke of Cornwall's Own)
Machine Gun Corps
Motor Machine Gun Battery
Norfolk Regiment
Northamptonshire Regiment
Northumberland Fusiliers
Northumberland Regiment
Notts & Derby (Sherwood Foresters)
Oxford & Bucks Light Infantry
The Prince Consorts Own Regiment
Rifle Brigade
Royal Air Force
Royal Army Medical Corps
Royal Artillery
Royal Artillery (Salisbury Plain)
Royal Engineers
Royal Field Artillery
Royal Flying Corps
Royal Garrison Artillery
Royal Flying Corps (Wings)
Royal Fusiliers
Royal Fusiliers (10th Battalion)
Royal Horse Artillery
Royal Irish Regiment
Royal Military College (Camberley)
Royal Scots (Lothian Regiment)
Royal Staff College (Camberley)
Royal Tank Corps
School of Musketry (Hythe)
Scots Fusiliers
Scottish Borderers
Scottish Horse
Seaforth Highlanders
Shropshire Light Infantry
Somerset Light Infantry
South Wales Borderers
Staffordshire Regiment (The Prince of Wales' North)
Staffordshire Regiment (South)
Suffolk Regiment
Surrey Regiment (East)
Surrey Regiment (Royal West)
Sussex Regiment (Royal)
St. John's Ambulance
Warwickshire Regiment (Royal)
Welsh Regiment
Welsh Fusiliers (Royal)
Wiltshire Regiment
Woman's Auxiliary Army Corps
Worcestershire Regiment
Yorks & Lancaster Regiment
Yorkshire Regiment
Yorkshire Regiment (West Riding)
Yorkshire Regiment (West)
Yorkshire Regiment (East)
King's Own Yorkshire Light Infantry
Alexandra, Princess of Wales' Own Yorkshire Regiment

Overseas Dominions
Australian Commonwealth Military Forces
Canadian General Service
Canadian Engineers
Canadian Royal (The Leinster Regiment)
Royal Highlanders of Canada
New Zealand General Service
New Zealand 1st (Canterbury)
New Zealand 3rd (Auckland)
New Zealand 4th (Otago)
New Zealand 9th (Hawkes Bay)
New Zealand 11th (Taranaki)
New Zealand 15th (Nth Auckland)
New Zealand Engineers
South African Artillery
South African General Service

Naval Crests
Royal Navy
Royal Naval College (Dartmouth)
Royal Naval Air Service
Royal Naval Air Force
Royal Naval Volunteers
HMS: Achilles
Africa
Agamemnon
Antrim

Argyll
Audacious
Bellerophon
Britannia
Centurion
Collingwood
Colossus
Commonwealth
Conqueror
Cornwallis
Dominion
Dreadnought
Dublin
Fortune
Hercules
Hindustan
Indefatigable
Indominatable
Inflexible
Invincible
Iron Duke

King Edward VII
King George V
Lion
Liverpool
Lowestoft
Monarch
Neptune
Orion
Princess Royal
Queen Elizabeth
Queen Mary
Russell
St. Vincent
Superb
Surprise
Temeraire
Thunderer
Vanguard
Victorious
Warrior
Zealandia

Aynsley:
Argyll & Sutherland Highlanders
Army Service Corps
Black Watch
Connaught Rangers 88th & 94th Foot
2nd Dragoon Guards (Royal Scots Greys)
3rd Dragoon Guards
154th Dragoon Guards
Grenadier Guards
Highland Light Infantry 71st & 74th Foot
King's Dragoon Guards
King's Own Scottish Borderers
21st Lancers
Leeds Company; RAMC Volunteers
1st Middlesex Regiment (Victoria and Albert's Rifles)
4th Middlesex Regiment
13th Middlesex RV: (Queen's Westminsters)
18th Middlesex Regiment
Queen's Own Cameron Highlanders 79th Foot
The Queen's Surrey 4th Battalion
Royal Army Medical Corps
Royal Artillery
Royal Garrison Artillery - Southern Division
Royal Horse Artillery
Royal Irish Rifles 83rd & 86th Foot
Royal Irish Fusiliers
Royal Marine Artillery
Royal Scots; 1st Foot
Royal Scots Fusiliers; 21st Foot
Royal Scots Greys
Royal Welsh Fusiliers; 23rd Foot
Royal West Surrey Regiment (The Queens)
Seaforth Highlanders (72nd & 78th Foot)
South Notts Hussars
Staffs Imperial Yeomanry
Victoria & St. George's Rifles

Arcadian:
Army Service Corps
Black Watch
Cheshire Regiment
Denbighshire Regiment
Derbyshire Regiment
Devonshire Regiment
East Kent Regiment 'The Buffs'
East Surrey Regiment
Essex Regiment
Gloucestershire Regiment
Gordon Highlanders
Inns of Court OTC
Lancaster Regiment
Light Infantry
Lincolnshire Regiment
London Scottish
Machine Gun Corps
Manchester Regiment
Northumberland Fusiliers
North Staffs Regiment; 64th & 98th Foot
Oxfordshire & Buckinghamshire Light Infantry
Queens Royal West Surrey Regiment
Prince Albert's Somerset Light Infantry
Royal Artillery
Royal Aircraft Establishment
RAE Ewshott
Rifle Brigade - The Prince Consort's Own
Royal Air Force
Royal Army Medical Corps
Royal East Kent Mounted Rifles - Imperial Yeomanry
Royal West Kent (The Queen's Own)
Royal Engineers
Royal Field Artillery
Royal Flying Corps
Royal Irish; 5th Lancers
Royal Horse Artillery
Royal Marines
Royal Military College Camberley
Royal Shropshire Light Infantry
Staff College Camberley
Royal Sussex Regiment
Staffs Regimental Insignia (Staffordshire Knot)
York & Lancaster Regiment
H.M.S. Hercules
HMS Queen Mary
HMS Thunderer
H.M.S. Achilles (Transfer view of ship)

Alexandra:
Aldershot Command - Blackdown Camp
Aldershot Command - Deepcut Camp
Longmoor Camp
Cranwell

Anglo-Heraldic
Royal Military College, Camberley

Bow: (Savoy)
Army Service Corps
Gordon Highlanders
Royal Army Medical Corps
Seaforth Highlanders

British Manufacture
Army Cyclist Corps

Carlton
Coldstream Guards
Tank Corps
Whitley Camp
HMS Australia
HMS Carodox
HMS Conqueror
HMS Furious
HMS Inflexible
HMS Lion
HMS Queen Elizabeth
HMS Temeraire
HMS Tyrant
HMAS Sydney
HMS Warspite
RMS Lusitania
RMS Duchess

Duchess
Royal Engineers
12th Lancers

Clifton
RFA
Coldstream Guards
Royal Military College, Camberley
Royal Staff College, Camberley

Coronet Ware
King's Own Yorkshire Light Infantry

Etruscan
HMS Achilles

Florentine
RMC Camberley

JWR (Arcadian)
Devonshire Regiment

Kingsway Art (Willow)
HMS Ceres
HMS Hood
HMS Valiant

Patriotic China
11th Welsh
13th Manchester

Premier
Royal Military College, Camberley

Royal Doulton
RN Training School

Savoy
Royal Military College, Camberley
Royal Scots Greys
Worcestershire Regiment

Shelley
RGA

Swan
(see Arcadian)

Triood
Worcestershire Regiment

Tudor Arms
RFC

Victoria
1st Battalion Hertfordshire Regiment
5th Battalion Surrey (The Queens)
4th Battalion Northamptonshire Regiment
Royal Fusiliers, 1st City of London Brigade

Willow
Army Ordnance
Army Service Corps
Canadian General Service Corps (Maple Leaf)
King's Own Yorkshire Light Infantry
Leicestershire Regiment
2nd Life Guards
Lincolnshire Regiment
Loyal North Lancs Regiment
Northumberland Fusiliers
Royal Air Force
Royal Army Medical Corps
Royal Artillery
Royal Engineers
RE Longmore Camp
Royal Military College, Camberley
Royal Flying Corps
Royal Naval Air Service
Royal West Surrey Regiment
Somerset Light Infantry

iv
Notes on named ships

In the first years of the century the Navy underwent drastic reorganisation. Advances in ship-building technology made it possible to construct heavily armoured and heavily armed battleships. Designated 'Dreadnoughts' these ships formed the basis of all the Navies of the World.

Main armament consisted of 12in., 13.5in., 15in. or 18in. guns - the 12in. guns fired a projectile weighing 1,500 lbs and a broadside of eight guns carried a total weight of over five and a half tons over ten miles - backed up by 12 pounders, 3 pounders and others. Most were fitted with torpedo tubes.

In length they varied from 500 to 700 ft. with displacements ranging from 17,000 tons (HMS Dreadnought) to 32,000 tons (HMS Canada). Speed was approximately 22 knots for battleships and 30 knots for battlecruisers. All were coal fired although modifications were carried out at the outbreak of war to convert them to oil. Ships compliment in excess of 1,000 and cost of building in the region of £1 million (the Navy's latest Aircraft Carrier cost £147 million!).

	Dreadnought Battleships	Dreadnought Battlecruisers	Pre-Dreadnought Battleships	Armoured Cruisers	Protected Cruisers	Light Cruisers	Light Protected Cruisers	Destroyers	Torpedo Boats	Submarines
Britain	34	10	40	34	17	79	-	238	70	96
France	12	-	21	19	-	-	10	87	153	93
Germany	20	8	20	9	46	-	-	152	47	39
Austria-Hungary	4	-	12	3	9	-	-	18	85	11
Italy	10	-	8	10	-	11	-	46	75	20
Russia	7	-	9	10	12	-	-	140	25	43

BATTLESHIPS - 10 CLASSES TOTALLING 34 SHIPS

Name	*Class*	*No. of Ships in Class*	*Main Armament*	*Place Built*	*Date Completed*	*War Service*					*Remarks*	*Model by:*
						1914	*1915*	*1916*	*1917*	*1918*		
Dreadnought	Dreadnought	1	10 x 12″ 24 x 12 pdrs	Portsmouth Dockyard	October 1906	Flagship 4th BS	Sank Sub. U29	Flagship 3rd BS	Reserve	4th B.S.	Sold for £44,000 in 1920 Broken up at Inverkeithing in 1923	Carlto Grafto
Thunderer	Orion	4	10 x 13.5″ 16 x 4″ 4 x 3 pdrs	Thames Ironworks Blackwall	June 1912	2nd BS	-	Jutland	-	-	Cadet training ship 1920-26	Carlto
Iron Duke	Iron Duke	4	10 x 13.5″ 12 x 6″ 3 x 3″ 4 x 3 pdrs	Portsmouth Dockyard	March 1914	Flagship C-in-C	-	Jutland	Mediterranean	-	Gunnery training ship 1933. Depot ship Scapa Flow 1939-45. Broken up at Faslane 1946.	Grafto Carlto Savoy
Marlborough	Iron Duke	4	As above	Devonport Dockyard	June 1914	1st BS	-	Jutland 1.	Mediterranean	-	Broken up at Rosyth 1932.	Carlto
Queen Elizabeth	Queen Elizabeth	5	8 x 15″ 16 x 6″ (later 14) 4 x 3 pdrs (2 x 3 AA later)	Portsmouth Dockyard	January 1915	-	Flagship East Med. Squadron 2.	Flagship C-in-C 3.	-	Surrender of German Fleet signed on board 21.11.18	Reconstructed and served through WW2.	Arcadia Carlto Savoy
Warspite	Queen Elizabeth	5	As above	Devonport Dockyard	March 1915	-	5th BS	Jutland 4.	-	-	Served through WW2 and acquired longest battle record of any battleship; sold in 1947 and went aground in Prussia Cove, Cornwall on way to breaker's yard	Carlton
Barham	Queen Elizabeth	5	As above	John Brown Clyde	October 1915	-	-	Jutland 5.	-	-	Atlantic and Med. Fleets 1920-39. Served at Battle of Matapan and in the evacuation of Crete (WW2). Torpedoed and blew up 25.11.41	Savoy
Canada	Class of own	2	10 x 14″ 18 x 6″ (later 16) 3 x 3″ AA 4 x 3″ pdrs	Elswick 6.	Sept. 1915		4th BS	Jutland	-	-	Returned to Chilean Navy & renamed Almirante Latorre. Served until 1958. Broken up in Tokyo Bay 1959	Carlton

1. Torpedoed amidships but kept station; 3 months under repair.
2. Support ship for Allied troops in Dardanelles campaign; recalled in May.
3. Under refit during Jutland.
4. Hit by heavy shell.
5. Hit six times. 26 killed and 37 wounded.
6. Originally built for Chilean Navy but bought by RN at outbreak of war.

Abbreviations:
BS: Battleship Squadron
BCS: Battlecruiser Squadron
RAN: Royal Australian Navy
RN: Royal Navy

BATTLECRUISERS - 4 CLASSES TOTALLING 10 SHIPS

Name	*Class*	*No. of Ships in class*	*Main Armament*	*Place Built*	*Date Completed*	*War Service* 1914	1915	1916	1917	1918	*Remarks*	*Models by:*
Inflexible	Invincible	3	8 x 12″ 16 x 4″ (later 12) 3 x 4″ AA 1 x 3″	Clyde	October 1908	Flagship 2nd BCS Falkland Islands	Flagship Dardanelles Squadron 1.	Jutland 2.	-	-	Sold in 1922	Carlton
Lion	Lion	3	8 x 13.5″ 16 x 4″ 1 x 4″ AA 4 x 3pdr	Devonport Dockyard	May 1912	Flagship 1st BCS Battle of Heligoland Bight	Flagship Dogger Bank	Jutland 3.	-	-	Sold in 1926	Willow Carlton Savoy
Princess Royal	Lion	3	As Above	Barrow-in-Furness	Nov. 1912	1st BCS Heligoland Bight	Dogger Bank 4.	Jutland Flagship C-in-C 5.	-	-	Sold and scrapped (1926)	Carlton
Tiger	Lion	3	As above but: 12 x 6″ 2 x 3″ AA	Clyde	October 1914	1st BCS	Dogger Bank 6.	Jutland 7.	-	-	Sold and scrapped (1932)	Carlton
Australia	Indefatigable	3	8 x 12″ 16 x 4″ 1 x 4″ AA 4 x 3pdr		June 1913	Flagship RAN Taken over by RN Flagship West Indies Station	Flagship 2nd BCS	Collided with New Zealand. Under repair during Jutland	-	-	Returned to RAN in 1919. Towed out and sunk in Tokyo Bay (1924)	Carlton

NOTES:
1. Hit in the bridge and mined on 18th March: under repair for 3 months then joined 3rd BCS.
2. Sister ship Invincible blew up. Over 1,000 killed, only 5 survived.
3. Extensively damaged: 100 killed, 50 injured.
4. Succeeded Lion as Flagship 1st BCS.
5. Damaged.
6. Hit: 2 killed.
7. Hit 21 times: 24 killed, 37 injured.

TRAWLERS

Name	*Owner*	*Identification Number*	*Displacement*	*Armament*	*1914*	*1915*	*1916*	*1917*	*1918*	*Remarks*	*Models by:*
HMMS Gowan Lea	J.C. Richards Fraserborough	Admiralty No. 2102. Fishing Letter No. FR105	87 tons	1 x 3 pdr	Built	Portsmouth Patrol Area and Gibraltar	Taranto	Taranto 1.	Portsmouth and South South Coast Patrol Area	Demolished at Fraserborough 29.1.19	Carlton
HMMS Peggy	Jas Hay 23 Maiden St. Peterhead	Adm. No. 1315 Fishing No. PD 149	100 tons	1 x 3 pdr	-	-	Patrolled Peterhead Area 2.	Commissioned Officers	as Quarters	Built 1906 Demolished 8.1.19	Carlton 3.

NOTES:
1. Skipper Joseph Watt RNR awarded VC for action in Straits of Otrento against Austrian cruiser 15 May 1917. Model registered 3 September 1917; award gazetted 29.8.17.
2. Skipper James F. Buchan RNR.
3. Arcadian used same mould but did not name model.

MONITOR SHIP - Flat bottomed for inshore and river work

Name	*Built*	*Size & Displacement*	*Armament*	*War Service* 1914	1915	1916	1917	1918	*Remarks*	*Models by:*
HMS Humber	1914 for Brazil but taken over by RN at outbreak of war 1.	266′ x 49′ Beam 1,260 tons 12 knots	3 x 6″ 2 x 4.7″ Howitzer	English Channel 2.	Arrived Malta 26.3. Covered Gallipoli 3. operations & evacuation	Based in Alexandria Port Said	Eastern Med. & Suez Canal	Eastern Med. & Suez Canal	Sold in 1920 to F. Rijsdijks as a crane ship	Carlton

NOTES:
1. Two other Monitors also taken over: renamed Severn and Mersey.
2. Bombarded German front lines between Ostend and Middleberk 18th-31st October. Commander A.L. Snagge.
3. Inspected by Rt. Hon. Winston Churchill, 1st Lord of the Admiralty: 10th January 1915.

SUBMARINES - ALL OF THE 'E' CLASS 1.

Number	Built	Date Completed	War Service 1914	1915	1916	1917	1918	Remarks	Models by:
E1	Chatham Dockyard	May 1913	Battle of Heligoland Bight Sent to Baltic Oct.	Baltic based at Revel. Torpedoed Moltke 19.3.15. Torpedoed transport 30.7.15	Baltic	Baltic	Scuttled off Heligoland	Under command of Noel Laurence. With E9 and others it caused much havoc in Baltic during war years.	Bow 2. Porcelle Savoy
E4	Vickers of Barrow	April 1913	Heligoland Bight rescued British & German seamen off Heligoland Bight	May 3: attacked by Zep. LZ9 while attacking Norddeich wireless station.	Rammed & sunk while on exercise. Raised and refitted 28.7.16. Sunk Senator Van Berenberg Gossley.	-		Commander E.W. Leir DSO. Sold to Upnor Shipbreaking Co. in Feb. 1922.	Alexandra; 3. Arcadian Botolph Corona Crown Grosvenor Milton; Swan Rayleigh; Willow Sussex; Victoria.
E5	Vickers of Barrow	June 1913	Attacked by cruiser Strassburg	May 3: Attacked by LZ9, returned fire, crash dived. Sept. 25: sunk German auxiliary ship	June: Failed to return from patrol off Heligoland Bight. Believed sunk by mine.	-	-	Commander C.S. Benning DSO.	Arcadian 4. Botolph Corona Coronet
E9	Vickers of Barrow	June 1914	13.9.14 'Hela' sunk 6.10.14 S116 sunk	Baltic: sunk German destroyers 23.1.15 & 4.6.15	Baltic (with E1)	Baltic (with E1)	Scuttled at Helsingfors	Lieut. Commander Max K. Horton DSO.	Carlton 5. Cyclone Grafton Shelley Victoria

NOTES:

1. 'E' class was the largest of the six submarine classes at outbreak war. 700 tons: 4 x 18" torpedo tubes plus deck gun.
   All the above were based at Harwich with the 8th Sub Flotilla at beginning of war.
2. Model registered by Birks, Rawlins & Co. (Savoy) 18.9.15.
3. Model registered by H.T. Robinson (Arcadian 20.10.15
4. Model registered by H.T. Robinson (Arcadian) 6.12.16
5. Four different models made.

"Bounty Awards"

For sinking enemy warships crews of attacking ships received £5 per enemy head on ship at the time of attack. The awards made to these ships were as follows:

E9: 'Hela'	£1,050
S116	£ 350
Destroyers	£ 930
	£2,330

E5: German Auxiliary £1,000

E4: Senator Van Berenberg Gossley £135

E1 did not receive any bounty award because the ships torpedoed did not actually sink.

V
Notes on named War Memorials

Memorial	*Designer*	*Date Unveiled*	*Unveiled by:*	*Notes*	*Models Made by:*
Bishops Stortford (Herts)	-	1921	-	Commemorates the 200 local men who died in the war: proportionally more than any other town.	Arcadian
Black Watch				Scottish soldier standing on a stone base.	Regis; Podmore
Blackpool (Lancs)					Podmore Carlton
Brighton (Sussex)	J.W. Simpson President RSBA	7.10.22	Earl Beatty	Described as a... "quasi-collonade of square pillars carrying entablature of architrave and freize without cornice. The collonade is developed at the SE and SW ends as two flanking pergolas... and at the centre is a small domed shrine facing northwards."	Carlton
Brora (Sutherland)	J.A. Hosie Architect Brora	25.12.1922		Built by Mr. G. Murray of Brora with stone from nearby Glynelish Quarry	Arcadian
Burford (Oxon)					Arcadian
Burnham-on-Crouch (Essex)					Arcadian
Cavell, Edith (London)	Sir George Frampton RA	17.3.20	HRH Queen Alexandra	Stands 40′ high, comprises a full sized marble figure of Nurse Cavell backing onto a tall block of granite which ends in a cross surmounted by a half figure of woman and child. Ins: *Edith Cavell: Brussels Dawn Oct. 12 1915. Patriotism is not enough; I must have no hatred or bitterness for anyone: Humanity, Sacrifice, Fortitude and Devotion.*	Various factories (see Appendix ix
Cavell, Edith (Norwich)	Poss. by Frampton But is similar to Framptons marble bust in IWM.			Cenotaph with full length figure of soldier in relief holding up wreath to head and shoulders bust of Nurse Cavell atop.	Arcadian Podmore Willow
Cenotaph (London)	Sir Edwin Lutyens	19.7.19		Temporary structure built in 1919 for Peace celebrations. Permanent structure unveiled 11th Nov. 1920.	Various factories (see Appendix ix
Chatham Naval (Kent)	Sir Robert Lorimer	1924	-	Same design used for three Naval memorials at Chatham, Portsmouth and Plymouth.	Willow Art

Memorial	*Designer*	*Date Unveiled*	*Unveiled by:*	*Notes*	*Models made by:*
Cheddar (Avon)					Devonia Art
Cheltenham	R.L. Boulton & Sons. Ecclesiastical sculptors.	Oct. 1st 1921	Major-Gen. Sir Robert Robertson		Arcadian
Chesham (Bucks)		1921			Arcadian
Clacton-on-Sea (Essex)	Charles Hartnell ARA	-	-	Comprises a bronze angel standing on a stone plinth.	Saxony Foreign Carlton
Cranbrook (Sussex)	Local Committee	1922	-	Memorial in the form of a Cenotaph.	Carlton Leadbeater Art
Crich Stand (Notts & Derby)				Memorial to the Sherwood Foresters which stands atop the Crich Stand Hill.	Leadbeater Art
Cumberland & Westmoreland (Carlisle)	Sir Robert Lorimer	26.5.22	Lord Lieut. of Lancs Earl Lansdale	Built by Messrs Laing & Sons of Carlisle: in the form of a Cenotaph and made from local granite from Shap Fell. Commemorates 10,000 men and women of the two counties who died. The memorial was in 3 parts: the Cenotaph: purchase of Rickerby Park and Greeny Bank, and erection of a 330′ steel bridge over River Eden.	Leadbeater Art Coronet
Dartford	Mr. Arthur G. Walker ARA	May 7th 1922	Air Vice-Marshal, Sir H. Geoffrey Salmond KCMG CB DSC	Comprises a bronze figure of infantryman in full kit, standing atop a granite pedestal bearing the names of 345 local men who died. The figure was sketched by the designer from a Tommy whom he found walking the streets of Chelsea and is intended to represent the 'men who won the war'.	Coronet
Derby (Derby.)	A.G. Walker RA	11.11.24	The Mayor: Alderman Oswald Ling	Stands 14′ high and constructed from Blue Bristol Pennant stone with a figure of mother and child in front.	Leadbeater Art
Douglas (Isle of Man)	Mr. Ewart Crellin ARIBA	29.5.24	Rt. Hon. Lord Derby	Comprises a figure of an infantryman in full kit surmounting a rectangular granite pillar, 40′ high. The figure was designed and sculpted by Mr. Hemms of Exeter. Commemorates the 641 local men who died.	Carlton
Dover (Kent)	Mr. Reginald Golden	5.11.24		Comprises a bronze figure of youth holding a fiery cross and with feet surrounded by thorns. Stands on a stone base bearing panels with the names of those who died.	Arcadian
Dover Patrol (Kent & France)	Sir Ashton Webb President RA	27.7.21	Prince of Wales (later HRH Duke of Windsor)	Foundation stone laid on Nov. 19th 1919 by Prince Arthur of Connaught. Stands at Heathercote Point. Erected with others at Cap Blanc Nez (France) and New York to commemorate men of the Dover Patrol Force	Arcadian
Dunbar (East Durham)					Carlton
East Dereham (Norfolk)	-	22.10.22	HRH Prince Henry (later Duke of Gloucester)	Constructed in granite and resembling a Cenotaph.	Arcadian
Folkestone (Kent)	F.W. Blundestone RBS of Kensington	2.12.22		Cast by E. Parlenti: comprises an angel holding a cross surmounting a stone plinth.	Arcadian
Fryatt (Dovercourt Churchyard)	-	After 1919	-	After the war Captain Fryatt's body was brought back to England and after a ceremony at St. Pauls the body was taken to Dovercourt where it was buried. The memorial was erected by the Great Eastern Railway Co. (see Appendix ii for inscription).	Arcadian Wilton
Gravesend (Kent)	F.W. Doyle-Jones	11.1.22	General Lord Horne GCB,	Stands 30′ high and comprises a bronze figure representing Victory bringing peace standing on a granite pedestal. The original was shattered by a bomb in 1940 and restored in 1947.	Florentine

Memorial	*Designer*	*Date Unveiled*	*Unveiled by:*	*Notes*	*Models made by:*
Great Yarmouth (Norfolk)	Col. Hayward of Olley & Hayward: Architects: Gt. Yarmouth	7.1.22			Arcadian Willow Saxony Florentine
Harrogate (Yorks)	Col. Prestwick & Sons: Leigh: Lancs.	21.9.23	Earl of Hare wood, Lord Lieut. West Riding & Princess Mary & Viscount Lascelles	Foundation stone laid on 2nd June 1922 by Hon. Edward Wood MP. The site for the memorial was purchased by the Council on May 28th 1922 for £5,000.	Leadbeater Art
Ilkestone (Derby)	H. Tatham-Sudbury, Architect of Ilkestone	8.1.22	Maj. Gen. J.E.B. Sealey, MP for Ilkestone	Erected by Pask & Thorpe, Stone Masons of Nottingham. Stands 23' high and is made of Derbyshire stone from Stancliffe Quarries near Matlock.	Willow Art
Invergordon (Ross & Cromarty)					Arcadian
Killin (Perthshire)	-	27.10.20	Marquis of Breadalbane	Comprises the figure of a highland soldier standing on a stone base. Dedicated to the 20 local men who died.	Arcadian
Loughborough (Leics)	W. Tapper FRIBA Architect for York Minster & Eton Col.	22.7.23	Field-Marshal Sir William Robertson	The tower houses a carillon of 47 bells. It is made of Portland stone and was built by Wm. Moss & Sons for £10,000. The bells were cast by Messrs. John Taylor & Sons for £7,000.	Arcadian Willow
March (Cambs)		19.6.21			R & M China
Margate (Kent)		5.11.22			Arcadian
Matlock Bath (Derby)	Built by James Beresford & Sons of Matlock	Late 1920	-	Comprises two marble figures of a soldier and sailor holding a flag and standing on a base of Cornish granite. Dedicated to the 22 local men who died.	Podmore Willow Art Norfolk Victoria Shelley Saxony Foreign
Llandudno (Gwynedd)	Mr. Colwyn Foulkes	Nov. 11th 1922	-	Stands in Prince Edward Square and is built of Cornish granite with a reinforced concrete core. On top of the 50ft. shaft is a bronze grenade.	
Newhaven Transport (Sussex)	Mr. Charles Hooper Surveyor to Newhaven UDC.	13.8.20	-	Comprises a stone base with inscription; surmounted with a ship's lantern. Dedicated to the men who lost their lives on transports that sailed from the port.	Arcadian
Newnham (London)					Grosvenor
Northallerton (Yorks)					Carlton
Nottingham (Notts)	Mr. T. Wallis-Gordon, City Engineer & Surveyor	11.11.27	-	Consists of a gateway flanked on either side by collonades with terraces overlooking the River Trent. Made in Portland Stone. Dedicated to the men of Nottingham who died.	Leadbeater Art
Orkney Earl Kitchener Memorial	James Baikie Architect of Kirkwall	July 2nd 1926	Gen. Lord Horne of Stirkoke	Built of grey Orkney stone and stands on Marwick Head, the nearest point of land to where the Hampshire went down. At the ceremony HMS Royal Sovereign gave a 19 gun salute from the spot where the ship went down. The tower is 48ft. 6ins. high, has one door and no windows or staircase. A marble plaque carries an inscription (see Appendix ii)	Arcadian

Memorial	*Designer*	*Date Unveiled*	*Unveiled by:*	*Notes*	*Models made by:*
Plymouth Naval (Devon)	Sir Robert Lorimer	29.9.24	Sub-Lieut. HRH Prince George KC: GCVO: R.	See Chatham Naval	Arcadian Willow Art Devonia Art Leadbeater Art
Portsmouth Naval (Hants)	Sir Robert Lorimer	1920-24		See Chatham Naval	Willow Art Arcadian (Southsea)
RAF Memorial (London)	Sir Reginald Blomfield ARA	16.7.23	Prince of Wales later HRH Duke of Windsor	Bronze globe and eagle cast by E. Parlanti. Stone base sculpted by Mr. Reid Dick ARA of Messrs Dove Ltd. who erected the monument. Dedicated *'In memory of all ranks of the RNAS, RFC and RAF and those Air Forces from every part of the British Empire who gave their lives in winning victory for their King and Country 1914-1918; I bare you on eagle's wings and brought you unto myself'*	Alexandra
Ripon (Yorks)		1921		Comprises a simple obelisk with carved shield with the city's horn on it at the top.	Victoria
Romsey (Hants)		22.6.21	The Lord Lt. of Hampshire; Cllr. F. Freemantle		Corona
Rushdean (Northants)					Corona
Sheringham (Norfolk)					Arcadian
St. Annes (Lancs)	Sculpted by Walter Marsden MC	12.10.24	The Mayor: Alderman C.F. Critchley JP & the children of the men who fell	Comprises a column surmounted by a figure with arms outstretched. At the base is the figure of a mother and child and of a soldier. Bas-relief plaques around the base depict scenes of the feeling of the war. Dedicated to the 170 local men who died.	Wilton
St. Ives (Cambs)	-	2.11.22	Lady Hain (Wife of Sir Edward Hain)		R & M China
Thetford (Norfolk)	-	Dec. 1921	Maj.-General Sir C. Townsend	Comprises an octagonal shaft mounted on a base of pink granite Dedicated to the 115 local men who died.	Willow
Tunbridge Wells (Kent)	Sculpted by S. Nicholson RBS	11.2.23	Viscount Harding of Penshurst	Comprises a figure of an infantryman holding a rifle atop a stone base. The guard of honour for the unveiling ceremony was provided by the 4th Battalion Royal West Kent Regiment.	Carlton
Ulster (Thiepval, France)		11.11.21	Duchess of Abercorn	Erected to commemorate the 5,500 men of the 31st Ulster Division who were casualties on the first day of the Somme July 1st 1916. It is an exact copy of the memorial that stands in the Marquis of Dufferin's estate in Co. Down where the Division had its training ground.	Leadbeater Art
Ulverston					
Walsall (Staffs)	-	1.10.12	Earl of Dartmouth Lord Lieutenant of Staffordshire	Cenotaph in design, stands 26' high and made of Portland Stone The building cost £200.	Wilton
Weymouth (Dorset)	Mr. D. Jones	6.11.21	Ex. Rifleman Albert E. Whitby	Stands 17½ft. high and commemorates the 250 local men who died.	Regis
Woodhouse Eaves (Leics)	Sir Robert Martin (Chairman of the Quarry)	1920	-	Built from Mountsorrel Granite from Mountsorrel Quarry. The cross is made of granite and the name plaques are set into natural rocks. Commemorates the 32 men who died in the war and is inscribed: 'Their name liveth for evermore'	Arcadian
Worthing (Sussex)	Mr. F. Roberts Borough Surveyor	11.4.21	Field-Marshal Sir Wm. Robertson	Sculpted by Francis Tate of Worthing and comprises a bronze life-sized statue of a triumphant infantryman atop a stone base.	Foreign Willow

vi
HMLS Creme-de-Menthe at the Sugar Factory; Notes on Tanks and Armoured Cars

By the beginning of September 1916 the first of the new and top secret 'Tanks' had arrived in France. Amid great secrecy they were transported to the Front where they were confidently expected to break the deadlock that had been encountered. On the evening of the 14th the fifty tanks of 'C' and 'D' Companies of the newly formed Heavy Section Machine Gun Corps moved up to their starting points over a six mile front from Pozieres on the left to Leuze Wood, outside the village of Combles, on the right.

The four sections of 'D' Company (twenty-six tanks) were to support infantry divisions on the left flank in their attacks on the villages of Martinpuich, Flers and Gueudecourt while three sections of 'C' Company were to cover attacks by divisions of the XIV Corps on the Quadrilateral and Bouleaux Wood on the right. The remaining section had been allocated to the 2nd Canadian Division of the Reserve Army for their attack of a fortified sugar factory outside Courcelette.

The six tanks of No. 1 Section 'C' Company, namely Creme-de-Menthe, Cognac, Chartreuse, Chablis, Champagne and Cordon Rouge, took their places in the line outside the town of Pozieres. On the right, 800 yards from the town along the Bapaume Road waited Creme-de-Menthe (the command tank), Cognac and Cordon Rouge. A mile to their left were the remainder of the Section: Chablis, Champagne and Chartreuse. Their objective lay less than a mile away along the Le Sars Road. The three tanks on the right were to move along the road one on the road itself, the others either side of it, up to the sugar factory which one would attack while the others turned down Factory Trench. The tanks of the left were to move along Sugar Trench and enter the factory from the north.

At 6.20am, after a heavy bombardment, the tanks and infantry advanced. Battalions of the 4th and 6th Brigade, 2nd Canadian Division led the attack and, despite fierce fighting and heavy losses, made good headway. Soon after 7.00am the 20th (Central Ontario) and 21st (East Ontario) Battalions had secured the sugar factory taking 125 prisoners. As they consolidated the position Creme-de-Menthe and Cordon Rouge lumbered up (Cognac had been hit by a shell and failed to cross the Canadian lines although its commander, Lieut. Campbell, transferred to Creme-de-Menthe), having been overtaken by the Canadians in the initial rush. Nevertheless the Tanks did not miss all the action, a contemporary account reads: 'Creme-de-Menthe sparkled with blue fire as the German gunners whipped her vainly with bullets. Rising in weird toad-like fashion, she prowled around the sandbagged and concrete redoubt, with her guns sweeping every grey figure in sight. In addition Cordon Rouge succeeded in laying 400 yards ot telephone cable. Seeing that the Canadians were in position they returned to their lines.

The tanks on the left had met with less success. Only two of the three left the starting point and these followed the wrong trench line (MacDonnell Trench instead of Sugar Trench) in which they eventually ditched. Nevertheless they had a demoralising effect on the enemy; one comment from a prisoner being that the use of tanks was 'not war but bloody butchery'.

Similar stories to this came from most points of the attack. Of the thirty-two tanks that reached their starting points less than half proved to be of any use to the infantry, the remainder breaking down, ditching or getting lost in the advance. Hastily trained and with inadequate practice the crews became hopelessly lost in both where they were and what they should do. With the possibilities that the Tank offered not fully appreciated the overall effect had been, materially minimal, nevertheless they proved a great morale booster for the battle weary troops. One tank of 'D' Company (Dinnaken) was successful in reaching Flers and was immediately reported in the press as 'Tank walking up the High Street of Flers with the British Army behind'!

Further small attacks were made by the tanks and infantry in the days and weeks that followed during which there was much dash and gallantry shown by the Tanks crews. In these first attacks no fewer than seventeen MCs and thirteen Military Medals were won by the tank commanders and their crews. Captain Arthur Macculloch Inglis, commanding officer No. 1 Section 'C' Company and Creme-de-Menthe's commander received the DSO, his citation reading: ...'He brought his tanks forward over very difficult ground. Although one of the wheels of his own tank was blown off early by a shell he succeeded in reaching his objective and manoeuvering throughout the whole operation.' Second Lieutenant Geordie Osmond Lorne Campbell who had transferred to Creme-de-Menthe when his tank (Cognac) was hit, was awarded an MC and for his skill and courage in driving the tank during the action Pte (A/C) G.B. Shepherd received the DCM.

Battle of Flers Courcelette - Tank deployment (see Map 2)

NOTE: The Heavy Section Machine-gun Corps (formed in May 1916) comprised six companies (A, B, C, D, E & F) each of twenty-five tanks. The companies were divided into four sections commanded by a Captain. Tank commanders held the rank of Lieutenant or 2/Lieutenant. The establishment of a company was twenty-eight officers and 255 other ranks. For the attack on the 15th only 'C' and 'D' companies were used.

'C' Company: Officer commanding: Major Holford Walker.

No. 1 Section: (Capt. A.M.A. Inglis) plus a spare tank to the 2 *CANADIAN DIV.* to help in the attack on the fortified Sugar Factory outside Courcelette. Two tanks reached objective; two ditched; one hit; one failed to start. (See HMLS Creme-de-Menthe at the Sugar Factory).

No. 2 Section: (Capt. H. Hiscocks) plus three tanks from No. 3 Section plus one 'special duties' tank to the *GUARDS DIV.*
Two tanks failed to start (1 mechanical, 1 ditched). Of the starters two got lost but returned; one ditched; one started late but had some success; special duties tank succeeded in protecting the left flank of the Guards from a machine-gun nest. Three others started but broke down at first objective.

No. 3 Section: (Capt. R. Trevethick) less three tanks to the *56th DIVISION*
One tank helped in the taking of 'Combles Trench'; one broke down; one ditched.

No. 4 Section: (Temp. Major A. Holford Walker) less three tanks to the *6th DIVISION.*
Two failed to arrive at starting point; one lost but later found German trenches and returned.

Company Reserve: Three tanks from No. 4 Section.

MAP 1

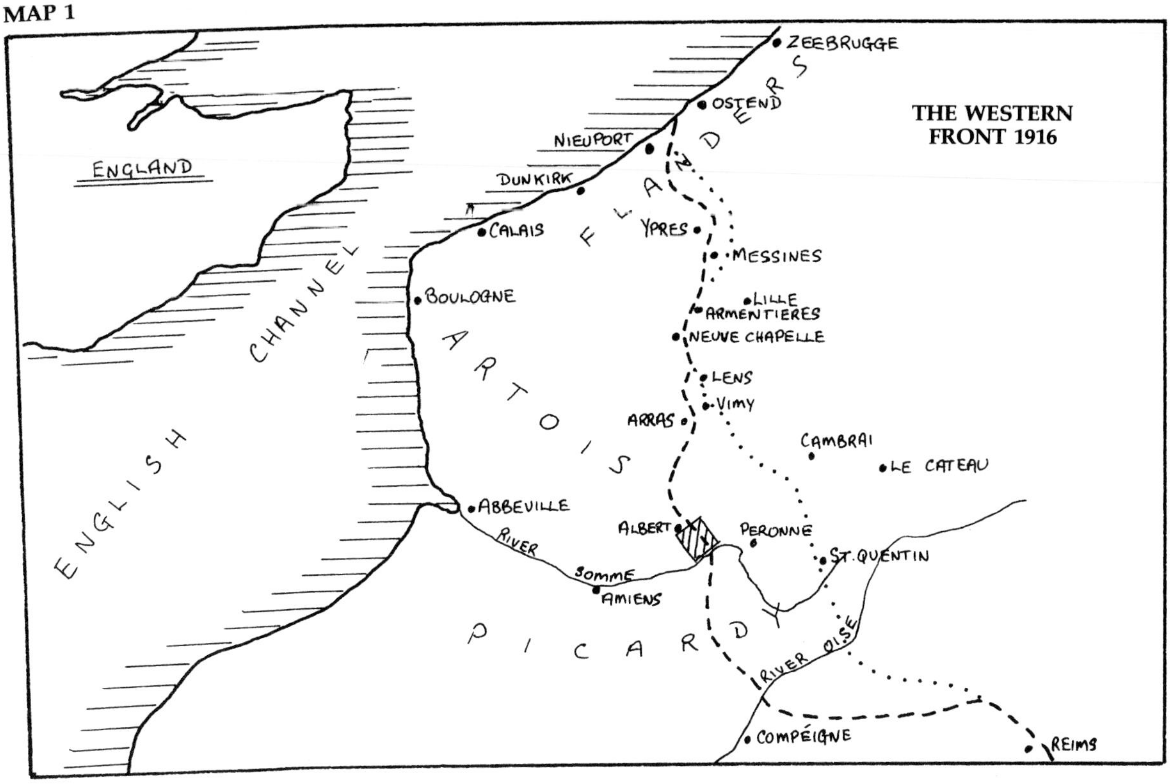

'D' Company: Officer commanding: Major Summers DSC.

No. 1 Section: (Capt. H.W. Mortimer) less two tanks to the *14th DIVISION.*
One failed to start; one started late and was disabled; one reached Gueudecourt after a late start; one started early (5.15am) in a preparatory attack.

No. 2 Section: (Capt. Nixon) less two tanks to the *NEW ZEALAND DIVISION.*
All started late; one disabled; one hit but managed to return; two were of use to the infantry.

No. 3 Section: (Capt. Sellick) plus four tanks to the *41st DIVISION.*
Three failed to start; four were hit or ditched; three reached Flers, one of which went on to Gueudecourt.

No. 4 Section: (Capt. Mann) less two tanks to the *47th DIVISION.*
All ditched or hit.

? Section: Two tanks to the *50th DIVISION* to help in the attack on Martinpuich.
One disabled; one reached final objective.

? Section: Two tanks to the *15th DIVISION* to help in the attack on Martinpuich.
One started late but was of help to the infantry; one failed to start.

SUMMARY OF BOTH COMPANIES

Failed to start	= 10
Hit or ditched	= 17
Broke down	= 4
Helped infantry	= 15
Got lost	= 2
Total deployed	= 48

KEY

------------	Allied Line before the Somme offensive (July)
....	Allied Line after the Somme offensive (November)
(hatched box)	Area covered by Maps 2 and 3: The Battle of Flers-Courcelette 15.9.16

Tank identification
The tanks in this first attack - Mark I - carried three forms of identification:

1. Factory production numbers. Either 700 series (Males) or 500 series (Females).
2. Company number. A number prefixed by the company letter e.g. C5; D22.
3. Tank name. Usually starting with the company letter e.g. Creme-de-Menthe, Donner Blitzen, Die-Hard.

Unfortunately, the early records of the HSMGC are incomplete and complete names and numbers are only known for the following:

Tank No. 540 (Female)	Co. No. D5; Name: Dolphin
Tank No. 546 (Female)	Co. No. D9; Name: Dolly
Tank No. 548 (Female)	Co. No. D13; Name: Delilah
Tank No. 759 (Male)	Co. No. D17; Name: Dinnaken
Tank No. 705 (Male)	Co. No. C19; Name: Clan Leslie

The six tanks of No. 1 Section 'C' Company were named: Creme-de-Menthe (command tank); Cordon Rouge; Chablis; Cognac; Champagne and Chartreuse.

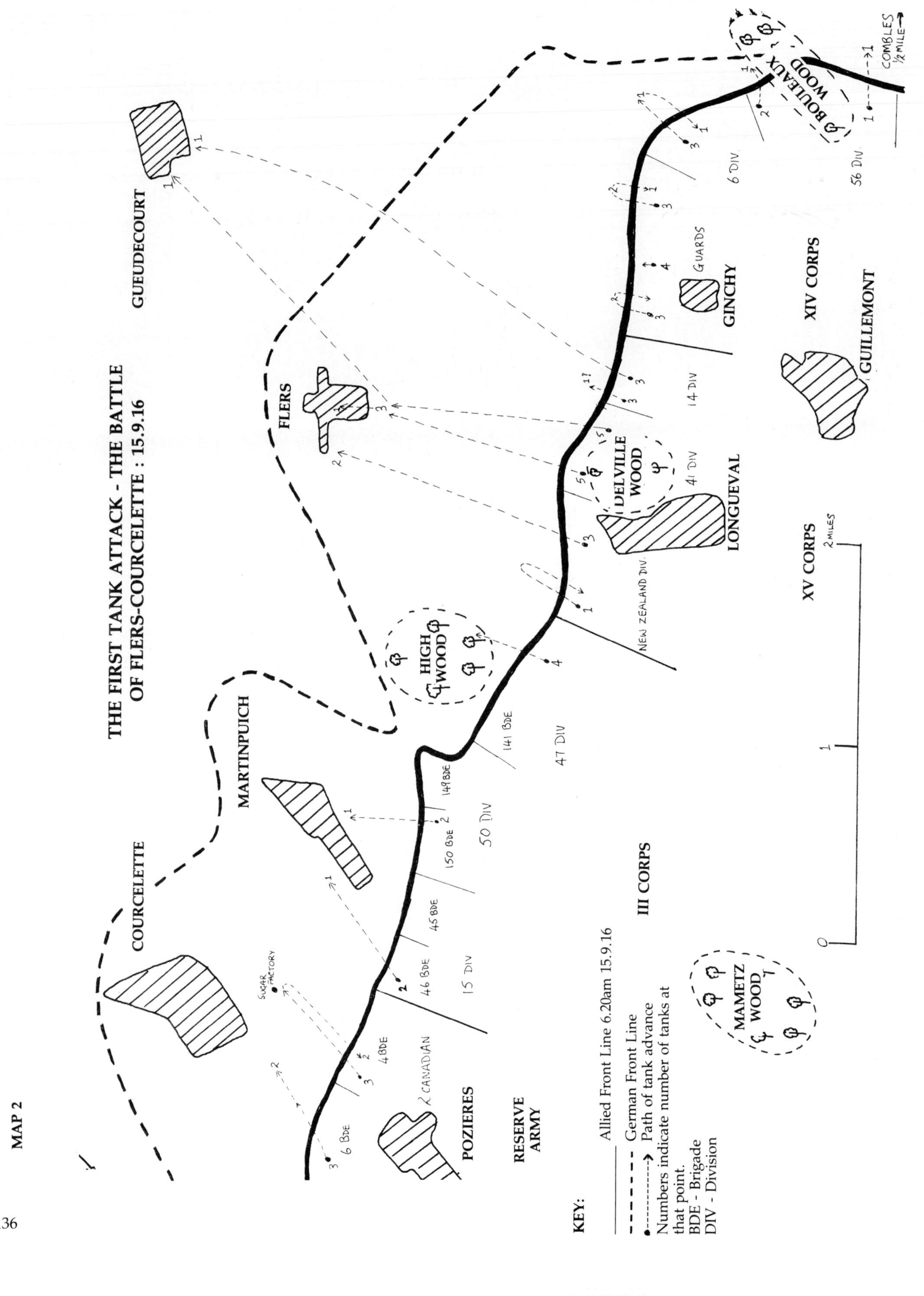
MAP 2
THE FIRST TANK ATTACK - THE BATTLE OF FLERS-COURCELETTE : 15.9.16
GUEUDECOURT
FLERS
MARTINPUICH
COURCELETTE
POZIERES
SUGAR FACTORY
HIGH WOOD
DELVILLE WOOD
LONGUEVAL
GINCHY
GUILLEMONT
BOULEAUX WOOD
COMBLES ½ MILE
MAMETZ WOOD
RESERVE ARMY
III CORPS
XV CORPS
XIV CORPS
6 BDE
2 CANADIAN
4 BDE
46 BDE
45 BDE
150 BDE
149 BDE
141 BDE
15 DIV
50 DIV
47 DIV
NEW ZEALAND DIV.
41 DIV
14 DIV
GUARDS
6 DIV
56 DIV
0
1
2 MILES
KEY:
Allied Front Line 6.20am 15.9.16
German Front Line
Path of tank advance
Numbers indicate number of tanks at that point.
BDE - Brigade
DIV - Division

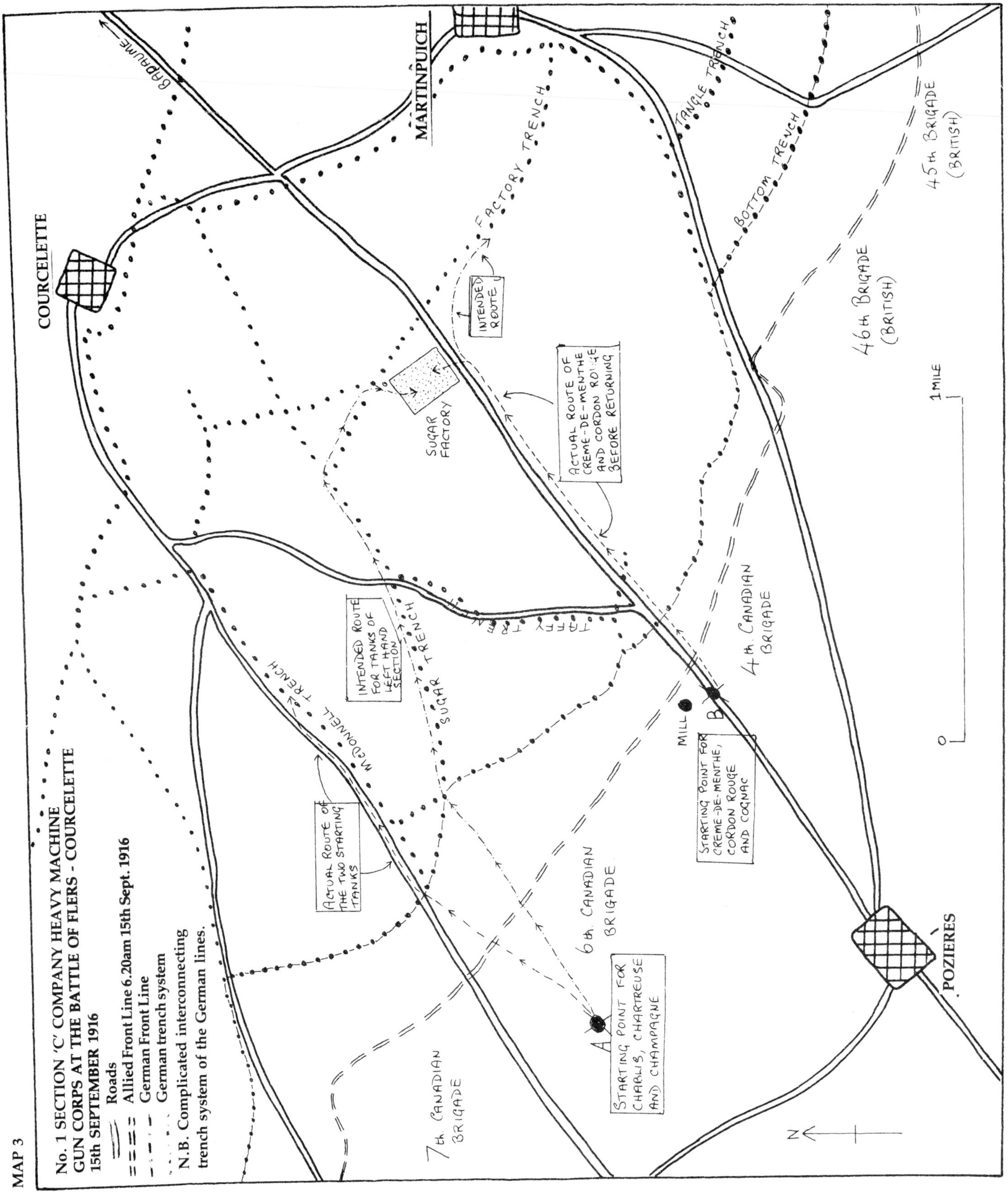
MAP 3
No. 1 SECTION 'C' COMPANY HEAVY MACHINE GUN CORPS AT THE BATTLE OF FLERS - COURCELETTE 15th SEPTEMBER 1916
Roads
Allied Front Line 6.20am 15th Sept. 1916
German Front Line
German trench system
N.B. Complicated interconnecting trench system of the German lines.
COURCELETTE
MARTINPUICH
POZIERES
BAPAUME
TANGLE TRENCH
FACTORY TRENCH
BOTTOM TRENCH
45th BRIGADE (BRITISH)
46th BRIGADE (BRITISH)
INTENDED ROUTE
ACTUAL ROUTE OF CREME-DE-MENTHE AND CORDON ROUGE BEFORE RETURNING
SUGAR FACTORY
1 MILE
0
INTENDED ROUTE FOR TANKS OF LEFT HAND SECTION
SUGAR TRENCH
McDONNELL TRENCH
MILL
B
4th CANADIAN BRIGADE
STARTING POINT FOR CREME-DE-MENTHE, CORDON ROUGE AND COGNAC
ACTUAL ROUTE OF THE TWO STARTING TANKS
6th CANADIAN BRIGADE
A
STARTING POINT FOR CHARLIS, CHARTREUSE AND CHAMPAGNE
7th CANADIAN BRIGADE
N

ARMOURED CARS

Name	*Chassis*	*Power*	*Armament*	*Crew*	*Speed*	*First Appearance*	*Remarks*	*Models by:*
Talbot (modified 1st Admiralty pattern) (Britain)	Clement-Talbot of North Kensington London	4 Cylinder 25/50hp	2 Maxim MGs	3		Nov. 1914	Shoulder high armour and open top allowing fire over sides and front and back. Few seem to have been made (at least 6). Succeeded by turreted pattern in Spring 1915.	Savoy Porcelle 1.
Automitrailleuse Sava (Belgium)	From: Societe Anversoise pour Fabrication de Voitures Automobiles of Antwerp		1 Hotchkis MG	3		Oct. 1914	One of the first enclosed armoured cars to appear. Revolving turret open at rear and curved armour in front of crew compartment enhanced protection. Side doors in hull gave access to interior.	Shelley
Autoblindata Lancia IZ (Italy)	Lancia IZ 2. Light Truck Chassis	35hp	3 St. Etienne MGs	4	70Kph	1915 Mark VI 1917	The most important Italian armoured car of the war. Used on NE Borders of Italy and in training of US troops in Italy. Used in WW2. 1917 model dispensed with small top turret and instead mounted gun in hull facing backwards.	Carlton 3.
Rolls Royce (Admiralty turreted pattern)	Rolls Royce 4. Derby	6 Cylinder 7,428cc	1 x .303 Vickers MG	3	60 mph	1914 mod. 1920 mod.	The most famous of all armoured cars. Served in many theatres of war and used in early part of WW2. The 1920 version differed only in size of turret and plated wheels.	Carlton 5.

NOTES:

MG - Machine Gun

1. Model registered by Birks, Rawlins & Co. 13.11.15.
2. The cars were made by the Ansaldo Engineering firm of Turin.
3. The china model would appear to have been based on the 1917 version although they were never used by the RNAS.
4. In September 1914 all 'Silver Ghost' chassis at Derby, with coachbuilders or with agents were requisitioned and converted.
5. The model resembles the 1920 version of the car and may have been brought out with the Vickers Tank (see 'Tanks').

NOTE:

The Arcadian 'Model of Armoured Car' (Reg. No. 657736) registered on 27th September 1916 (eleven days after the first tank attack) is ficticious in design although the tracks and suspension are good copies of the Roberts Chain Track suspension found on the Hornsby Tractors of the time. It is considered to be an attempt by a designer to model a tank from newspaper reports, in the absence of a photograph. The more accurate model of the tank (Reg. No. 658588) followed 2 months later when the first photographs appeared in the press - even this model was wrong having only one steering wheel instead of two.

TANKS

Name	Weight (Tons)	Dimensions (L x W x H)	Power Source	Max. Speed	Armament	Crew	First used	No. built	Remarks	Models made by
Mark I Heavy Tank (British)	28(M) 27(F) 1.	32'6" x 13'9" x 8'	Daimler 6 Cylinder 105hp	3.5-4 mph	(M): 2 x 6pdr Naval Guns + 4 MG (F): 5 MG	8 2.	Sept. 1916	150 3.	The direct descendant of 'Mother' designed by Wm. Tritton & Lieut. W.G. Wilson. Able to cross a 9' trench and 4'6" parapet. In November 1916 the two steering wheels were removed.	Arcadian:Alexandra Botolph:Caledonia: Carlton:Clifton: Corona: Esbeco Florentine: Grafton: Pearl Arms·Regis: Savoy:Shelley: Swan:Victory: Victoria:Waterfall: Willow
Mark IV Heavy Tank (British)	28(F) 26(M)	26'5" x 13'6" x 8'2" 26'5" x 10'6" x 8'2"	Daimler 6 Cylinder 105hp	3.5 mph	2 x 6pdr Naval Guns or 4. 6 MG	8	April 1917	1220 5.	First tanks to achieve dramatic success when on Nov. 20th 1917 381 tanks carved a hole 6 miles wide and 4,000 yards deep in the Hindenberg line. Superceded by the more manoeuverable Mark V.	Arcadian:Carlton: Botolph:Coronet: Caledonia:Cyclone: Clifton:Florentine: Goss:Grafton: Norfolk:Palatine: Savoy:Shelley: Willow:Victoria: Porcelle
Medium Tank Mark A (Whippet) (British)	14	20' x 8'7" x 9'	2 x 45hp Tylor Engines (1 on each track)	9mph	4 Hotchkiss MG	3	March 1918	200	Designed as a light, fast tank that could exploit openings made by the heavy tanks. Superceded by Mark B. Based on a design by Sir Wm. Tritton.	Arcadian: Swan: Grafton
Renault FT 17 (French)	6.5	16'5" x 5'7½" x 7'	Renault 4 cyl. (35bhp)	4.8 mph	1 x 37mm Purteaux Cannon	2	Spring 1917	Over 3,500	The most advanced and most reliable of all WW1 tanks. One was issued to each Tank Battalion in 1917 for use as a command/reconnaisance vehicle. Main tank of French Army until 1936. Designed by Louis Renault.	Carlton: Corona: Grafton: Victoria
Carro-Fiat Tipo 2000	40	Approx. 26' x 10'	Fiat 6 cyl. (240hp)	4.5 mph	1 x 65mm Gun + 7 Revelli MGs	10	End of 1918	2	Designed and built by Fiat Co. of Turin and was first heavy tank to have a cannon armed turret. The second tank made differed slightly from the first.	Carlton
Vickers Medium Tank Mark I	12(?)			20 mph	1 x 3pdr Cannon + 4 Hotchkiss MGs	5(?)	1922		First fast tank to come into operational use. Its armament was placed in the turret which enabled all round traverse fire. Remained standard tank of British Army until 1938.	Carlton

NOTES:
M.G. - Machine Gun
1. Two models - Male and Female differing in armament: built by Messrs. Fosters, Agricultural Implement Manufacturers of Lincoln.
2. Viz: Commander, Gearsmen, 2 Brakesmen, 2 6pdr Gunners, 2 Lewis Machine Gunners.
3. Of the first 50 ordered by Haig in 1916, only 36 arrived at Front line; of these 9 proved to be of any use.
4. Lewis Guns replaced by Hotchkiss Machine Guns.
5. 205 were modified as tank tenders.

vii
The Wrecking and the wreck of the Zeppelin LZ33

On the night of September 24th 1916 the L33 was brought down by the combined efforts of the London defences and 2nd Lieut. A de B Brandon of 39 Squadron, flying his BE2c. Landing in an almost intact state in a field near the Essex village of Little Wigborough, it provided an ideal opportunity (and the first) for British aviation scientists to study the intricacies and details of Zeppelin technology at first hand. The information gathered was then used to improve the designs and structure of the 'R' series airships that appeared at the end of the war.

The account (unsigned) of the wrecking of the L33 is the official report, written at the time and can be found in the archives of the Imperial War Museum, London. The description of the wrecked ship is extracted from 'The Great War' by H.W. Wilson & J.A. Hamerton; Vol. 8 p.220-222 which appeared in February 1917. Although lengthy it is interesting for its detail, available for public release only six months after the ship's crash.

The Wrecking of the L33

There can be little doubt that during the bombardment over East London one propeller had been damaged and a shell passed through her body. She also began to lose gas, though not rapidly, through punctures caused by shell splinters. In getting out of the rays of searchlights at Kelvedon Common she attempted to climb rapidly and appeared to release a smoke cloud. At about 12.30 she was attacked by 2nd Lieut. (now Captain) A. de B. Brandon, Royal Flying Corps, but his bullets failed in their purpose of bringing her down. The majority of prisoners of the L33 were vague as to the aeroplane attack which passed off more or less unnoticed by them, but were unanimous that the ship was pierced by a shell shortly after leaving the river i.e. over East London.

The aviator continued his close pursuit of the airship which at 12.35am passed south of Ongar, and at 12.45am north of Chelmsford. There she began to jettison cargo. At Broomfield spare parts, two aluminium cartridge boxes and a leather machine gun case were thrown out and at Boreham, a mile or two further, a machine gun followed. At 12.55am the airship was between Witham and Maldon. She now began to labour considerably as her height and speed diminished. About 1am she dropped her second machine gun in the grounds of 'Monckton', Wickham Bishops. A third machine gun followed at Gate House Farm, Tiptree. About 1.15am she went out to sea at West Mersea, but her commander, who in view of her condition, preferred to be taken prisoner rather than to run the risk of drowning with his crew like the men of the L15, almost immediately returned to the coast, and at 1.20am brought his ship down to earth in a field between Little Wigborough and Peldon, some three miles inland, north east of Mersea. There a slight explosion took place and the ship took fire, but owing to her great loss of gas comparatively little damage was inflicted upon her, only the outer casing being destroyed and the front gondola suffering severe damage. The framework partly collapsed amidships when the casing took fire. She probably dropped a good many bombs (HE) at the mouth of the River Thames on the way over as the number dropped by her in this country, 26, is much less than that usually carried by an airship of her type'.

The Wreck of the L33

....'The Super Zeppelin was of immense bulk, little inferior to the Lusitania. It displaced 50 tons weight of air and contained 2,000,000 cu. ft. of gas. It's outer surface was not of goldbeaters skin which in the past was commonly employed for airships, but of a finely woven Manchester cotton. On this cotton, delicate wavy lines were printed in black or dark blue. The colour effect of the envelope seen from a distance was grey. Closely examined it looked like newspaper covered with very fine print of a microscopic fount. This material was perhaps adopted to make the airship less visible, though it is also possible that the lines may have been printed to make the fabrics resemble shirting and to enable them to pass the blockade. It was not varnished or treated in any way except, it may be, by a solution rendering it non-flammable. It played in the airship the same part as the thin outer steel plating of a seafaring vessel. It was tough and very hard to tear, while it would offer no resistance to artillery projectiles unless they had a very sensitive fuse.

As the outer steel plating of a sea-going vessel is carried on frames so was the cotton covering of the airship. But whereas the frames of a sea vessel are of steel and are ponderous, in the airship they were of the lightest metal available, an alloy of aluminium, and of a lattice work design, with an air of extraordinary fragility about them that made them seem almost fantastic. Besides these frames there were longitudinal girders running the length of the ship. The enormous skeleton of metal 680ft long and 72ft beam, covered an acre of ground and looked as large as a fairy-like Crystal Palace. In shape the hull was streamlined, which means that the forward end was comparatively blunt and was larger in diameter than the mid-ships portion. Astern it tapered down and terminated in a fine point at the tail. The general shape of the hull was that of a cigar with 25 sides. In this respect it differed from the earlier Zeppelins, which were not streamlined and had a bow shaped similar to the stern, and 17 or 18 sides. The Super Zeppelin's hull was far more favourable to high speeds. It seems possible that she may have attained 80mph in fine weather conditions although her average speed would not have been more than 50mph.

Within the great cigar shaped hull were 24 gas-bags made of silk fabric coated with india-rubber varnish and gas-proof. Each bag was shaped like a Cheddar Cheese and probably each was fitted with valves, one of which was hand operated, while the other, an automatic valve for releasing gas when the pressure rose dangerously, was placed in the side of the hull. Passing through the gas bags by a gas tight valve and running from end to end of the hull was a great hawser. From this radial wires were carried to each aluminium transverse frame, as the spokes of a cycle wheel run from the hub to the rim of the wheel. These radial wires kept the gas-bags apart and when the great central cable was tightened - for which a very simple device was fitted - the tension of them was tautened too, and the whole of the framework of the ship braced, exactly as the sails of a sailing ship are braced at sea by tightening the stays and rigging. The great cable, the existence of which no-one in this country suspected, thus served to keep the hull of the ship together and to relieve the strain on it when it was exposed to gun, fire or wind.

On the top of the hull forward was a small platform on which were two 5ins guns, firing a little shell of nearly a pound in weight. Right astern, not far from the apex of the tail, was another station for a single 5ins gun, in a yet lonelier and more dangerous position. These were the weapons to which the designers of the Super Zeppelin trusted for repelling aeroplane attack. These remote stations in the great rusting hulk were reached by ladders or by climbing a cat walk which ran along the keel. This walk gave a means of passing from end to end of the hull, but it was so perilously narrow that it must have strained any but the steadiest nerves. The width of the gangway was only 9ins. of the thinnest plywood, laid directly on the girder framing. If a man missed his footing he would shoot through the flimsy cotton cover and fall to a certain death, though there was a handhold in the form of a rope to enable him to grope his way in the darkness of the ship's interior.

In this dim alleyway, abaft the forward gondola was the bomb chamber where were hooks for 60 bombs, which may have weighed one and a half tons or more. The hooks were electrically operated by the sixty buttons on the murder keyboard which was placed in the forward gondola. In form the buttons resembled bell pushes. When the button was pressed the hook released the bomb, a lever was previously moved which opened a sliding shutter which allowed the bomb to fall. This device was the crudest possible, and it made accurate aiming out of the question. Anyone who examined it would realise why Zeppelins never hit their targets. A lavatory was also placed in the cat-walk but there were no arrangements for cooking.

The gondolas were four in number. Two of these were like large boats about fifty feet long, placed forward and astern. The two others were smaller and placed abreast on either side of the hull, nearer the centre of the ship. The forward one contained the Captain's cabin with wheels controlling the two rudders for horizontal and vertical movement and other controls for the petrol tanks and water ballast. The gondolas were covered with fabric but had non-flammable celluloid windows. Abaft the Captain's cabin was the wireless room which was little more than a cupboard, six feet by four feet and abaft that again was a 240hp Mercedes Maybach Engine with dynamo and two machine guns. The engine drove a propeller immediately behind the gondola and underneath the hull. The two small amidships gondolas each contained a similar engine driving a similar propeller with dynamo and machine gun. The large gondola astern carried three engines, two of which drove propellers at the side of the airship by level gearing, and a third propeller astern of the gondola and underneath the hull. Each engine was fitted with a dynamo and in the gondola there were two machine guns. Thus there were six engines each of 240hp, totalling 1440hp in all, 6 dynamos, 6 propellers (four under and two at the sides of the airship) and six machine guns, besides that three .5ins weapons at the bow and stern.

The petrol tanks of the Super Zeppelin carried 2,000 gallons and were placed in or near the cat-walk so as to keep them well away from the engines. There were many ingenious contrivances, among them an apparatus for releasing the mooring rope by pressing a button. The exhaust from the engines appeared to be carried out through the hull so as to keep the gas warm when cruising in the frightful cold of the upper air. A smoke producing apparatus was fitted. Like other Zeppelins this airship was probably equipped with an observation car capable of containing one man which could be lowered 1,000 yards and was connected with the airship by telephone cable.

The report that the gondolas were armoured was explained by the appearance of the aluminium of which they were made, and which looked like burnished steel. The metal was very tough sheeting about a fifth of an inch thick and was strongly stayed. The gondolas appeared watertight and would probably have floated but for the heavy weights they contained.

The crew numbered 23 men of all sizes and not chosen for their lightness. They wore very heavy and warm clothing and many of them had special knowledge of East Anglia, indeed one had worked in Colchester.

The engines were fitted with silencers and despite these the noise they made was very great and was noticed all over the place that they landed. Such were these 'Super Zeppelins' of which the first seems to have been completed in June. L33 on her tanks bore the mark: 'H14 7 16' which probably stood for 'Herbst (summer) 14th day, 7th month (July) 1916....'

viii Biographies of Personalities

Allenby: Edmund Henry Hynmans; 1st Viscount Allenby of Megiddo and Felixstowe in the county of Suffolk.
b. 23.4.1861; d. 1936.

Entered Army (1879) served with Inniskilling Dragoons; Bechuanaland Expedition (1884-5); Zululand (1888); Commander 5th Lancers (1902); Commander 4th Cavalry Brigade (1905-09); Inspector-General of Cavalry at Aldershot (1914); Commander of the Cavalry Division at Mons (and later when it became a Corps); Commander 5th Corps (1915); Commander 3rd Army at Arras (1917); led Egyptian Expeditionary Force (June 1917-1918); Appointed High Commissioner for Egypt and Sudan (Oct. 1919); retired 1925.

Promotion: General (1917); G.C.B. (1918); Field Marshal (1919). Granted sum of £50,000 for War Service and created Viscount.

Beatty: David; 1st Earl Beatty
b. 17.1.1871 Howbeck Cheshire; d. 1936.
Entered Navy Jan 1884; Mediterranean (1896); Khartoum Expedition (1898); China (1900); Mediterranean (1904-05); Naval Adviser to the Army Council (1906); ADC to King (1908); Naval Adviser to 1st Lord of the Admiralty (1910); Naval Secretary to the 1st Lord (1912); Commander Battlecruiser Squadron (1913-16); succeeded Sir John Jellicoe as Commander of Grand Fleet (Nov. 1916); received surrender of German High Seas Fleet at Rosyth (Nov. 21st 1918); 1st Sea Lord (Oct. 1919-July 1927).

Promotion: Sub-Lieutenant (1890); Lieutenant (1892); Commander (1898); Captain (1900); Rear Admiral (1910); at 39 the youngest to achieve flag-rank since Nelson; Admiral (1919).

Fought with his Battlecruisers at Heligoland Bight, Dogger Bank (where his Flagship, the Lion, was disabled, Beatty being on the bridge for most of the time); Jutland when his Battlecruiser force engaged the enemy High Seas Fleet. In 1919 he was granted £100,000 and an Earldom for his services during the war.

Foch: Ferdinand
b. 4.10.1851 Tarbes; d. 20.3.1929.
Enlisted 1870, entered Engineering and Artillery School at Fontainbleau, left (1874) as a 2nd Lieutenant; 10th Regiment of Artillery (1878); picked for School of War (1885); appointed General Staff (1894) and later Professor of Military History, Strategy and Applied Tactics at the Ecole Superieure de Geurre (staff college); wrote 'The Conduct of War' and 'The Principles of War'; commanded a regiment (1901); appointed Chief of Staff 5th Army Corps (1905); General Staff (1907); command of Ecole de Guerre (1907-11); General of Division (1911); General 8th Army Corps (1912); General 20th Army Corps (1903); formed 9th Army at Joffre's request in August 1914; reached

age limit in September 1916 but kept on active list; voted Generalissimo of French, British, American and Belgian Forces on the Western Front; elected Marshal of France (1918); Head of Peace Delegation (11.11.18); organised conferences between German and Allied leaders after the war.

Promotion: 2nd Lieutenant (1874); Captain (1878); Colonel (1903); Brigadier-General (1907); General (1911); Marshal of France (1918).

Distinguished himself as a leader in the defence of Nancy (August 1914); the Battle of the Marne (Sept. 1914); with the British at Ypres (Oct. 1914) and on the British Right at the Somme (July 1st 1916). Largely responsible for the preliminary peace terms and for post-war German settlement.

French: John Denton Pinkstone; 1st Earl of Ypres and High Lake, Roscommon.
b. 28.9.1852 Ripple, Kent; d. 22.5.1925.

Entered Navy (1866); transferred to militia (1870); commissioned into 8th Hussars later transferring to 19th (1874); Egyptian Expedition (1884); Commander 19th Hussars (1889); Assistant Adjutant General of Cavalry (1893); Commander 2nd Cavalry Brigade at Aldershot (1897); Commander 1st Cavalry Brigade (1899); Commander Cavalry Division in South African War (1900); Aldershot command (1902-07); Inspector-General (1907); ADC to King (1911); Chief of Imperial General Staff (1912); Resigned in 1914 over Ulster troubles but selected to lead BEF; surrendered command of BEF to Haig (Dec. 1916); Commander British Forces in Britain (1917-18); Viceroy of Ireland (1918); retired (1921) as the Earl of Ypres.

Promotion: Commissioned (1874); Captain (1880); Major (1883); Lieut-Colonel (1885); Maj-General (1900); General (1907); Field Marshal (1913).

Haig: Douglas 1st Earl of Bemersyde
b. Edinburgh 19.6.1861; d. 29.1.1928
Educated Clifton; Brasenose College, Oxford; Sandhurst.
Gazetted 1885 to 7th Hussars; Khartoum campaign (1898); South African War (1900-02); Inspector General Cavalry in India (1903-06); Director Military training in Britain (1906-07); Director of Staff duties at headquarters (1907-08); Chief of Staff Indian Army (1909-12); Aldeshot Command (1912-14); Commander 1st Corps BEF (1914); Commander 1st Army (1915); Commander in Chief British Armies in France (Dec. 1915-1918)
Promoted Field Marshal Jan. 1st 1917; Earldom (1919) and a grant of £100,000; Knight of the Thistle (1917); Order of Merit (1919).

Jellicoe: John Rushworth; 1st Earl Jellicoe
b. 5.12.1859 Southampton; d. 1935.
Entered Navy (1872); Egyptian War (1882); won prize for Gunnery Lieutenants at RNC Greenwich (1883); Board of Trade Silver Medal for Gallantry in saving life at sea (1886); China (1900); Admiralty (1902-7); 2nd in Command Atlantic Fleet (1907-8); 3rd Sea Lord and Controller (1908-10); 2nd Sea Lord (1910-14); Commander Grand Fleet (1914-16); 1st Sea Lord (1916-17); Admiral of the Fleet (1919); Governor of New Zealand (1920-24).

Promotion: Lieutenant (1880); Commander (1891); Captain (1907); Vice-Admiral (1914); Admiral (1915); created Viscount Jellicoe of Scapa (Jan. 1918); Earldom conferred 1925.

Awarded K.C.V.O. (1907); O.M. and G.C.V.O. (1916) and £50,000 for war services (1919).

Joffre: Cesaire Joseph Jacques
b. 12.1.1852 Rivesaltes in the Pyreenes; d. 3.1.1931.
Subaltern in Franco-Prussian War (1870) engaged in plans for new fortifications of Paris, Versailles and Montpellier; served Far-East (1884-88); appointed to Staff (1889); lecturer on fortifications at Fontainbleau Artillery School (1891); Senegal and Timbuctoo (1892); Madagascar (1897); Chief of Command Corps of Engineers (1904); General of Division (1905); Commander 6th Infantry Division (1906); Chief of 2nd Army Corps (1908); French General Staff (1909); Supreme Commander French Army (1911-16); went to America with French Mission (1917); retired.

Promotion: Subaltern (1870); Major (1889); Colonel (1897); Brigadier-General (1901); Marshal of France (1916).

Awards: Commander of Legion of Honour (1903); Grand Officer of Legion of Honour (1909); Order of Alexandra Nevski (1913); G.C.V.O. (1917).

Kitchener: Horatio Herbert; 1st Earl of Khartoum and Aspal.
b. 24.6.1850 Ballylongford, Co. Kerry; d. 5.6.1916 in sinking of HMS Hampshire.

Passed out of Woolwich (1870) and joined Royal Engineers; Staff of Palestine Exploration fund (1874-78), surveyed in Palestine and Cyprus; Egyptian Army (1882-85); Suakin operations (1888); Toski Campaign (1889); Commander Egyptian Army (1892); Dongola operations (1896); Khartoum Campaign (1898); Chief of Staff to Lord Roberts in South Africa and later Commander-in-Chief (1899-1902); Commander-in-Chief in India (1902-09); British Agent in Egypt (1911); Appointed Secretary of State for War (August 5 1914) started the building of a 'New Army' comprising 70 Divisions (1,400,000 men). Went down with the HMS Hampshire en route for Russia, body never found.

Raised to the peerage as Baron (1898) and awarded £30,000 for services; made Viscount (1902) and awarded Order of Merit and £50,000 for services in South African War; Earldom conferred 1914.

ix
Trade Names and Factories of China Manufacturers

At the time of the Great War the main Heraldic China manufacturers were trading from the following places:

Arcadian:
J.A. Robinson & Sons Ltd., Wolfe St., Stoke-on-Trent.

Carlton:
Wiltshaw & Robinson Ltd., Carlton Works, Copeland St., Stoke-on-Trent.

Savoy:
Birks, Rawlins & Co. Ltd., Vine Pottery, Summer St., Stoke.

Shelley:
Wileman & Co., King St., Fenton, Stoke-on-Trent.

Grafton:
A.B. Jones & Sons Ltd., Grafton China, Marlborough Rd., Longton.

Willow:
Hewitt & Leadbeater, The Willow Pottery, Longton.

Goss:
William Henry Goss Ltd., Falcon Pottery, Stoke.

Corona:
Sampson Hancock & Sons, Bridge Works, Stoke.

For further details of these and other manufacturers see *Crested China by Sandy Andrews* (see bibliography).

x
Catalogue of First World War Heraldic China

NOTES:
1. The models encompassed within the term 'Great War Crested China' are a small part of the total output of the Crested China industry during its fifty years of existence. Other models of a martial nature were produced before and after the war and are technically out of the scope of this catalogue. However, where confusion may arise they have been included.

2. **Dating:** The only accurate way of dating the origin of models is from registration marks. Other models can only be dated by indirect, less accurate means e.g. by tracing the original photograph from which the model was taken or by referring to the factory marks on some makes of china (see Appendix 1)

This form of dating gives the earliest date for a model. Some of the more popular lines were made until the mid-twenties while others, less popular, were discontinued soon after their appearance.

3. **Scarcity:** Although made in their thousands the numbers of some of the models surviving today may be counted in tens and hundreds - damaged, broken or simply thrown away over the years, because they lacked the inherent value of some of the finer types of chinaware. The rare models of today are those which for some reason failed to sell whether it be because they lacked aesthetic appeal or were produced in the twenties when interest in the china was waning. Another group of rareties are those that were made in small numbers for a particular retailer. Such models invariably carry a 'Made for ....' inscription.

4. Prices: In the past few years the demand and thus the value, of this china has increased dramatically and it would be misleading to include exact values as they would very soon be out of date. However, a guide to approximate values at the time of going to press is appended to the scarcity scale given below. The reader who wishes to learn more about current values is directed to *The Price Guide to Crested China by Nicholas Pine (Milestone)* and *The Price Guide to Goss China by Nicholas Pine (Milestone)* both being the standard references on the subject.

5. **Measurements:** Sizes of models are given in millimetres. The measurement given in that of the longest aspect of the model unless otherwise stated. Variations of less than 5mm in a particular model are caused by shrinkage during firing and can be ignored. Larger differences between similar models are due to variations between moulds and do not necessarily indicate a different model.

6. **Inscriptions:** Inscriptions are omitted unless they provide some form of identification. A full list of inscriptions appearing on the china will be found in Appendix ii.

7. **Registration Numbers:** Registration numbers and manufacturers stock numbers are listed where known. These are correct for the models listed. Any other numbers on a particular model may be considered as an error.

8. **Plate references:** Numbers in brackets refer to page numbers where a photograph of the model may be found. Identical models from different factories are listed with the number of their 'parent' model.

9. The following scale is used to indicate scarcity and approximate value:

A =	Very Rare	£100+
B =	Rare	£75-£100
C =	Scarce	£50-£75
D =	Common	£25-£50
E =	Very Common	0-£25

10. The china is listed by chapter.

1. FIGURES

a. British Soldiers

D	*Arcadian*	100mm	'Model of Tommy on Sentry Duty' 657213
D	*Arcadian*	100mm	'Model of Tommy and his machine gun' 657214
D	*Arcadian*	115mm	'Model of Despatch Rider' 657737
A	*Arcadian*	120mm	'To Berlin' (Tommy driving steamroller over the Kaiser)
A	*Arcadian*	120mm	'Model of British Cavalry Soldier' 658680
B	*Arcadian*	124mm	'Model of Tommy in Bayonet Attack' 658676
B	*Arcadian*	125mm	'Model of Tommy throwing grenade' 658681
B	*Arcadian*	128mm	'Model of British Soldier'
A	*Arcadian*	155mm	'Model of Bugler'
A	*Arcadian*	135mm	'Model of Drummer Boy' 658737
D	*Carlton*	80mm	'Tommies dugout' 660631
B	*Carlton*	125mm	Tommy with bandolier (no ins.)
B	*Carlton*	132mm	'Old Bill'
D	*Carlton*	155mm	'Are we downhearted? No!'
B	*Coronet*	130mm	'Tommy in bayonet attack' 658676
D	*Clifton*	115mm	'Model of Despatch Rider' 657737
D	*Elite*	132mm	'Our Brave Defender'
A	*Grafton*	120mm	'Over the top'
A	*Grafton*	140mm	'The Bomb Thrower'
D	*J.W.R.*	100mm	'Model of Tommy and his machine gun' 657214
A	*Savoy*	85mm	Tommy in dugout
D	*Willow*	130mm	'Our Brave Defender'
D	*W & R*	144mm	'Our Brave Defender'
B	*Swan*	100mm	'Model of British Soldier'
D	*Swan*	100mm	'Model of Tommy and his machine gun' 657214
D	*Swan*	125mm	'Model of Despatch Rider' 657737

b. Scottish Soldiers

A	*Arcadian*	135mm	'Model of Scottish Soldier' 767734
B	*Caledonia*	165mm	
B	*Carlton*	155mm	651139
B	*Savoy*	165mm	
A	*Shelley*	111mm	Shelley 402 *'Scotland For Ever'*

c. Foreign Soldiers

A	*Arcadian*	122mm	'Model of Russian Cossack' 658684
A	*Arcadian*	135mm	'Model of Colonial Soldier' 656885
A	*Arcadian*	135mm	'Model of French Soldier' 657733
A	*Grafton*	80mm	American Soldier (Grafton 85)

d. Sailors

C	*Arcadian*	95mm	Coloured sailor 'HMS Lion'
D	*Arcadian*	130mm	Sailor with hands on hips 652243
C	*Arcadian*	105mm	'Model of Sailor winding capstan' 658675
C	*Carlton*	70mm	Squatting sailor holding submarine
D	*Carlton*	130mm	'Handy Man'
D	*Crown*	130mm	'Our Brave Defender'
D	*Elite*	130mm	'Our Brave Defender'
C	*Grafton*	79mm	Squatting sailor
A	*Grafton*	100mm	Diver in diving suit
D	*Porcelle*	130mm	Sailor with hands on hips 652243
D	*Willow*	130mm	'Our Brave Defender'
C	*Wilton*	70mm	Squatting sailor holding submarine
D	*Wy Not*	130mm	'Our Brave Defender'

e. Airman

A	*Willow Art*	140mm	Arms straight
A	*Willow Art*	140mm	right arm holding a medal

f. Nurses

D	*Arcadian*	125mm	'A Soldier's Friend'
C	*Arcadian*	140mm	'Model of Nurse with wounded Tommy' 658674
D	*Botolph*	125mm	'A Soldier's Friend'
D	*Carlton*	150mm	'A Friend in Need'
D	*Clifton*	133mm	'A Friend in Need'
D	*Disa Art China*	133mm	'A Friend in Need'
D	*Milton*	133mm	'A Friend in Need'
D	*Royal Crown*	133mm	'A Friend in Need'
D	*Willow*	133mm	'A Friend in Need'

g. Other Figures

B	*Carlton*	140mm	'Doing her bit' Munitions Worker 662105
B	*Mother Shipton*	140mm	'Doing her bit' Munitions Worker 662105
B	*Shelley*	105mm	'Vive La France' Shelley 406
B	*Shelley*	105mm	'Rule Britannia' Shelley 403
B	*Grafton*	88mm	'British Territorial Bulldog' Grafton 262
C	*Podmore*	160mm	HRH Prince of Wales

2. BUSTS AND PART FIGURES

a. Soldiers

D	*Arcadian*	90mm	'Tommy Atkins' or 'Territorial'
A	*Arcadian*	80mm	'Model of Belgian Soldier'
A	*Arcadian*	93mm	'Model of new gas mask' 657652
D	*Swan*	90mm	'Tommy Atkins'
D	*Wembley*	95mm	'Tommy Atkins'

b. Sailors

D	*Arcadian*	92mm	'HMS Dreadnought/Lion/Queen Elizabeth 652244

D	*Carlton*	85mm	'HMS Dreadnought or Handyman'
D	*Clifton*	95mm	'HMS Dreadnought'
D	*Savoy*	126mm	'HMS Lion/Iron Duke/Warspite'
D	*Swan*	92mm	
D	*Victoria*	90mm	

c. Airman

A	*Swan*	93mm	'Arry' ...Bust of Airman

3. PERSONALITIES

B	General Allenby	Grafton	140mm	'Allenby'
C	Lord Beatty	Regis	165mm	
C	Lord Beatty	Savoy	150mm	+ ins.
A	John Travers Cornwell	Savoy	110mm	+ ins.
D	Foch	Grafton	140mm	'Foch'
D	Sir John French	Grafton	140mm	'French'
D	Sir John French	Shelley	120mm	+ ins.
D	Admiral Jellicoe	Arcadian	170mm	
D	Admiral Jellicoe	Grafton	135mm	'Jellicoe'
D	Admiral Jellicoe	Shelley	118mm	+ ins
C	Admiral Jellicoe	H & L	174mm	
D	General Joffre	Arcadian	170mm	
D	General Joffre	Grafton	150mm	'Jellicoe'
D	General Joffre	Shelley	130mm	+ ins.
D	Lord Kitchener	Arcadian	150mm & 175mm	
D	Lord Kitchener	Grafton	100mm & 130mm	Grafton 395
D	Lord Kitchener	Grafton	125mm	
D	Lord Kitchener	Savoy	125mm	
D	Lord Kitchener	Shelley	120mm	+ ins.
D	Lord Kitchener	Carlton	130mm	
A	Count Zeppelin	German	165mm	

4. ROYALTY AND CIVILIANS

D	Albert I of Belgium	Grafton	127mm	
C	Albert I of Belgium	Savoy	150mm	
C	Albert I of Belgium	H & L	170mm	
D	Alexandra	Arcadian	140mm	
D	Alexandra	Carlton	140mm	
D	George V	Arcadian	135mm	+ ins.
D	George V	Grafton	130mm	
D	George V	Shelley	130mm	
D	Lloyd George	Arcadian	127mm	
C	Lloyd George	Carlton	155mm	Figure on plinth
D	Lloyd George	Grafton	135mm	659418 Grafton 415
D	Lloyd George	Shelley	118mm & 130mm	
D	Queen Mary	Arcadian	135mm	
C	Prince of Wales	Arcadian	135mm	583045

5. TOMMIES KIT

a. Caps and Headware

E	Airmans Cap	Queens	72mm	
E		Savoy	80mm	
E		Carlton	78mm	
E	Colonial Hat	Arcadian	90mm	'Model of Colonial Hat' 637738
E		Carlton	90mm	'Colonial Hat'
E		Clifton	88mm	'Model of Colonial Hat' 637738
E		Grafton	87mm	
E		Porcelle	90mm	
E		Queens	92mm	
E		Savoy	81mm	
E		Swan	87mm	
E	Despatch Riders hat with goggles	Gemma	65mm	
D	Forage Cap	Aynsley	90mm	445680
E		Regis	83mm	
D	French Helmet	Caledonia	82mm	'French trench helmet' + ins.
D		Queens	82mm	'French trench helmet'
D		Savoy	82mm	'French trench helmet'
E	Glengarry	Arcadian	90mm	
D		Aynsley	93mm	
E		Carlton	78mm	
E		Caledonia	85mm	
E		Craven	78mm	
E		Diamond	78mm & 100mm	
E		Porcelle	70mm & 100mm	
E		Queens	90mm	
E		Savoy	70mm	'Scots Bonnet' 661741
E		Shelley	86mm	Shelley 176
E		Waterfall	90mm	
E		Willow	97mm	
E	Peaked Cap	Arcadian	70mm	
E		Carlton	78mm	'Territorial's hat'
E		Coronet	63mm	
E		Pearl Arms	70mm	
E		Savoy	73mm	
E		Wembley	65mm	
E		Willow	80mm	
E	Military Helmet	Arcadian	60mm	
E	Pickelhaube	Dainty		
E		Pearl Arms	55mm	
E		Willow	50mm	
E	Pith Helmet	Arcadian	88mm	
D		Aynsley	42mm	
D	Rumanian Helmet	Savoy	82mm	'Rumanian soldiers steel helmet'
D	Steel Helmet	Arcadian	69mm	'Tommy's Steel Helmet'
D		Clarence	76mm	
D		Clifton	76mm	
D		Porcelle	82mm	
D		Savoy	82mm	
		Willow	75mm	
D	Sailors Hat	Savoy	70mm	

b. Drums

E	Arcadian	55mm x 50mm high	
D	Aynsley	55mm	444367
E	Botolph	58mm x 30mm high	
E	Carmen	51mm high	
E	Clarence	56mm high	
E	Corona	53mm x 68mm high	
E	Cyclone	32mm	
E	Florentine	55mm	
E	Grafton	50mm x 45mm high	
E	Shelley	30mm	412407
E	Swan	55mm x 52mm high	
E	Universal	57mm	

c. Kit-bags

E	Carlton	70mm	(two varieties)
E	Clarence	70mm	
E	Clifton	74mm	
E	Craven	70mm	
E	Disa Art	70mm	
E	Kingsway	70mm	
E	Milton	70mm	
E	Pearl Arms	70mm	
E	Norfolk Crest	72mm	
E	Regis	70mm	
E	Tudor Arms	70mm	
E	Willow Art	70mm	

d. Knives

D	Arcadian	108mm	'Model of Trench dagger' 657649
D	Arcadian	108mm	'Model of Gurkha's knife' 657698
D	Alexandra	140mm	'Model of Gurkha's knife'
D	Corona	140mm	'Model of Gurkha's knife'
D	Coronet	110mm	'Model of Gurkha's knife' 657698
D	Grosvenor	140mm	'Model of Gurkha's knife'
D	Sussex	108mm	Model of trench dagger 657649
D	Victoria	140mm	Model of Gurkha knife

e. Sandbags

E	Arcadian	74mm	'Model of sandbag' 658678
E	Clifton	70mm	
E	Coronet	70mm	
E	Sussex	76mm	
E	Swan	74mm	

f. Tents

E	Alexandra	90mm x 70mm base	
D	Aynsley	70mm	444368
E	Arcadian	65mm	'Camping out'
E	Carlton	70mm	'Tommy's bungalow'
E	Corona	85mm	
E	Coronet	65mm	
E	Clifton	60mm x 65mm	
E	Empire China	67mm	
E	Grafton	65mm x 140mm	Grafton 239
E	Herald Series	57mm	
E	Sussex SP & Co.	80mm	
E	Triood	85mm	
D	Willow	70mm	
D	Shelley	100mm	664306 Shelley 341 + ins.
C	Arcadian	105mm	657215 'Model of Tommies Hut'
C	Coronet	105mm	657215
C	Swan	105mm	657215

g. Telescopes/Field glasses

E	Arcadian	62mm	(FG) 'Model of pair of field glasses'
E	Swan	62mm	(FG)
E	Crown	70mm	(T)
E	Florentine	70mm	(T)
E	Coronet	70mm	
E	Wilton	80mm	(T)

h. Trench lamp/Torch

E	Arcadian	70mm	657696 'Model of Trench Lamp'
E	Corona	88mm	
E	Shelley	85mm	Shelley 342
E	Shelley	70mm	Shelley 191
E	Regency Ware	85mm	

i. Water bottles

E	Arcadian	62mm	'Model of Water Bottle' 657549
D	Aynsley	80mm	444365
E	Corona		
E	Coronet	62mm	
E	Royal Vale	70mm	

j. Bugles

E	Milton	70mm	
E	Kingsway	70mm	
D	Shelley	112mm	Shelley 354
E	Willow Art	70mm	
D		115mm	

CHAPTER 2
AMBULANCES, TANKS AND ARMOURED CARS

a. Ambulances

E	Alexandra	100mm	
E	Arcadian	85mm	
A	Arcadian	160mm	
E	Botolph	88mm	
E	Carlton	98mm	
E	Corona	100mm	
E	Coronet	90mm	
E	Elite	88mm	
E	Florentine	88mm	
D	Grafton	100mm	+ ins. Grafton 397
E	Leadbeater Art	54mm	
D	Porcelle	110mm	
E	Panorama	88mm	
D	Queens	110mm	
D	Savoy	110mm	652655
E	Shelley	98mm	Shelley 330
E	Sussex SP & Co.	85mm	
E	Swan	88mm	
E	Victoria	102mm	
E	Waterfall	88mm	
E	Willow	88mm	
E	Willow Art	57mm	

b. Armoured Cars

D	Arcadian	95mm	'Model of Armoured Car' 657736
D	Caledonia	125mm	
C	Carlton	115mm	'Model of British Anti-aircraft Motor'
B	Carlton	116mm	'RNAS' (Lancia)
B	Carlton	120mm	(Rolls Royce)
E	Coronet	100mm	
B	Grafton	80mm	'Model of Motor Tractor used on Western Front' Grafton 456
D	Porcelle	124mm	
D	Savoy	124mm	652656 (Talbot)
D	Shelley	115mm	Shelley 329

c. Tanks: Mark I

E	Alexandra	100mm & 153mm	
A	Arcadian	144mm	'Model of Tank' 668588 (1 wheel)
E	Arcadian	144mm	'Model of Tank' 668588 (2 wheels)
E	Arcadian	115mm	'Model of Tank'
E	Botolph	105mm	658588
D	Carlton	130mm & 160mm	'HMLS Creme-de-Menthe' + ins.
D	Caledonia	140mm	'HM Bonner Blitzen' + ins.
E	Clifton	127mm	658588
E	Corona	105mm	
E	Esbeco	95mm	658588 'Model of British Tank'
E	Florentine	125mm	
D	Grafton	120mm	658588 'HMLS Creme-de-Menthe'
E	Pearl Arms	130mm	658588 'Model of Tank'
D	Porcelle	160mm	'HM Donner Blitzen' + ins.
E	Regis	127mm & 95mm	
E	Royal Stafford		
E	Triood	100mm	
D	Savoy	162mm & 132mm x 35mm wide	'HM Donner Blitzen
E	Shelley	115mm	658588 'Model of British Tank' 400
E	Swan	120mm	
E	Victoria	105mm	
E	Waterfall	125mm	658588
E	Willow Art	120mm	658588
E	British Manufacture	125mm x 95mm	

d. Tanks: Mark IV

E Arcadian 100mm; 115mm; 160mm 658588
D Arcadian 180mm 658688
A Arcadian 325mm 658588
D Carlton 80mm; 100mm; 134mm & 156mm 'HMLS Creme-de-Menthe'
D Carlton 156mm 'Tank Bank'
E Coronet 110mm
D Caledonia 135mm 'HM Donner Blitzen' + ins.
E Cyclone 130mm
E Clifton 110mm 'Model of Tank'
E Botolph 155mm 'Model of Tank'
E Florentine 120mm
D Goss 115mm 'Model of British Tank' + ins.
E Grafton 100mm
E Norfolk 102mm
E Palatine 115mm 'Model of Tank' 658588
D Savoy 110mm; 130mm & 150mm 'HM Donner Blitzen'
E Shelley 140mm Shelley 400a
D Shelley 135mm x 100mm 'Tank Bank' Shelley 413
E Willow 90mm
E Willow Art 100mm
E Victoria 120mm
D Porcelle 145mm 'HM Donner Blitzen'

e. Other Tanks

C Corona 100mm (Renault)
C Grafton 100mm (Renault)
C Carlton 120mm 'HM Whippet Tank' (Renault)
C Grosvenor 100mm (Renault)
C Victoria 80mm (Renault)

C Arcadian 172mm (Whippet)
C Grafton 115mm 'Model of Whippet Tank' Grafton 449
C Swan 172mm (Whippet)

B Carlton 126mm (Vickers)

A Carlton 100mm (Fiat)

f. Miscellaneous

B Omnibus:
Arcadian 130mm

CHAPTER 3
GUNS AND GRENADES

a. Field guns:

i. 18 pounders

E Alexandra 120mm
E Arcadian 100mm 'Model of New Field Gun with screen 658586
E Corona 120mm
E Coronet
E Regis 110mm
E Royal Crown 110mm
E Willow Art 115mm
E Waterfall 120mm

ii. Without screen

E Arcadian 150mm 652245
E Arcadian 120mm 'Model of RFA gun'
E Caledonia 150mm 'Model of field gun'
E Carlton 130mm
E Corona 120mm
E Clifton 115mm
E Porcelle 170mm
E Queens 150mm
E Rayleigh 125mm
E Swan 120mm
E Triood 127mm
E Botolph 120mm
E Warwick 65mm high

b. Howitzers

E Arcadian 135mm
E Arcadian 140mm & 115mm 'Model of German Howitzer'
E Botolph 135mm
E Caledonia 163mm
E Corona 140mm
E Clifton 70mm
E Grafton 75mm 'Trench Howitzer' Grafton 404
E Porcelle 168mm & 140mm
D Shelley 145mm Shelley 340
D Shelley Shelley 331
E Sussex SP & Co.
D Savoy 163mm & 140mm
E Waterfall 112mm
E Willow 112mm

c. Mortars

E Arcadian 70mm 'Model of Trench Mortar' 657212
E Arcadian 70mm
E Arcadian 90mm
E Botolph 70mm 661741
E Carlton 70mm 'Model of British Trench Mortar'
E Carlton 60mm
E Clifton
E Diamond 105mm
D Savoy 90mm 661741 'British Trench Mortar Gun'
E Victoria 70mm
E Shelley 50mm high Shelley 327
E Shelley Shelley 179
D Queens 110mm
D Porcelle 95mm 'British Trench Mortar Gun'

d. Miscellaneous named guns

E 'French 75' Carlton 140mm
E Carlton 125mm
E Grafton 153mm Grafton 403
D 'French 75' on sled Grafton 93mm base Grafton 412
A Alpine Gun Grafton 105mm 'Model of Alpine Gun' 394
D Desert Gun Grafton 160mm 'Desert Gun' Grafton 430
D German Gun captured by British Grafton 145mm Grafton 403
A Naval Gun Carlton 95mm x 54mm high 662103

e. Machine guns

D Carlton 100mm 'Model of British Machine Gun' (2 versions)
D Carlton 100mm 661446 'British Machine Gun'
D Crown 100mm
B Porcelle 130mm (gun) 'British Machine Gun' 661446
B Savoy 130mm (gun) 'British Machine Gun' 661446
D W & R London 100mm

f. Small arms

D Arcadian 83mm 657653 'Model of revolver'
D Botolph 83mm 657653

g. Grenades

Mills Bomb

E Arcadian 60mm 657211 'Model of Mills Hand Grenade'
E Carlton 83mm 'British Hand Grenade'
E Grafton 80mm 'Mills Hand Grenade' 657211 no. 411
E Shelley 80mm Shelley 334
E Sussex SP & Co. 60mm

A 'Model of Hairbrush grenade' Arcadian 105mm 657702
B 'Model of Plum Pudding Bomb' Arcadian 75mm 657699
A 'Model of German stick grenade' Arcadian 76mm 657697
A 'Model of Trench pig' Arcadian 95mm 657701
D Hand bomb Aynsley 90mm
B 'Model of Trench Mortar Bomb' Savoy 82mm
D Spiggot Mortar Bomb Arcadian 80mm 657651
E 'Cannister Bomb' Arcadian 56mm 657700
E Clifton
E Swan 56mm

E		Victoria	56mm	
E	'German incendiary bomb'	Arcadian	78mm	
E		Carlton	75mm	
E		Grafton	80mm	Grafton 405

h. Shells

E	Albion China	75mm	
D	Arcadian	135mm	'Jack Johnson'
E		90mm & 70mm	
E	Arcadian	96mm	'Model of Anti-aircraft shell'
E	Caledonia	68mm	'Iron Rations for Fritz'
E	Carlton	90mm	'Model of British 15ins. shell'
E	Carlton	75mm	'Model of cannon shell'
E	Clifton	70mm	
E	Corona	70mm	
E	Craven	75mm	
E	C & S China	73mm	
E	Florentine	75mm	
E	Herald	90mm	'Jack Johnson'
E	Goss	112mm	'Russian shrapnell shell'
E	Goss	112mm	'British 6ins. shell'
E	Grafton	95mm	Grafton 399
E	Grafton	88mm & 72mm	
E	Porcelle	76mm	
E	Queens	60mm	
E	Savoy	60mm; 70mm & 80mm	
E	Waterfall	100mm	
E	Wembley	64mm	
E	Shelley	90mm	Shelley 175
D	Aynsley	104mm	444369
E	Victoria	75mm	

i. Clip of bullets

E	Arcadian	55mm	657648	'Model of clip of bullets'
E	Swan	55mm	657648	
E	Botolph	55mm		
E	Iceni	62mm		

D Cartridge case Aynsley 444366

CHAPTER 5
AEROPLANES

i. Monoplanes

D	Alexandra	142mm	
D	Arcadian	153mm	'Model of New Aeroplane'
D	Arcadian	120mm	607828
B	Botolph	175mm	(Sim-Victoria)
D	Carlton	136mm	
D	Carlton	134mm	
D	Corona	150mm	
D	Coronet	170mm	(Arcadian)
D	Coronet	145mm	(Arcadian)
D	Caledonia	178mm	(Savoy)
D	Devonia Art	145mm	(Willow Art)
D	Florentine	165mm	
D	Grafton	135mm	
D	Pearl Arms	145mm	(Willow Art)
D	Podmore	140mm	
D	Savoy	125mm	
D	Shelley	152mm	Shelley 311
D	Thistle	150mm	(Willow Art)
D	Waterfall	145mm	(Willow)
D	Willow Art	145mm	
B	Victoria	170mm	(Sim. Botolph)
E	Foreign	95mm	
E	Foreign	130mm	
E	Unmarked	90mm	
E		125mm	
E	Germany	80mm	

ii. Biplanes

B	Arcadian	122mm	'Model of New Aeroplane'	658683
A	Carlton	165mm		
A	Carlton	135mm	657607	
B	Grafton	145mm	Grafton 450	
A	Savoy	165mm		
C	Shelley	145mm	Shelley 344	
C	W & R London	145mm		
C	Unmarked	145mm		

iii. Aeroplane propellers

D	Willow	150mm	(usually found with RFC, RNAS or RAF cre
D	Savoy	150mm	
D	Milton	150mm	
D	Arcadian	150mm	

CHAPTER 6
AIRSHIPS AND ZEPPELINS

i. Non-rigid

J	Arcadian	125mm	'Model of British Airship' (Blimp) 658679
D	Diamond	80mm	'Beta'
D	Regis	80mm	'Beta'
D	Willow Art	80mm	'Beta'

ii. Balloons

D	Arcadian	80mm	'Model of Observer sausage balloon'	66858
D	Botolph	80mm	'Model of Observer'	

iii. Rigid Airships

E	Alexandra	130mm		
E	Arcadian	130mm	'Model of British Airship'	652241
E	Arcadian	127mm	'Model of Super Zeppelin'	657735
E	Carlton	120mm		
E	Corona	130mm		
E	Coronet	130mm		
E	Porcelle	130mm		
E	Queens	170mm		
E	Regency	153mm		
B	Savoy	175mm	+ ins.	659483 (with movable propeller)
B	Shelley	155mm	'L33'	Shelley 332
E	Sussex	130mm		
E	Swan	130mm	652241	
E	Swan	125mm	657735	
E	Triood	130mm		
E	Victoria	130mm		
E	Warwick	130mm		

iv. Bombs

Goldschmidt bombs:

E	Arcadian	80mm	'Model of bomb dropped from Zeppelin'
E	Carmen	80mm	
E	Clifton	80mm	
E	Coronet	78mm	
D	Goss	75mm	
D	Goss	75mm	
E	Grafton	80mm	
E	J & S China	80mm	
E	Iceni	75mm	
E	Shelley	80mm	Shelley 177

Miscellaneous

A	Arcadian	115mm	'Model of bomb dropped on Loftus' (with movable propeller)
C	Arcadian	115mm	'Model of bomb dropped on Sheringham' 664837
		115mm	'Model of bomb dropped on Loftus' (with movable propeller)
D	Arcadian	75mm	'Model of British aerial bomb' 657694

v. Searchlights

D	Arcadian		
D	Carlton	75mm	'Model of British Searchlight' + ins.
D	Craven	70mm	
B	Savoy	100mm	'Model of British Motor Searchlight'
B	Diamond	105mm	'Model of British Motor Searchlight'
B	Caledonia	100mm	'Model of British Motor Searchlight'
B	Porcelle	100mm	'Model of British Motor Searchlight'

vi. Miscellaneous

E	Anti-Zeppelin Candlestick	Arcadian	65mm	
D	Anti-Zeppelin Candlestick	Shelley	83mm	Shelley 348

CHAPTER 7
SHIPS AND SUBMARINES

i. Named ships

C	HMS Australia	Carlton	162mm	
C	HMHS Anglia	Carlton	162mm	662104
B	HMS Barham	Savoy	165mm	
C	HMS Canada	Carlton	162mm	
C	HMS Dreadnought	Carlton	140mm	
C	HMS Dreadnought	Grafton	140mm	Grafton 408
C	HMS Humber	Carlton	140mm	
C	HMS Inflexible	Carlton	155mm	
C	HMS Iron Duke	Grafton	155mm	
C	HMS Iron Duke	Savoy	165mm	
C	HMS Iron Duke	Carlton	160mm	
C	HMMS Gowan Lea	Carlton	115mm	+ ins. 661565
C	HMS Lion	Bow	168mm	
E	HMS Lion	Caledonia	140mm	
E	HMS Lion	Devonia Art	140mm	
C	HMS Lion	Carlton	160mm	
E	HMS Lion	Norfolk	140mm	
E	HMS Lion	Waterfall	140mm	
E	HMS Lion	Willow	140mm	
E	HMS Lion	W & R London	140mm	
E	HMS Lion	H & SP China	140mm	
C	HMS Lion	Savoy	160mm	659327
E	HMS Lion	Regis	138mm	
C	HMS Marlborough	Carlton	162mm	
B	HMMS Peggy	Carlton	115mm	+ ins. 661565
C	HMS Princess Royal	Carlton	160mm	
C	HMS Queen Elizabeth	Arcadian	162mm	
E	HMS Queen Elizabeth	Arcadian	115mm	
C	HMS Queen Elizabeth	Carlton	162mm	
C	HMS Queen Elizabeth	Porcelle	165mm	
C	HMS Queen Elizabeth	Savoy	165mm	
C	HMS Ramilies	Bow	168mm	
C	HMS Renown	Carlton	165mm	
C	HMS Thunderer	Carlton	160mm	
C	HMS Tiger	Carlton	160mm	
C	'Victory'	Grafton	140mm	
C	HMS Warspite	Carlton	155mm	
C	HMS Warspite	Savoy	155mm	
C	RMS Lusitania	Carlton	162mm	
C	RMS Lusitania	Corona	160mm	
C	RMS Lusitania	Sussex	165mm	
C	RMS Lusitania	Alexandra	160mm	

ii. Unnamed ships

E	Arcadian	160mm, 120mm & 106mm
D	Bow	165mm
E	Botolph	115mm
D	Carlton	165mm
E	Carlton	155mm, 140mm, 120mm & 112mm
E	Carmen	106mm
E	Clifton	115mm
E	Corona	120mm
E	Coronet	115mm
E	Devonia Art	116mm
E	Pearl Arms	127mm
E	Swan	160mm, 120mm & 106mm
E	Shelley	120mm Shelley 319
E	Sussex	120mm
E	Waterfall	140mm
E	Warwick	120mm
E	Willow Art	140mm
E	Wilton	115mm
E	Triood	115mm

iii. Other named ships

Torpedo boat destroyer

E	Arcadian	115mm	'Model of Torpedo boat destroyer' 658677
E	Botolph	115mm	'Model of Torpedo boat destroyer'
E	Carmen	115mm	'Model of Torpedo boat destroyer'
A	Caledonia	140mm	'Model of Torpedo boat destroyer'
E	Coronet	105mm	658677
A	Porcelle	140mm	
A	Savoy	140mm	'Model of Torpedo boat destroyer'
E	Swan	110mm	658677
E	Victoria	110mm	658677

Minesweeper

D	Arcadian	126mm	
D	Carlton	112mm	661565 + ins.
A	Savoy	146mm	'Model of British Minesweeper'

Liner converted to troop carrier

A	Willow	135mm
A	Devonia Art	135mm
A	Disa Art	135mm
A	Pearl Arms	135mm

iv. Submarines

E1

D	Bow	150mm	
D	Porcelle	150mm	
D	Savoy	147mm	651546 + ins.

E4

E	Alexandra		
E	Arcadian	95mm	658687
E	Botolph	95mm	
E	Corona	110mm	
E	Crown	120mm	
E	Grosvenor		
E	Milton	120mm	
E	Swan	95mm	
E	Rayleigh		
E	Willow	120mm	
E	Sussex	105mm	
E	Victoria		

E5

E	Arcadian	125mm	'Model of New Submarine' 658687
E	Botolph	125mm	
E	Corona	146mm	'Model of New Submarine'
E	Coronet	131mm	

E9

D	Carlton	140mm	'Model of British Submarine'
D	Carlton	144mm	
D	Carlton	122mm	'Model of British Submarine' (half submerged)
D	Cyclone	147mm	
D	Grafton	148mm	Grafton 406
D	Shelley	144mm	Shelley 328
D	Victoria	147mm	

v. Mines and Torpedoes

Floating mine

D	Carlton	80mm	'Model of floating mine' 662106
D	Arcadian		
C	Shelley	67mm	

Contact mine

B Goss 73mm Issued only to members of 'The International League of Goss Collectors'

Torpedo

D Arcadian 100mm 'Model of British Aerial Torpedo' 657210
D Corona 135mm & 150mm 'Model of Torpedo'
D Alexandra 150mm
D Grosvenor 155mm
C Shelley 70mm Shelley 187 Model of Head of German Torpedo
D Victoria 155mm

vi. Miscellaneous

Ships capstan

E Arcadian 58mm
E Wembley 58mm
E Carlton 70mm 'Model of Dockside capstan'

Scarborough Lighthouse damaged by shellfire

B Willow 132mm

Scarborough Coastguard Station and Lighthouse damaged by shellfire.

B Willow 130mm
B Carlton 95mm

CHAPTER 8
MEMORIALS

i. Named Memorials

C	Bishops Stortford	Arcadian	145mm
C	Black Watch	Willow	130mm
C	Black Watch	Regis	130mm
D	Blackpool	Podmore	145mm
C	Brighton	Carlton	55mm & 105mm across
B	Brora	Arcadian	155mm
C	Burford	Arcadian	128mm
C	Burnham-on-Crouch	Arcadian	146mm
D	Chatham Naval	Willow	160mm
C	Cheddar	Devonia Art	148mm
C	Chesham	Arcadian	159mm
C	Cheltenham	Arcadian	150mm & 185mm
E	Clacton-on-Sea	Saxony	137mm
E	Clacton-on-Sea	Foreign	118mm
C	Cranbrook	Carlton	130mm
B	Crich Stand	Notts & Derby	150mm (Leadbeater)
C	Cumberland & Westmoreland	Leadbeater Art	148mm
C	Derby	Leadbeater Art	150mm
C	Dartford	Coronet	163mm
C	Dunbar	Carlton	122mm
C	Dover	Arcadian	142mm
D	Dover Patrol	Arcadian	128mm
C	East Dereham	Arcadian	
C	Folkestone	Arcadian	160mm x 145mm base
C	Folkestone Remembrance Stone	Wilton	78mm
C	Fryatt	Arcadian	125mm
C	Gravesend	Florentine	140mm
E	Great Yarmouth	Arcadian	148mm
E	Great Yarmouth	Florentine	178mm
E	Great Yarmouth	Saxony	130mm
E	Great Yarmouth	Willow	166mm (and Willow Art)
C	Harrogate	Leadbeater Art	153mm
C	Ilkeston	Willow Art	132mm
C	Invergordon	Arcadian	148mm
C	Killin	Arcadian	145mm
C	Llandudno		180mm
D	Loughborough	Arcadian	155mm
D	Loughborough	Willow Art	155mm
C	March	R & M China	174mm
D	Margate	Arcadian	160mm
E	Matlock Bath	Norfolk	172mm
E	Matlock Bath	Podmore	199mm
E	Matlock Bath	Foreign	150mm
E	Matlock Bath	Foreign	120mm
E	Matlock Bath	Saxony	150mm
E	Matlock Bath	Shelley	180mm
E	Matlock Bath	Victoria	120mm
C	Newhaven Mercantile	Willow Art	180mm
B	Newnham	Arcadian	
C	Northallerton	Grosvenor	138mm
C	Norwich	Carlton	110mm
C	Nottingham	Arcadian	134mm
C	Orkney Earl Kitchener Memorial 5 June 1916	Leadbeater Art	150mm
D	Plymouth Naval	Arcadian	110mm
D	Plymouth Naval	Devonia Art	140mm & 160mm
D	Plymouth Naval	Leadbeater Art	168mm
D	Plymouth Naval	Arcadian	180mm
D	Portsmouth Naval	Willow	160mm
C	RAF (London)	Willow Art	160mm
D	Ripon	Alexandra	170mm
C	Rushden	Victoria	118mm
C	Romsey		158mm
D	Southsea Naval	Corona	155mm
C	St. Annes	Arcadian	162mm & 140mm
C	St. Ives	Wilton	152mm
C	Tunbridge Wells	R & M China	135mm
C	Thetford	Carlton	170mm
B	Ulster	Wilton	150mm
C	Ulverston	Leadbeater Art	140mm
B	Weymouth	Carlton	148mm
		Regis	152mm
C	Walsall	Wilton	130mm
C	Woodhouse Eaves	Arcadian	
E	Worthing	Foreign	

ii. Edith Cavell Memorials

D	Arcadian	175mm (Norwich Memorial)
E	Arcadian	160mm & 147mm
E	Alexandra	95mm
E	Botolph	160mm & 115mm
E	Carlton	163mm & 140mm
B	Goss	180mm
E	Kingsway	145mm
E	Podmore	142mm & 170mm
D	Podmore	102mm, 138mm & 168mm (Norwich Memorial)
E	Savoy	168mm
E	Strand	140mm
E	Willow	110mm, 150mm & 175mm (London)
E	Willow	115mm & 155mm
D	Willow	175mm (Norwich)
D	Leadbeater Art	200mm
E	Mother Shipton	163mm

iii. Cenotaphs

E	Arcadian	80mm, 100mm, 140mm & 180mm
E	Botolph	80mm, 102mm & 140mm
E	Carlton	105mm & 146mm
E	Corona	140mm
E	Coronet	100mm
E	Cyclone	100mm & 140mm
E	Florentine	140mm
D	Goss	145mm & 85mm
E	Grafton	135mm & 155mm
E	Kingsway	145mm
E	Podmore	84mm, 130mm & 160mm
E	Regis	145mm
E	Savoy	130mm
E	Shelley	130mm & 152mm Shelley 368
E	Victoria	135mm
E	Willow	70mm, 145mm & 184mm

Miscellaneous Items

E	Bulldog in Kennel; 'The Black Watch'	Willow Art	63mm x 60mm
E	Bulldog in Kennel; 'The Black Watch'	Shelley	95mm x 42mm

'Keep the Home Fires Burning'

E	Arcadian	90mm	
E	Arcadian	62mm x 76mm x 27mm	
E	Botolph	110mm high	
E	Carlton	86mm x 100mm x 45mm	659352
E	Carlton	92mm x 100mm	
E	Carlton	79mm x 87mm	
E	Devonia Art	63mm high	
E	Podmore	93mm x 93mm	
E	Porcelle	70mm high	
E	Shelley	71mm x 95mm	Shelley 338
E	Sylvan		
E	Pearl Arms	65mm	

D	Bear with ins. 'War Edition 1914-16'			
D	Bulldog with ins. 'War Edition 1914-16'			
D	Lion 'Another Dreadnought'	Savoy	130mm	
D	Charabanc 'Dreadnought'	Grafton	97mm	Grafton 975
A	Desert Sled	Carlton	661566 (to date unseen)	
E	Top hat with flags of the Allies and General French	Corona		
D	Map of Blighty	Carlton		
D	Grandfather clock	Corona	128mm + peace ins.	

xi
Notes for the Collector

As the First World War recedes into the past so the objects, artifacts and ephemera that belong to that period become of interest to the historian and collector alike. Recent years have seen a tremendous upsurge in interest in things pertaining to the war. Heraldic China has been no exception to this.

Hitherto collecting Great War China has generally been regarded as a collecting theme in itself; the purpose being to collect as many different models as possible. However, faced with such an apparently daunting task the intending collector may do well to start by concentrating on one particular aspect confining himself to, for example, tanks or aeroplanes or memorials. An interesting collection could be made of the variations in type, size, detail and colours of a particular design. A relatively inexpensive start could be made by collecting the different varieties of caps and headware from the war.

Another avenue for the collector is provided by the crests that appear on the china. Models carrying the crests of related towns should be of added interest to the discerning collector. Ships bearing the crests of their home ports, Zeppelins with the crests of places they bombed, bombs with the crests of places where they fell, tanks and armoured cars with the crests of places where they were made and for those lucky enough to find them, military models carrying the crests of places in France and Belgium which formed part of the Western Front. I have, in my own collection, a model of a Carlton Biplane bearing the crest of La Boiselle, a small village in France which was the scene of heavy fighting during the Somme offensive. Unusual in itself, but to me, one of the creme-de-la-creme. Regimental crests, notably those of W.H. Goss are already sought after and highly prized items, nevertheless those on military models have an added interest.

The next question that faces a new collector is how to set about collecting the pieces. If you enjoy the search... the 'hunt' and the 'kill'... and the satisfaction of finding a 'snip' then undoubtedly your collection will grow slowly. Searching through the many antique shops and markets is a time-consuming albeit interesting pastime and many collectors may decide to put themselves in the hands of the specialist dealer from the beginning. Whichever course is taken the time will come when the collector finds himself looking for a particular elusive piece and in such an instance one would be well advised to approach one of the main dealers. Most are all too eager to help collectors in their search and will often keep 'wants' lists for interested customers.

Once a collection is started, and with an eye to the future, the collector will have to decide what standards of workmanship and condition will be acceptable. Certainly, as interest and prices increase so those models in pristine condition... the 'uncirculated' of the coin world... will command a better price and thus be a better investment. At some stage the collector will be faced with the problem of whether or not to accept a damaged model, may it be pre- or post-firing damage. Personally I consider firing flaws, within reason, to add extra interest to the model for they give us some idea of what standard of workmanship was allowed to pass out of the factory. Manufacturers differed greatly in their criteria for acceptability and it is a wonder that anybody bought the 'seconds' from certain factories with low standards. Nevertheless it should be borne in mind that they are sub-standard and should be judged accordingly. Damaged pieces, those with parts broken off and those with cracks in them fetch a small percentage of their perfect price and can usually be bought for a few pounds or less and will, at least, provide the collector with an example of the model. As prices increase so it becomes economical to have some of the more expensive pieces repaired if damaged. Repairs vary greatly in extent and quality and a piece that has been well repaired (i.e. so that it is not immediately visible to the naked eye) may be expected to fetch as much as 50% of its perfect price.

Obviously this leads on to the next point, that of examining pieces before purchase. Anyone who has bought such china will know how difficult it is to spot damage, especially in a darkened shop or when hidden by a judiciously placed price tag! To avoid disappointment and ill-feeling I advise any prospective buyer to examine any pieces very carefully before purchase... even a small chip will give you extra bargaining power and may have slipped the dealers gaze when the piece was priced. For the specialist dealer, with a reputation to maintain, pieces will generally be sold as perfect or damaged; nevertheless no-one is infallible and checking still applies.

It would be pointless to include a list of prices in this book for no sooner are they written than they become out of date, however general values at the time of going to press are given in Appendix x. For current price trends I can only recommend collectors firstly to *The Price Guide to Crested China by Nicholas Pine* (see Bibliography) which is the definitive priced list of all crested china wares and secondly to *Goss & Crested China*, the monthly catalogue produced and published by Milestone Publications. Suffice it to say that while the more common pieces may still be acquired for a few pounds more and more pieces are breaking the fifty pounds barrier while a handful of the extreme rarities fetch in excess of one hundred.

Ultimately the price will be governed by the collector and how much he or she is prepared to pay.)

xii
Further reading

Books on Heraldic China:
ANDREWS, S. *Crested China: The History of Heraldic Souvenir Ware* Published by Milestone 1980
GORDON-PUGH, Surgeon-Captain P.D.; *Heraldic China Mementoes of the First World War;* published by The Ceramic Book Co. 1972.
GOSS RECORD; *War Edition 1917;* reprinted Milestone 1979.
PINE, N. *Goss China, Arms, Decorations, and Their Values* published by Milestone 1979
PINE N. *The Price Guide To Crested China* published by Milestone 1981
PINE N. *The Pine Guide To Goss China* published by Milestone 1981

Books on World War I ephemera

HOLT, Toni and Valmi	*Till the boys come home;* Picture postcards of the First World War; Macdonald and Janes 1977.
HOLT, Toni and Valmi	*The Best of the Fragments from France;* pub. Phin 1978 (Bruce Bairnsfathers cartoons)
HOWELLS, BILL & JONES, BARBARA	*Popular Arts of the First World War;* pub. Studio Vista 1972.
RICKARDS, M & MOODY, M.	*The First World War: Ephemera, Mementoes and Documents;* pub. Jupiter 1975.

General Books on the First World War
This, of course, is a vast subject about which much has been written. Below are listed a small number of the more recent works on the subject that contain information of interest to the china collector. A good insight into the conditions, welfare and experiences that confronted the common soldier can be gained by reading some of the many personal accounts that have been published.

CAREW, T.	*Wipers;* pub. Hamish Hamilton 1974
CLARK, A.	*Aces High;* pub. Fontana/Collins 1974
COOK, G.	*Silent Marauders: British Submarines of the First World War;* pub. Hart-Davies 1976
COOMBES, R.E.	*Before Endeavours Fade - the Battlefields of the Western Front;* pub. Imperial War Museum
HARRIS, J.	*The Somme;* pub. White Lion 1975
HART, Liddel	*The History of the First World War;* republished Pan 1970
LANCE, D.	*The Tank: Theory and Practice 1916-1919;* pub. Imperial War Museum
MacDONALD, L.	*They Called It Passchendaele;* pub. Michael Joseph 1978
MIDDLETON, M.	*The First Day of the Somme 1916;* pub. Allen Lane 1971
MIDDLETON, M.	*The Kaisers Battle: the first day of the German spring offensive 1918;* pub. Allen Lane 1978
Ed. MOYNIHAM, M.	*A Place Called Armageddon: Letters from the Great War;* pub. David & Charles 1975
Ed. MOYNIHAM, M.	*People at War 1914-1918;* pub. David & Charles
SIMKISS, P.	*Air Fighting 1914-18;* pub. Imperial War Museum
TAYLOR, A.J:P.	*The First World War: An Illustrated History;* Penguin 1966
WILLIAMS, J.	*The Home Fronts 1914-18;* pub. Constable 1972
WHITEHOUSE, A.	*The Zeppelin Fighters;* pub. Robert Hale 1968

xiii

Leading Events of the War

1914
June 28th: Archduke Ferdinand and Duchess Sophia assasinated.
August 3rd: Great Britain declares war on Germany.
August 9th: First troops of the BEF arrive in Boulogne.
August 23rd: Battle of Mons.
August 25th: Retreat from Mons begins.
September 5th-9th: 1st Battle of the Marne.
October 21st-November 22nd: 1st Battle of Ypres.
November 1st: Battle of Coronel.
December 8th: Battle of the Falkland Isles.
December 16th: German Naval attack on Yorkshire coast.

1915
January 19th: First Zeppelin raid on Britain; Norfolk bombed.
March 10th: Battle of Neuve Chapelle.
April 22nd-May 24th: 2nd Battle of Ypres.
April 22nd: First gas attack.
April 25th: Landings at Gallipoli.
May 7th: Lusitania sunk.
September 8th: First Zeppelin raid on London.
September 25th: Battle of Loos

1916
February 21st: Battle of Verdun starts.
May 31st: Battle of Jutland.
July 1st: British Somme Offensive begins.
September 2nd: SL11 shot down over Cuffley, Herts.
September 15th: Tanks first used; Battle of Flers-Courcelette.
September 24th: L33 shot down at Little Wigborough, Essex.
November: Somme Offensive ends.

1917
April 6th: United States enters war.
July 31st: Battle of Passchendaele (3rd Ypres).
November: Battle of Cambrai.

1918
March 3rd: Treaty of Brest Litovsk; Russian peace with Germany.
March 21st: German spring offensive on the Somme begins.
July 18th-August 2nd: 2nd Battle of the Marne.
August 8th: Battle of Amiens.
November 11th: Armistice signed.

Index

Italic figures indicate a photograph.

Illustrations Acknowledgements

The illustrations in this book are supplied by or reproduced by courtesy of the following:
Imperial War Museum, London: 10, 16 bottom, 17, 21 top, 29 bottom, 30 (Tank), 34 top, 37 bottom, 38 bottom left and above, 39 top and bottom, 43 top right, 44 top, 46 bottom right, 49 top right and below, 50 top, 51 top right, 53, 54 middle and bottom, 56 bottom, 57 bottom, 58 bottom, 59 bottom, 61 left, 63, 70 bottom, 71 bottom, 72 top, 74 bottom, 89 top, 92 top, 112 bottom left and the three posters illustrated in colour.
Royal Tank Museum, Bovington: 27 top, 36 bottom.
Musee Royal de L'Armee et d'Histoire Militaire, Brussels: 27 bottom.
Illustrated London News Picture Library: 21 bottom right, 48 top.
Syndications International, London: 30 headline.
British Library, Colindale, London: Frontispiece.
The Registrar, Patent Office, London: 116, 117, 118, 119.
J. Mitchie: 48 top. P. Riley: 35 bottom left. R. Gough: 55 bottom left. R. Coombs: 104 inset top left. 'After the Battle' magazine: 104 aerial view.

The sketches were drawn by Trevor Glover.
The maps and sketches on pages 65, 66, 84 and 94 are adapted from those on pages 296, 284, 269 and 243 respectively of: 'A Military Atlas of the First World War'; Arthur Banks: Heinemann Educational 1975.

Illustrations on pages 20 top left, 25 bottom left, 45 bottom right, 57 middle, 69 bottom right, 85 bottom right, 96 bottom, 98 bottom, are from the Author's collection.

The written extracts on pages 68 and 140 are reproduced by courtesy of the Keeper, Public Records Office, London.

All possible care has been taken in tracing the ownership of copyright material used in this book and making acknowledgement for its use. If any owner has not been acknowledged, the author and publishers apologise and will be glad of the opportunity to rectify the error.